SAVAGE DRAGON

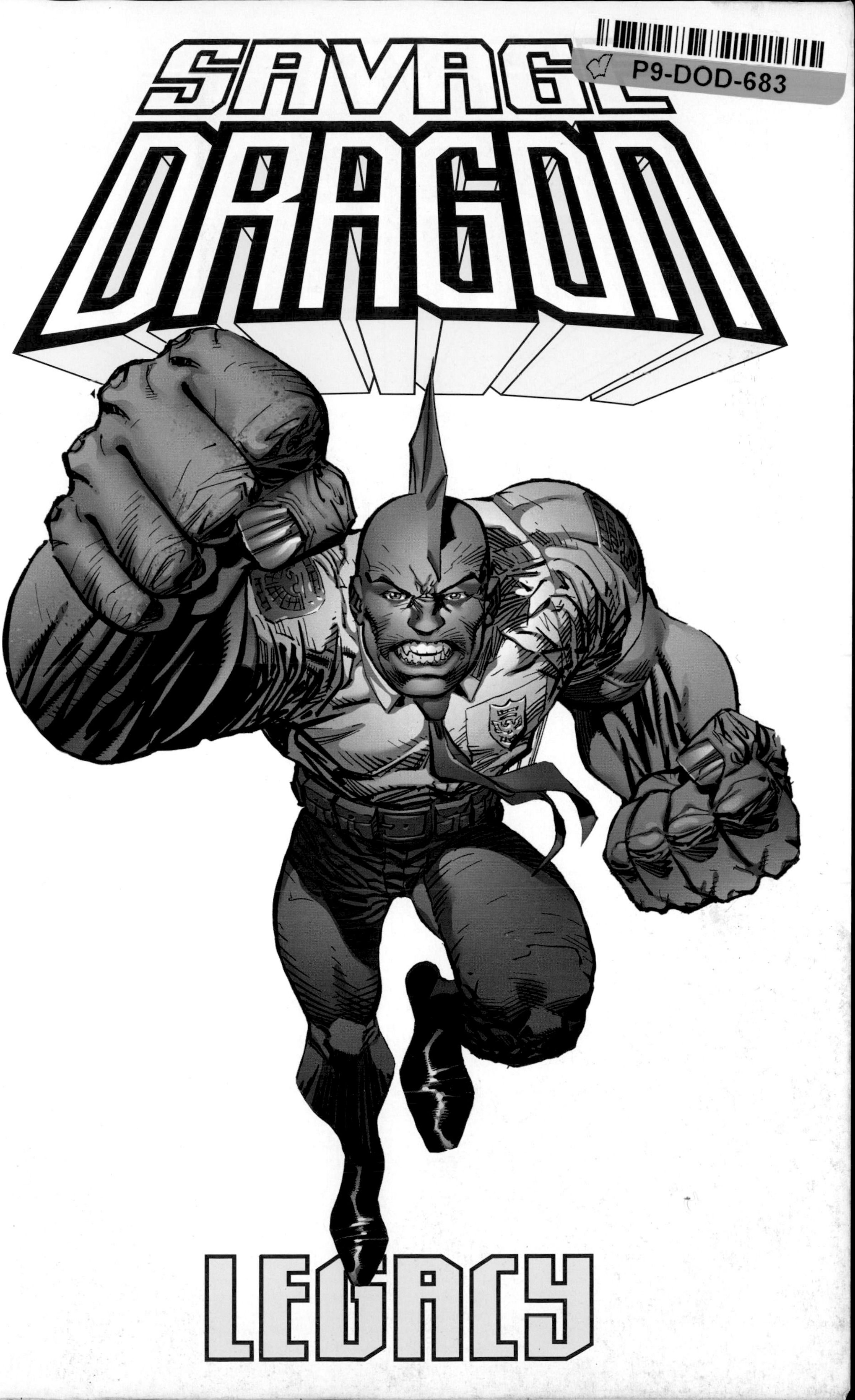

LEGACY

SAVAGE DRAGON®

BY

ERIK LARSEN

CHRIS ELIOPOULOS
letters

NIKOS KOUTSIS
colors

MIKE TORIS
flats

GAVIN HIGGINBOTHAM
editor

JOSH EICHHÖRN

Do not disturb without proper training and equipment.

Ant created by Mario Gully

IMAGE COMICS, INC.
Robert Kirkman – Chief Operating Officer
Erik Larsen – Chief Financial Officer
Todd McFarlane – President
Marc Silvestri – Chief Executive Officer
Jim Valentino – Vice-President
Eric Stephenson – Publisher
Corey Murphy – Director of Sales
Jeff Boison – Director of Publishing Planning & Book Trade Sales
Jeremy Sullivan – Director of Digital Sales
Kat Salazar – Director of PR & Marketing
Bramwyn Bigglestone – Controller
Drew Gill – Art Director
Jonathan Chan – Production Manager
Meredith Wallace – Print Manager
Briah Skelly – Publicist
Sasha Head – Sales & Marketing Production Designer
Randy Okamura – Digital Production Designer
David Brothers – Branding Manager
Olivia Ngai – Content Manager
Addison Duke – Production Artist
Vincent Kukua – Production Artist
Tricia Ramos – Production Artist
Jeff Stang – Direct Market Sales Representative
Emilio Bautista – Digital Sales Associate
Leanna Caunter – Accounting Assistant
Chloe Ramos-Peterson – Library Market Sales Representative
IMAGECOMICS.COM

SAVAGE DRAGON LEGACY TP. First printing. November 2016. Published by Image Comics, Inc. Office of publication: 2001 Center Street, Sixth Floor, Berkeley, CA 94704. Copyright © 2016 Erik Larsen. All rights reserved. Contains material originally published as SAVAGE DRAGON #211-216. "SAVAGE DRAGON," its logos, and the likenesses of all characters herein are trademarks of Erik Larsen, unless otherwise noted. "Image" and the Image Comics logos are registered trademarks of Image Comics, Inc. No part of this publication may be reproduced or transmitted, in any form or by any means (except for short excerpts for journalistic or review purposes), without the express written permission of Erik Larsen or Image Comics, Inc. All names, characters, events, and locales in this publication are entirely fictional. Any resemblance to actual persons (living or dead), events, or places, without satiric intent, is coincidental. Printed in South Korea. For international rights, contact: foreignlicensing@imagecomics.com. ISBN 978-1-63215-946-5.

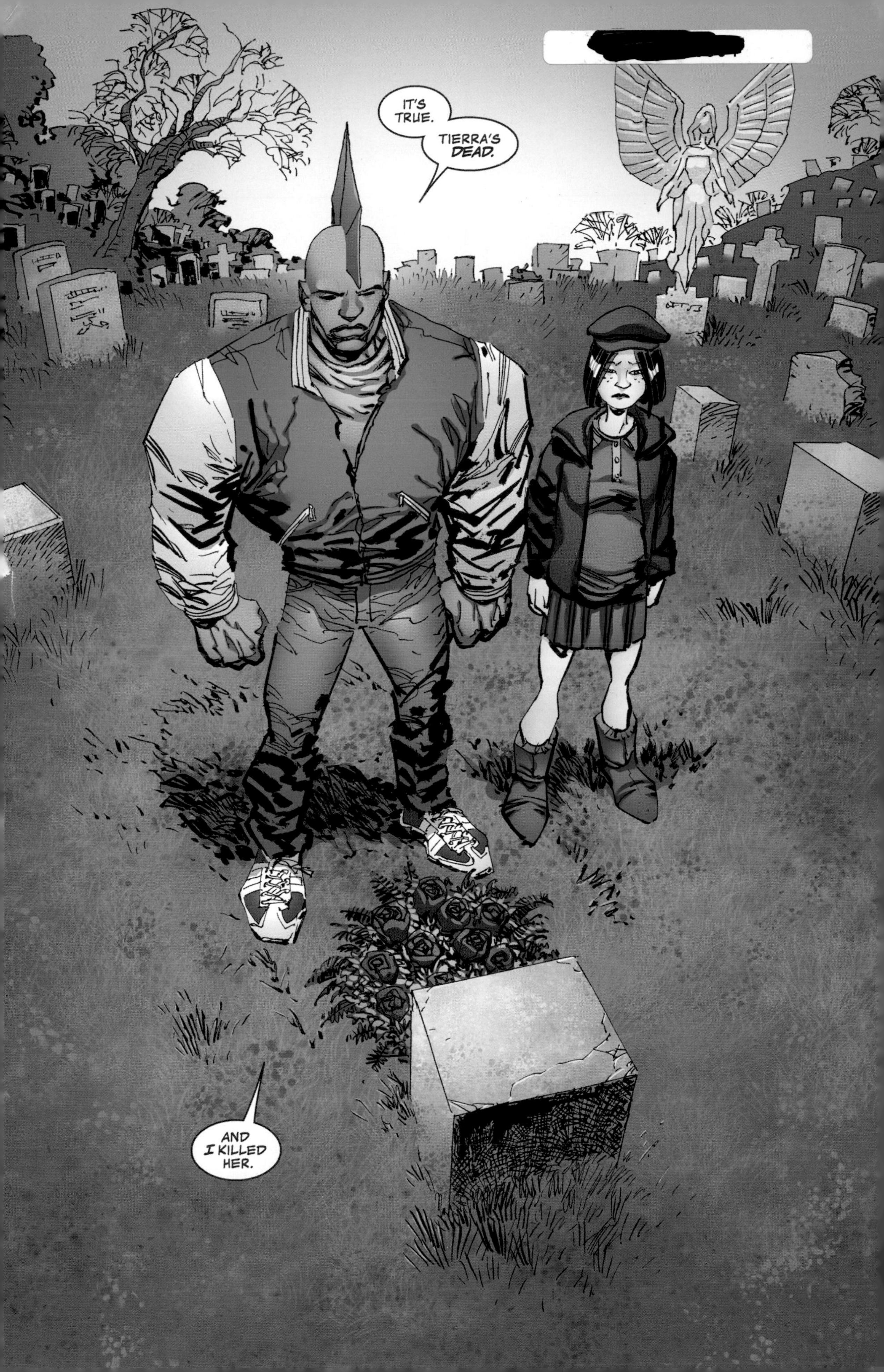
[redacted]
IT'S TRUE.
TIERRA'S DEAD.
AND I KILLED HER.

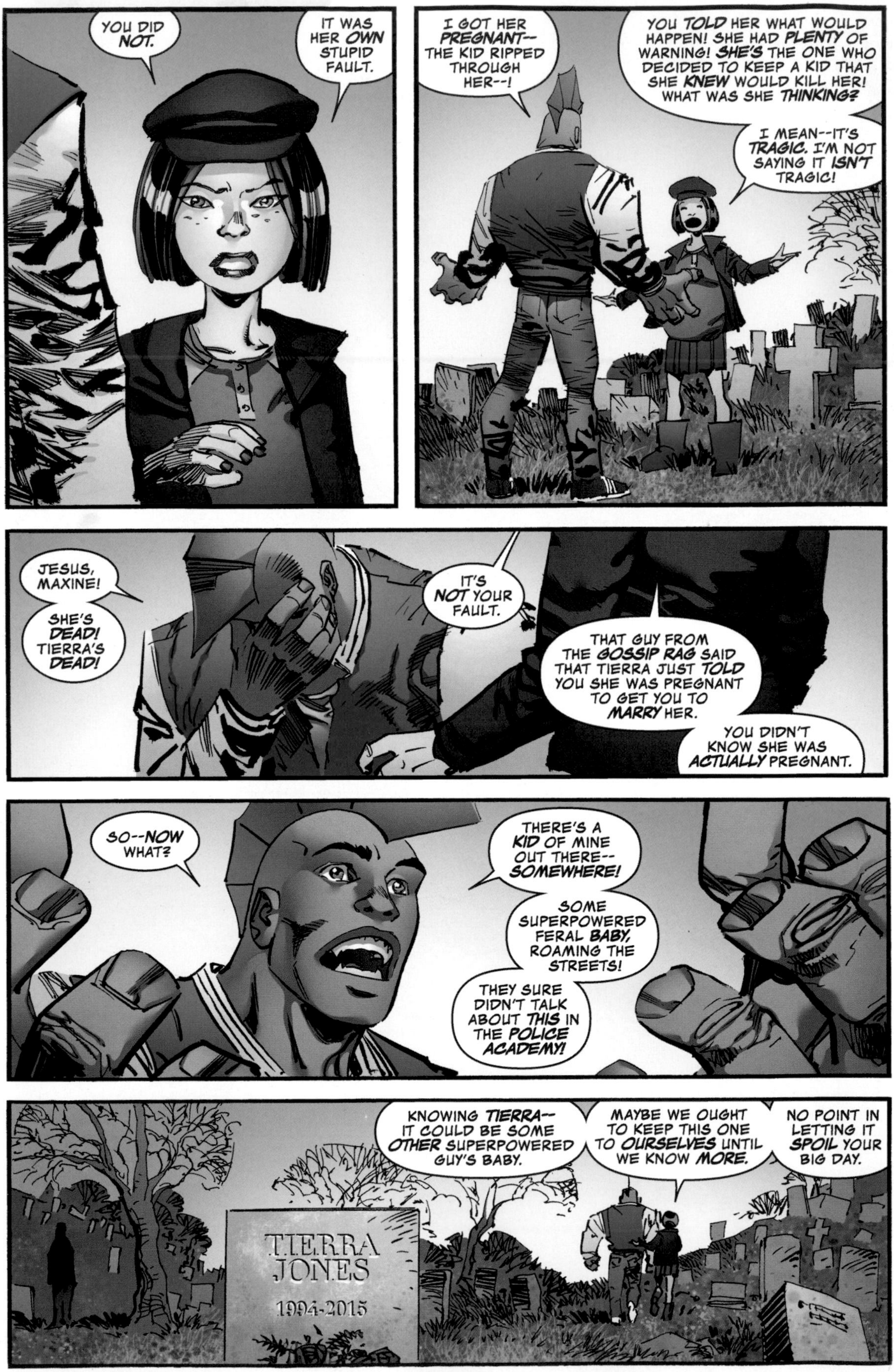
YOU DID NOT.
IT WAS HER OWN STUPID FAULT.
I GOT HER PREGNANT-- THE KID RIPPED THROUGH HER--!
YOU TOLD HER WHAT WOULD HAPPEN! SHE HAD PLENTY OF WARNING! SHE'S THE ONE WHO DECIDED TO KEEP A KID THAT SHE KNEW WOULD KILL HER! WHAT WAS SHE THINKING?
I MEAN--IT'S TRAGIC. I'M NOT SAYING IT ISN'T TRAGIC!
JESUS, MAXINE!
SHE'S DEAD! TIERRA'S DEAD!
IT'S NOT YOUR FAULT.
THAT GUY FROM THE GOSSIP RAG SAID THAT TIERRA JUST TOLD YOU SHE WAS PREGNANT TO GET YOU TO MARRY HER.
YOU DIDN'T KNOW SHE WAS ACTUALLY PREGNANT.
SO--NOW WHAT?
THERE'S A KID OF MINE OUT THERE-- SOMEWHERE!
SOME SUPERPOWERED FERAL BABY, ROAMING THE STREETS!
THEY SURE DIDN'T TALK ABOUT THIS IN THE POLICE ACADEMY!
KNOWING TIERRA-- IT COULD BE SOME OTHER SUPERPOWERED GUY'S BABY.
MAYBE WE OUGHT TO KEEP THIS ONE TO OURSELVES UNTIL WE KNOW MORE.
NO POINT IN LETTING IT SPOIL YOUR BIG DAY.
TIERRA JONES
1994-2015

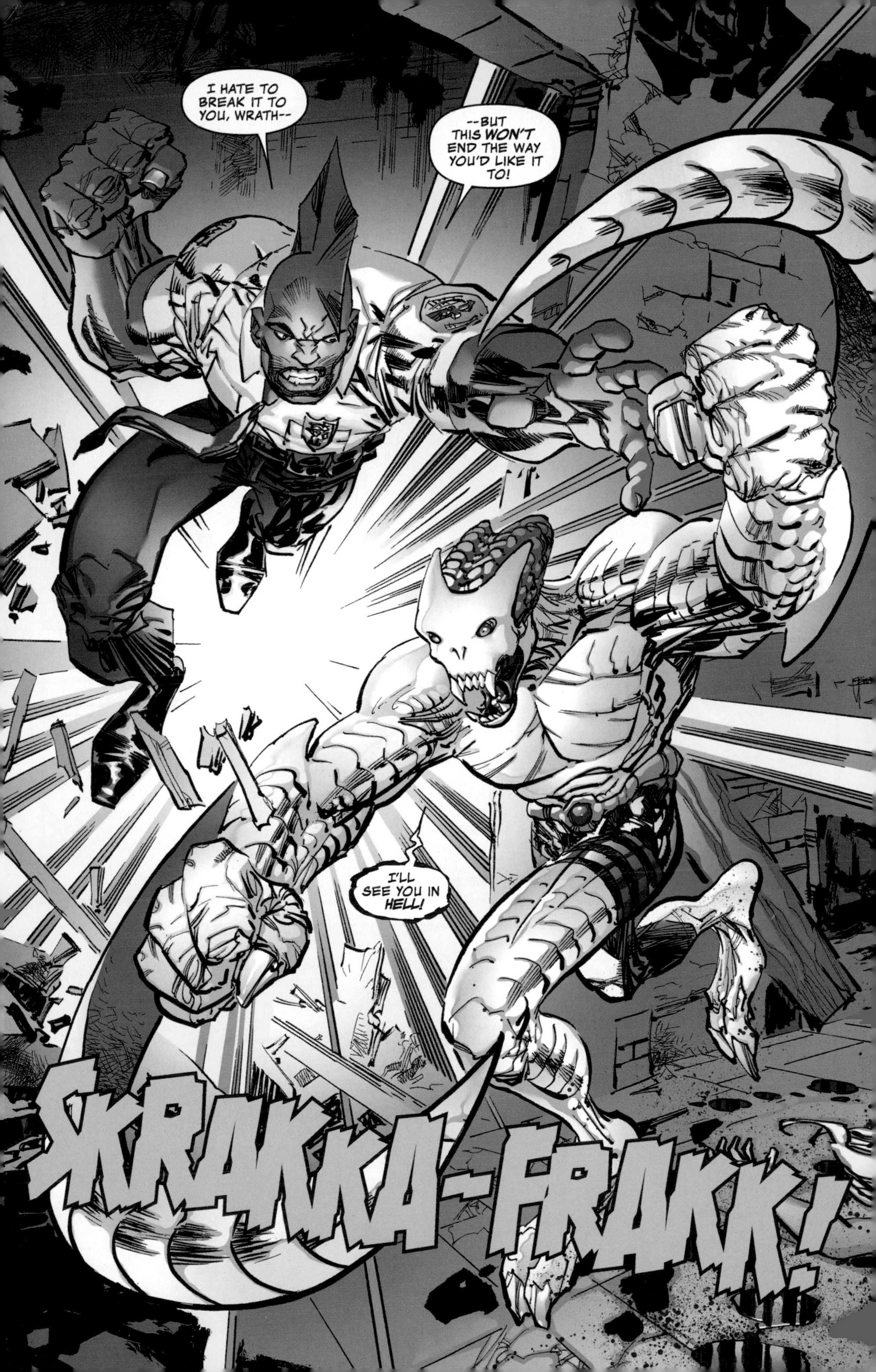
I HATE TO BREAK IT TO YOU, WRATH--
--BUT THIS WON'T END THE WAY YOU'D LIKE IT TO!
I'LL SEE YOU IN HELL!
KRAKKA-FRAKK!

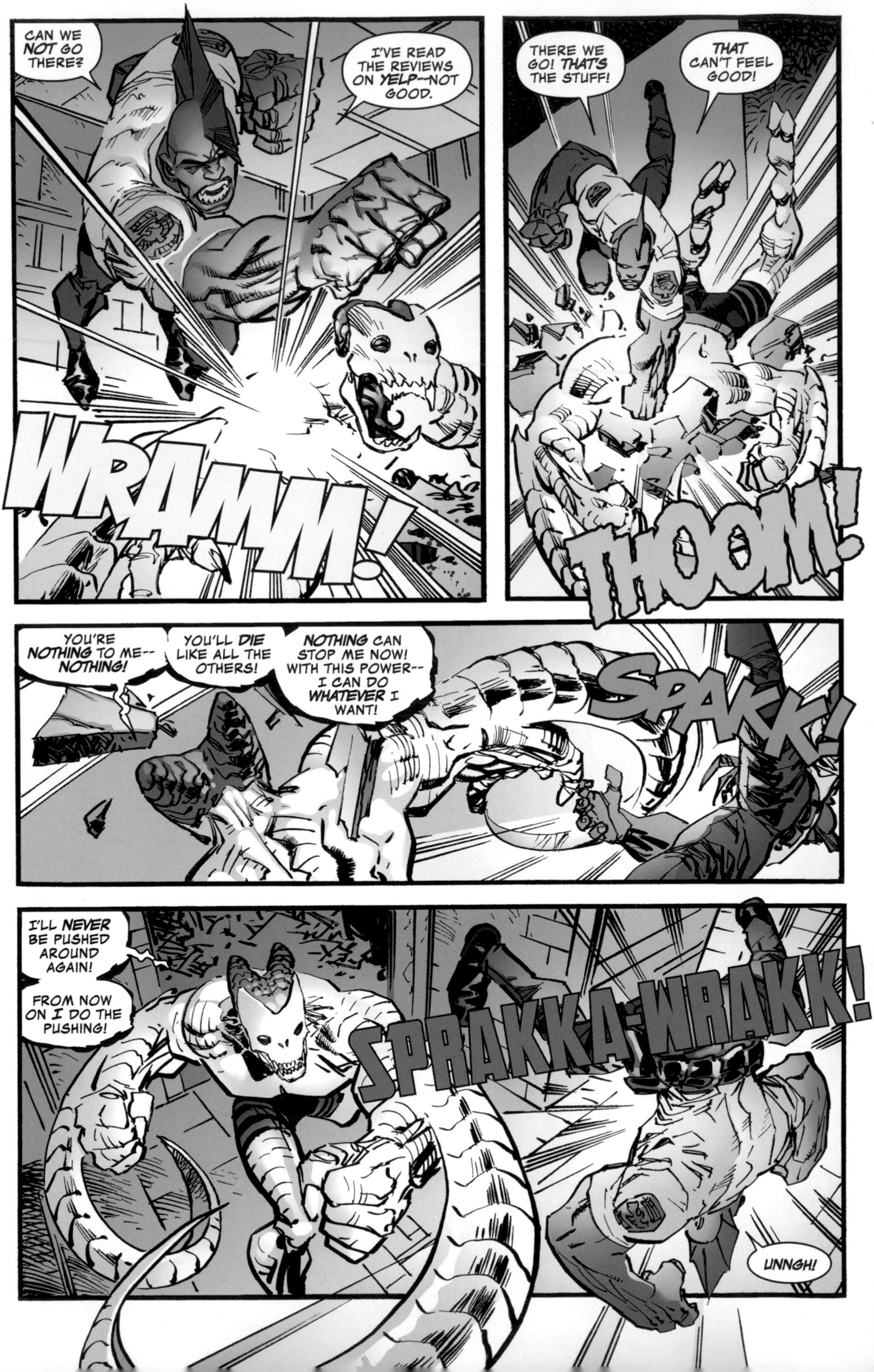
CAN WE NOT GO THERE?
I'VE READ THE REVIEWS ON YELP--NOT GOOD.
WRAMM!
THERE WE GO! THAT'S THE STUFF!
THAT CAN'T FEEL GOOD!
THOOM!
YOU'RE NOTHING TO ME-- NOTHING!
YOU'LL DIE LIKE ALL THE OTHERS!
NOTHING CAN STOP ME NOW! WITH THIS POWER-- I CAN DO WHATEVER I WANT!
SPAKK!
I'LL NEVER BE PUSHED AROUND AGAIN!
FROM NOW ON I DO THE PUSHING!
SPRAKKA-WRAKK!
UNNGH!

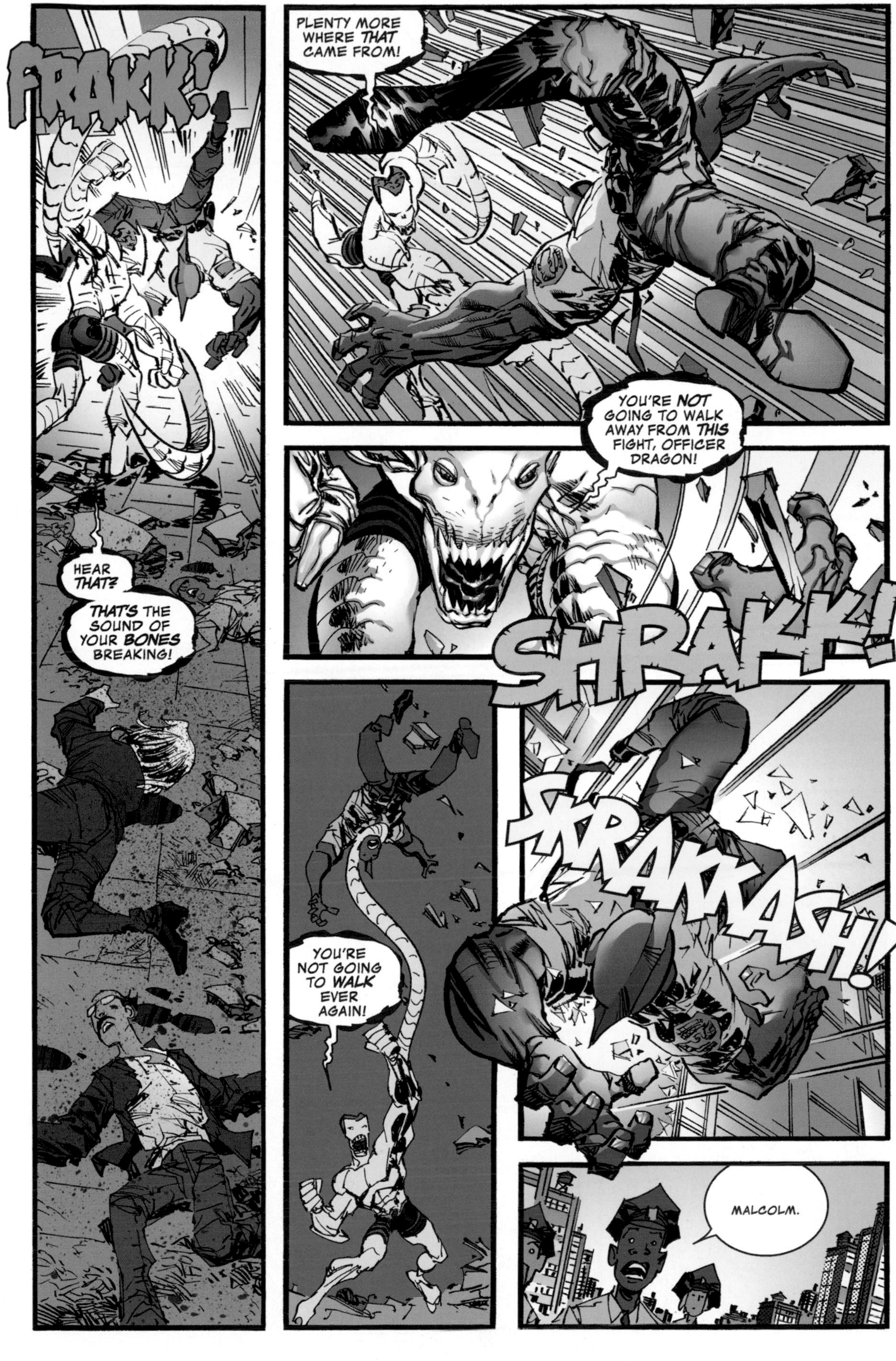
FRAKK!
HEAR THAT?
THAT'S THE SOUND OF YOUR BONES BREAKING!
PLENTY MORE WHERE THAT CAME FROM!
YOU'RE NOT GOING TO WALK AWAY FROM THIS FIGHT, OFFICER DRAGON!
SHRAKK!
YOU'RE NOT GOING TO WALK EVER AGAIN!
SKRAKKASH!!
MALCOLM.

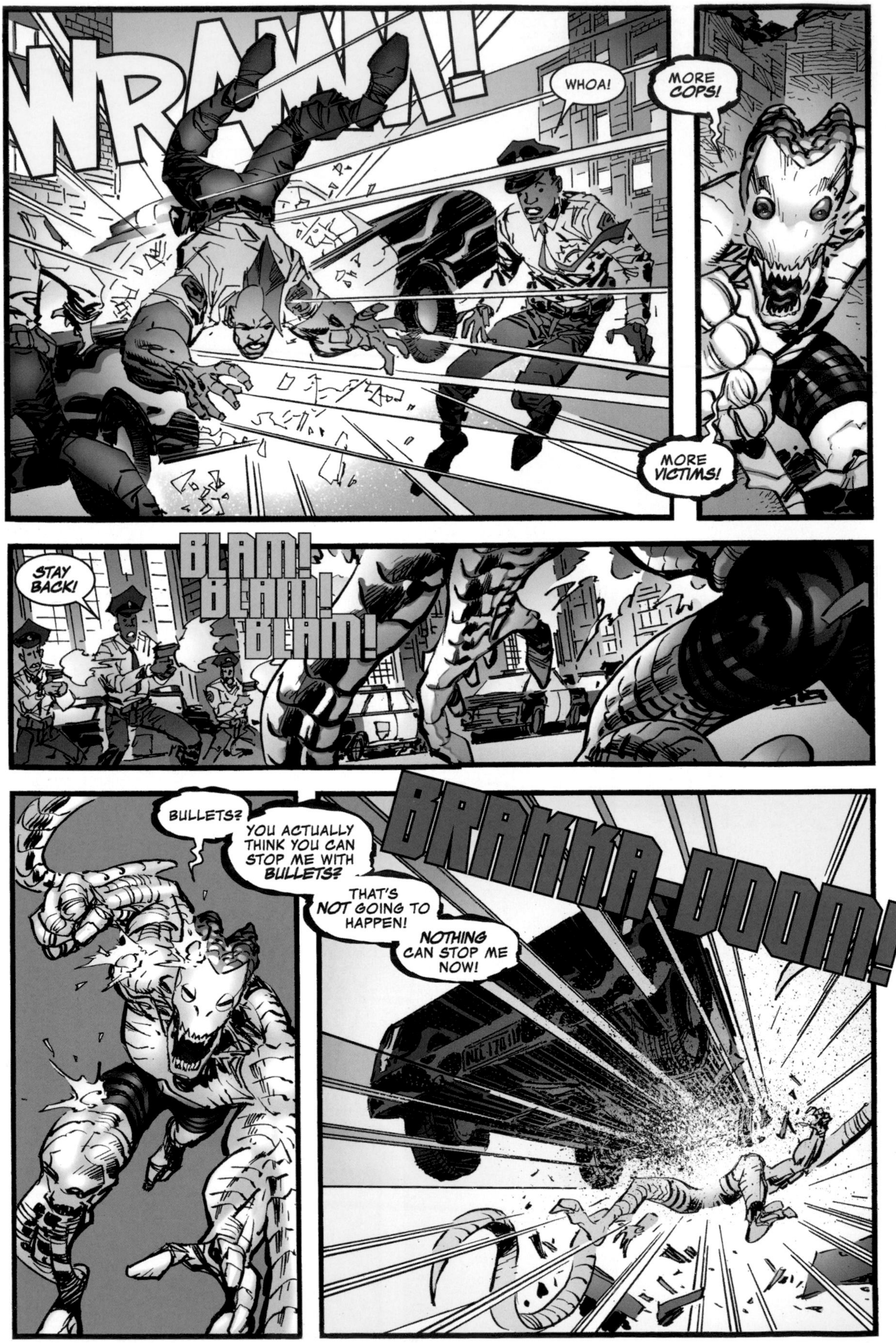
WRAMM!
WHOA!
MORE COPS!
MORE VICTIMS!
STAY BACK!
BLAM! BLAM! BLAM!
BULLETS?
YOU ACTUALLY THINK YOU CAN STOP ME WITH BULLETS?
THAT'S NOT GOING TO HAPPEN!
NOTHING CAN STOP ME NOW!
BRAKKA-DOOM!

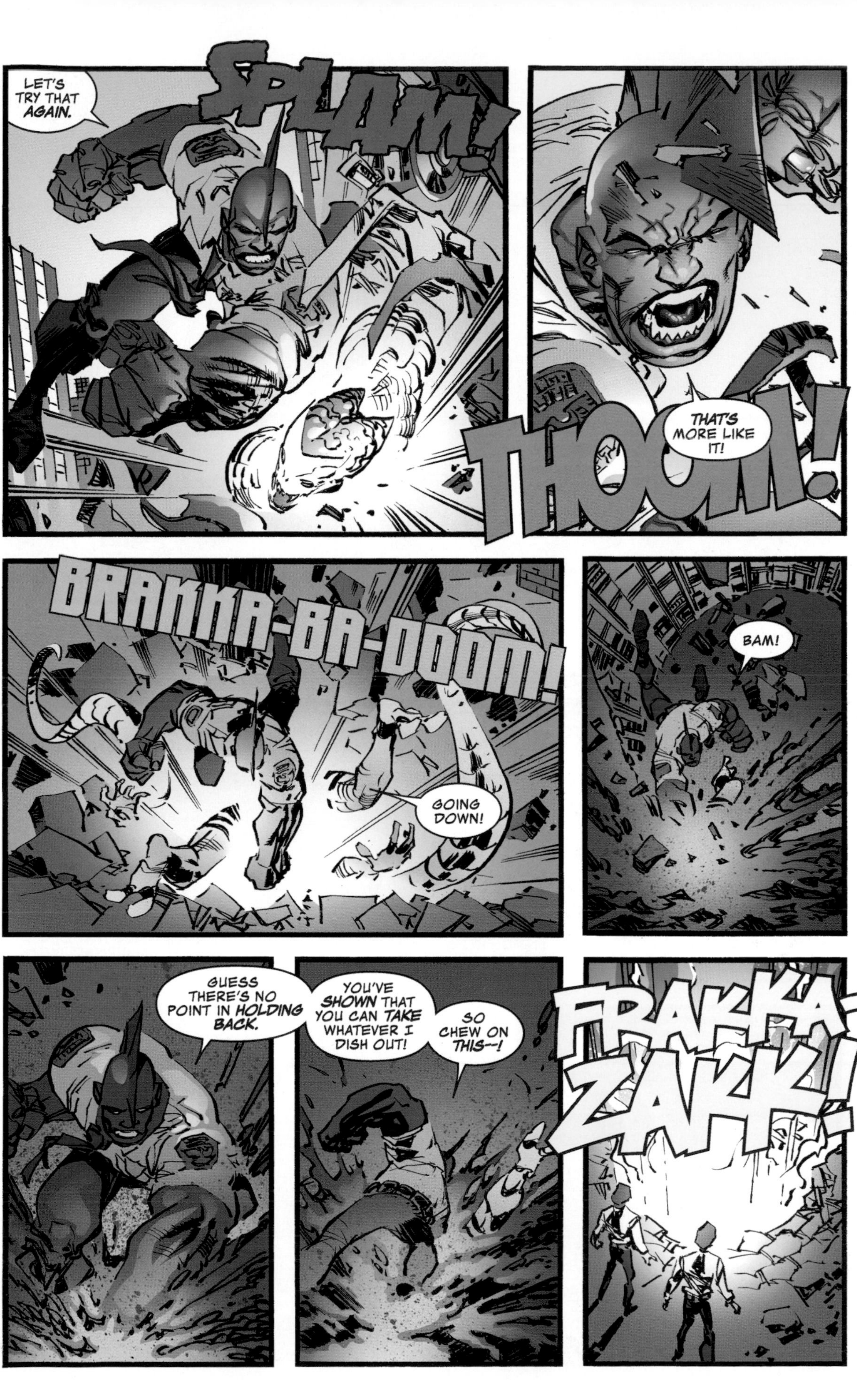

LET'S TRY THAT AGAIN.
SPLAM!
THOOM!
THAT'S MORE LIKE IT!
BRAKKA-BA-DOOOM!
GOING DOWN!
BAM!
GUESS THERE'S NO POINT IN HOLDING BACK.
YOU'VE SHOWN THAT YOU CAN TAKE WHATEVER I DISH OUT!
SO CHEW ON THIS--!
FRAKKA-ZAKK!

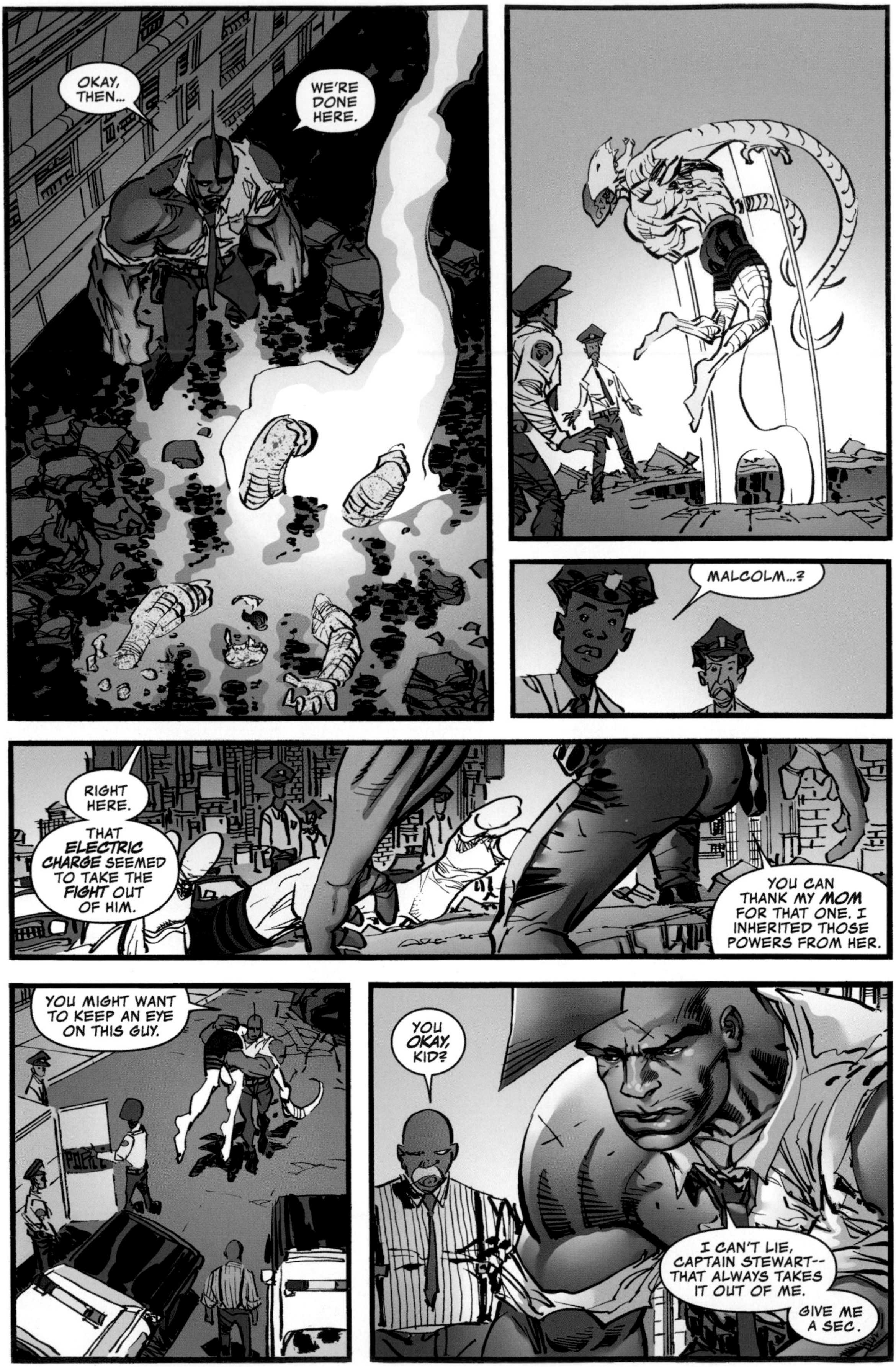
OKAY, THEN...
WE'RE DONE HERE.
MALCOLM...?
RIGHT HERE.
THAT ELECTRIC CHARGE SEEMED TO TAKE THE FIGHT OUT OF HIM.
YOU CAN THANK MY MOM FOR THAT ONE. I INHERITED THOSE POWERS FROM HER.
YOU MIGHT WANT TO KEEP AN EYE ON THIS GUY.
YOU OKAY, KID?
I CAN'T LIE, CAPTAIN STEWART-- THAT ALWAYS TAKES IT OUT OF ME.
GIVE ME A SEC.

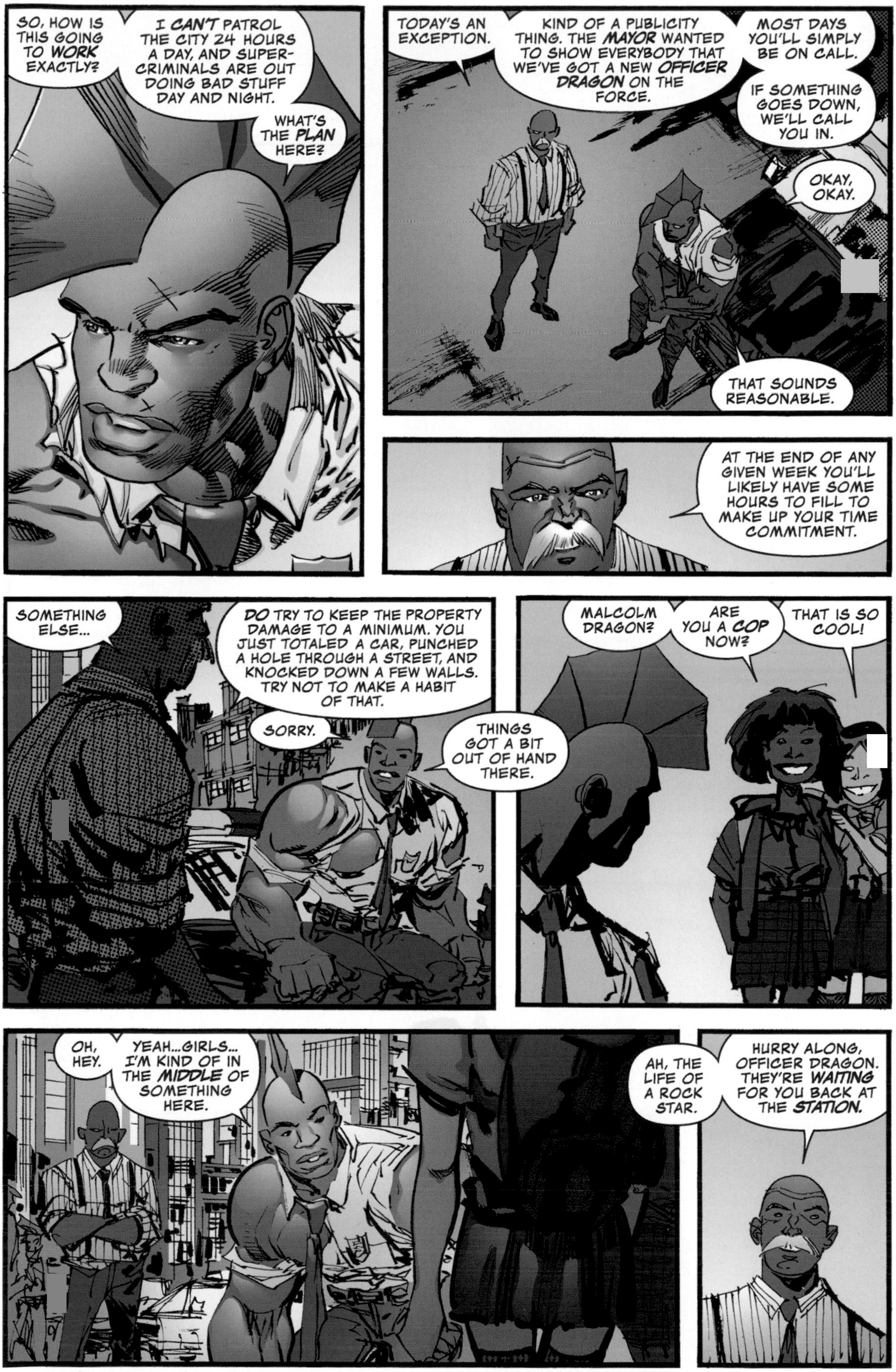
SO, HOW IS THIS GOING TO WORK EXACTLY?
I CAN'T PATROL THE CITY 24 HOURS A DAY, AND SUPER-CRIMINALS ARE OUT DOING BAD STUFF DAY AND NIGHT.
WHAT'S THE PLAN HERE?
TODAY'S AN EXCEPTION.
KIND OF A PUBLICITY THING. THE MAYOR WANTED TO SHOW EVERYBODY THAT WE'VE GOT A NEW OFFICER DRAGON ON THE FORCE.
MOST DAYS YOU'LL SIMPLY BE ON CALL.
IF SOMETHING GOES DOWN, WE'LL CALL YOU IN.
OKAY, OKAY.
THAT SOUNDS REASONABLE.
AT THE END OF ANY GIVEN WEEK YOU'LL LIKELY HAVE SOME HOURS TO FILL TO MAKE UP YOUR TIME COMMITMENT.
SOMETHING ELSE...
DO TRY TO KEEP THE PROPERTY DAMAGE TO A MINIMUM. YOU JUST TOTALED A CAR, PUNCHED A HOLE THROUGH A STREET, AND KNOCKED DOWN A FEW WALLS. TRY NOT TO MAKE A HABIT OF THAT.
SORRY.
THINGS GOT A BIT OUT OF HAND THERE.
MALCOLM DRAGON?
ARE YOU A COP NOW?
THAT IS SO COOL!
OH, HEY.
YEAH...GIRLS... I'M KIND OF IN THE MIDDLE OF SOMETHING HERE.
AH, THE LIFE OF A ROCK STAR.
HURRY ALONG, OFFICER DRAGON. THEY'RE WAITING FOR YOU BACK AT THE STATION.

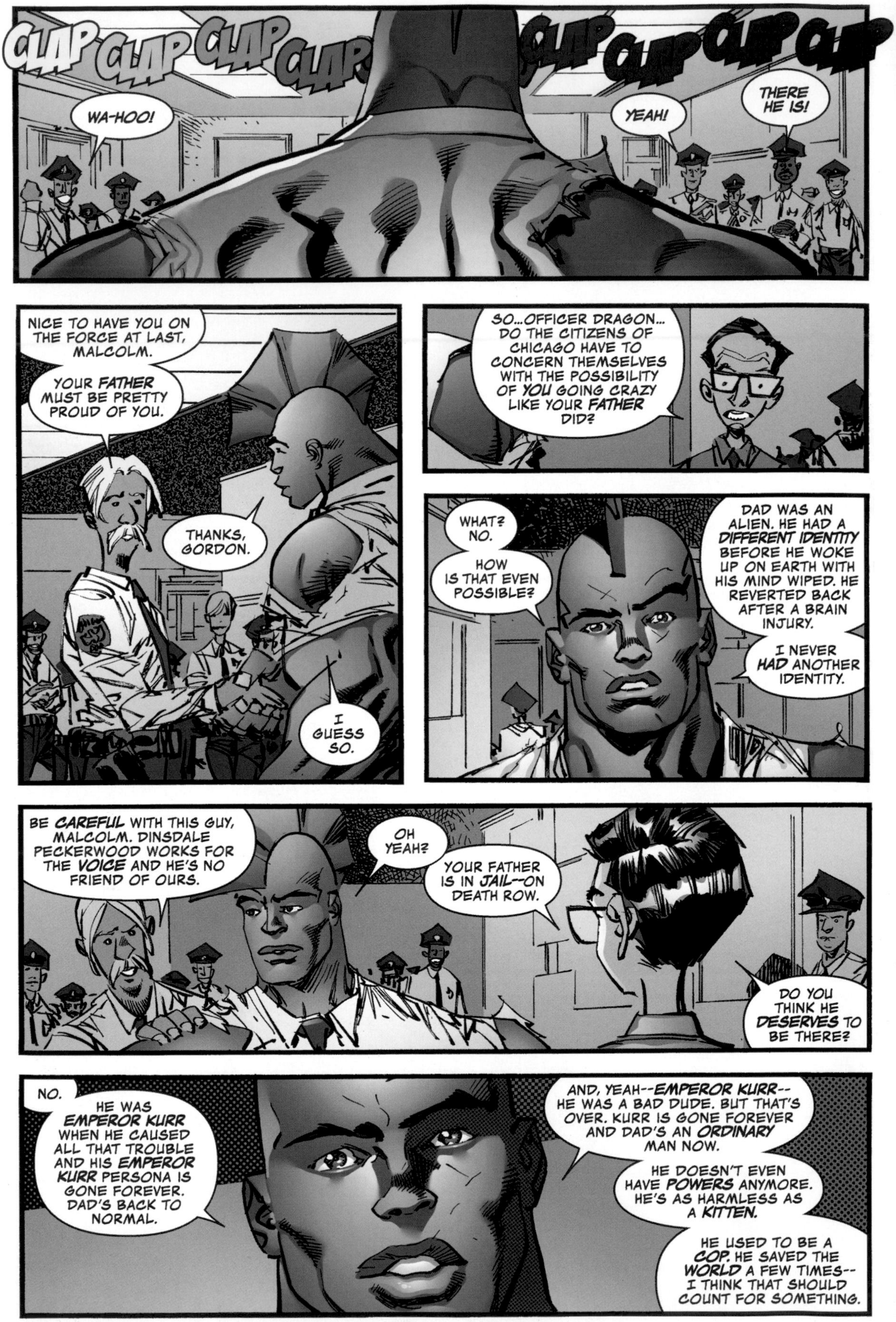
CLAP CLAP CLAP CLAP
CLAP CLAP CLAP CLAP
WA-HOO!
YEAH!
THERE HE IS!
NICE TO HAVE YOU ON THE FORCE AT LAST, MALCOLM.
YOUR FATHER MUST BE PRETTY PROUD OF YOU.
THANKS, GORDON.
I GUESS SO.
SO...OFFICER DRAGON... DO THE CITIZENS OF CHICAGO HAVE TO CONCERN THEMSELVES WITH THE POSSIBILITY OF YOU GOING CRAZY LIKE YOUR FATHER DID?
WHAT? NO.
HOW IS THAT EVEN POSSIBLE?
DAD WAS AN ALIEN. HE HAD A DIFFERENT IDENTITY BEFORE HE WOKE UP ON EARTH WITH HIS MIND WIPED. HE REVERTED BACK AFTER A BRAIN INJURY.
I NEVER HAD ANOTHER IDENTITY.
BE CAREFUL WITH THIS GUY, MALCOLM. DINSDALE PECKERWOOD WORKS FOR THE VOICE AND HE'S NO FRIEND OF OURS.
OH YEAH?
YOUR FATHER IS IN JAIL--ON DEATH ROW.
DO YOU THINK HE DESERVES TO BE THERE?
NO.
HE WAS EMPEROR KURR WHEN HE CAUSED ALL THAT TROUBLE AND HIS EMPEROR KURR PERSONA IS GONE FOREVER. DAD'S BACK TO NORMAL.
AND, YEAH--EMPEROR KURR-- HE WAS A BAD DUDE. BUT THAT'S OVER. KURR IS GONE FOREVER AND DAD'S AN ORDINARY MAN NOW.
HE DOESN'T EVEN HAVE POWERS ANYMORE. HE'S AS HARMLESS AS A KITTEN.
HE USED TO BE A COP. HE SAVED THE WORLD A FEW TIMES-- I THINK THAT SHOULD COUNT FOR SOMETHING.

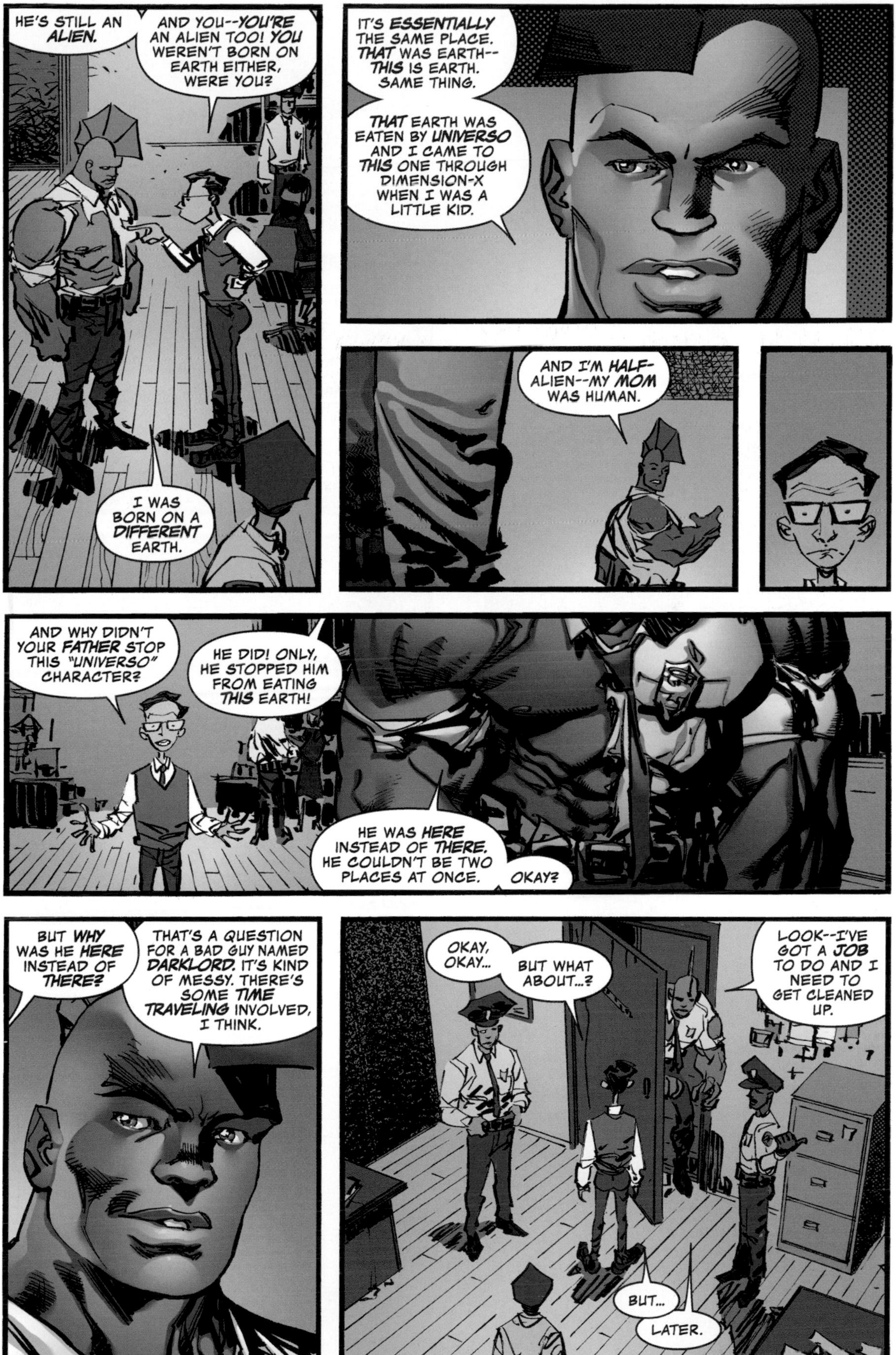

HE'S STILL AN ALIEN.
AND YOU--YOU'RE AN ALIEN TOO! YOU WEREN'T BORN ON EARTH EITHER, WERE YOU?
I WAS BORN ON A DIFFERENT EARTH.
IT'S ESSENTIALLY THE SAME PLACE. THAT WAS EARTH-- THIS IS EARTH. SAME THING.
THAT EARTH WAS EATEN BY UNIVERSO AND I CAME TO THIS ONE THROUGH DIMENSION-X WHEN I WAS A LITTLE KID.
AND I'M HALF-ALIEN--MY MOM WAS HUMAN.
AND WHY DIDN'T YOUR FATHER STOP THIS "UNIVERSO" CHARACTER?
HE DID! ONLY, HE STOPPED HIM FROM EATING THIS EARTH!
HE WAS HERE INSTEAD OF THERE. HE COULDN'T BE TWO PLACES AT ONCE.
OKAY?
BUT WHY WAS HE HERE INSTEAD OF THERE?
THAT'S A QUESTION FOR A BAD GUY NAMED DARKLORD. IT'S KIND OF MESSY. THERE'S SOME TIME TRAVELING INVOLVED, I THINK.
OKAY, OKAY...
BUT WHAT ABOUT...?
LOOK--I'VE GOT A JOB TO DO AND I NEED TO GET CLEANED UP.
BUT...
LATER.

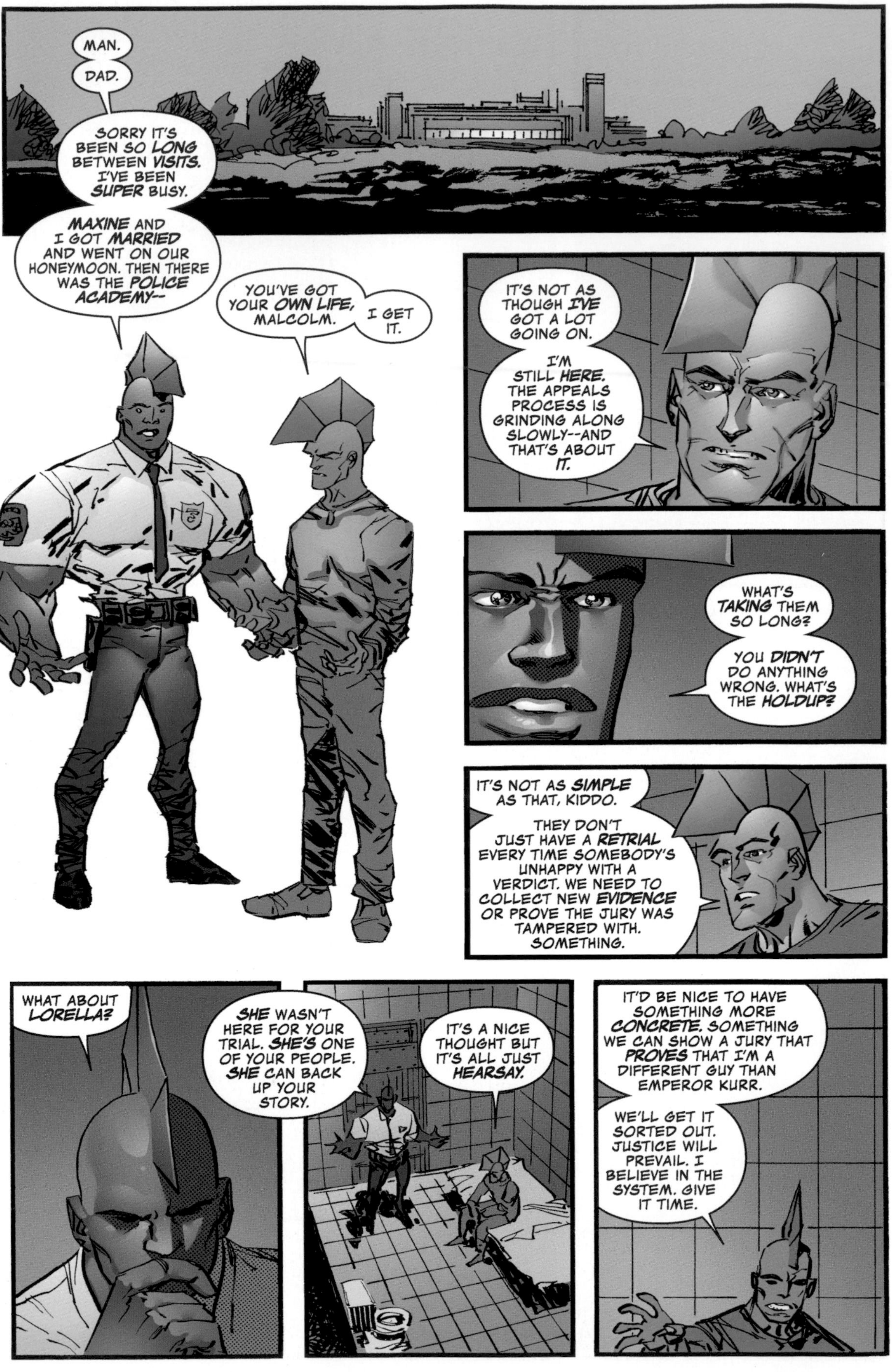
MAN.
DAD.
SORRY IT'S BEEN SO LONG BETWEEN VISITS. I'VE BEEN SUPER BUSY.
MAXINE AND I GOT MARRIED AND WENT ON OUR HONEYMOON. THEN THERE WAS THE POLICE ACADEMY--
YOU'VE GOT YOUR OWN LIFE, MALCOLM.
I GET IT.
IT'S NOT AS THOUGH I'VE GOT A LOT GOING ON.
I'M STILL HERE. THE APPEALS PROCESS IS GRINDING ALONG SLOWLY--AND THAT'S ABOUT IT.
WHAT'S TAKING THEM SO LONG?
YOU DIDN'T DO ANYTHING WRONG. WHAT'S THE HOLDUP?
IT'S NOT AS SIMPLE AS THAT, KIDDO.
THEY DON'T JUST HAVE A RETRIAL EVERY TIME SOMEBODY'S UNHAPPY WITH A VERDICT. WE NEED TO COLLECT NEW EVIDENCE OR PROVE THE JURY WAS TAMPERED WITH. SOMETHING.
WHAT ABOUT LORELLA?
SHE WASN'T HERE FOR YOUR TRIAL. SHE'S ONE OF YOUR PEOPLE. SHE CAN BACK UP YOUR STORY.
IT'S A NICE THOUGHT BUT IT'S ALL JUST HEARSAY.
IT'D BE NICE TO HAVE SOMETHING MORE CONCRETE. SOMETHING WE CAN SHOW A JURY THAT PROVES THAT I'M A DIFFERENT GUY THAN EMPEROR KURR.
WE'LL GET IT SORTED OUT. JUSTICE WILL PREVAIL. I BELIEVE IN THE SYSTEM. GIVE IT TIME.

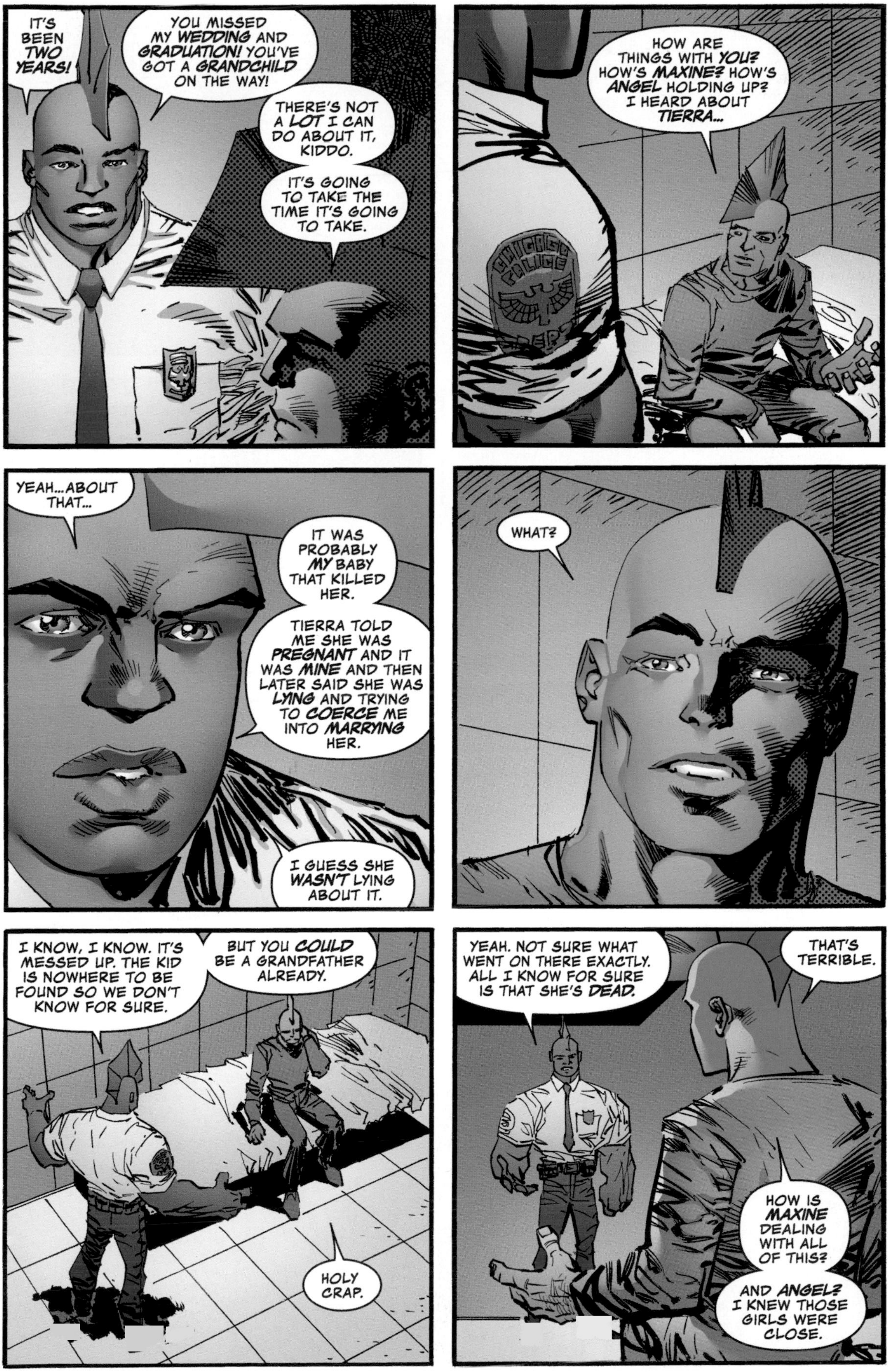
IT'S BEEN TWO YEARS!
YOU MISSED MY WEDDING AND GRADUATION! YOU'VE GOT A GRANDCHILD ON THE WAY!
THERE'S NOT A LOT I CAN DO ABOUT IT, KIDDO.
IT'S GOING TO TAKE THE TIME IT'S GOING TO TAKE.
HOW ARE THINGS WITH YOU? HOW'S MAXINE? HOW'S ANGEL HOLDING UP? I HEARD ABOUT TIERRA...
YEAH...ABOUT THAT...
IT WAS PROBABLY MY BABY THAT KILLED HER.
TIERRA TOLD ME SHE WAS PREGNANT AND IT WAS MINE AND THEN LATER SAID SHE WAS LYING AND TRYING TO COERCE ME INTO MARRYING HER.
I GUESS SHE WASN'T LYING ABOUT IT.
WHAT?
I KNOW, I KNOW. IT'S MESSED UP. THE KID IS NOWHERE TO BE FOUND SO WE DON'T KNOW FOR SURE.
BUT YOU COULD BE A GRANDFATHER ALREADY.
HOLY CRAP.
YEAH. NOT SURE WHAT WENT ON THERE EXACTLY. ALL I KNOW FOR SURE IS THAT SHE'S DEAD.
THAT'S TERRIBLE.
HOW IS MAXINE DEALING WITH ALL OF THIS?
AND ANGEL? I KNEW THOSE GIRLS WERE CLOSE.

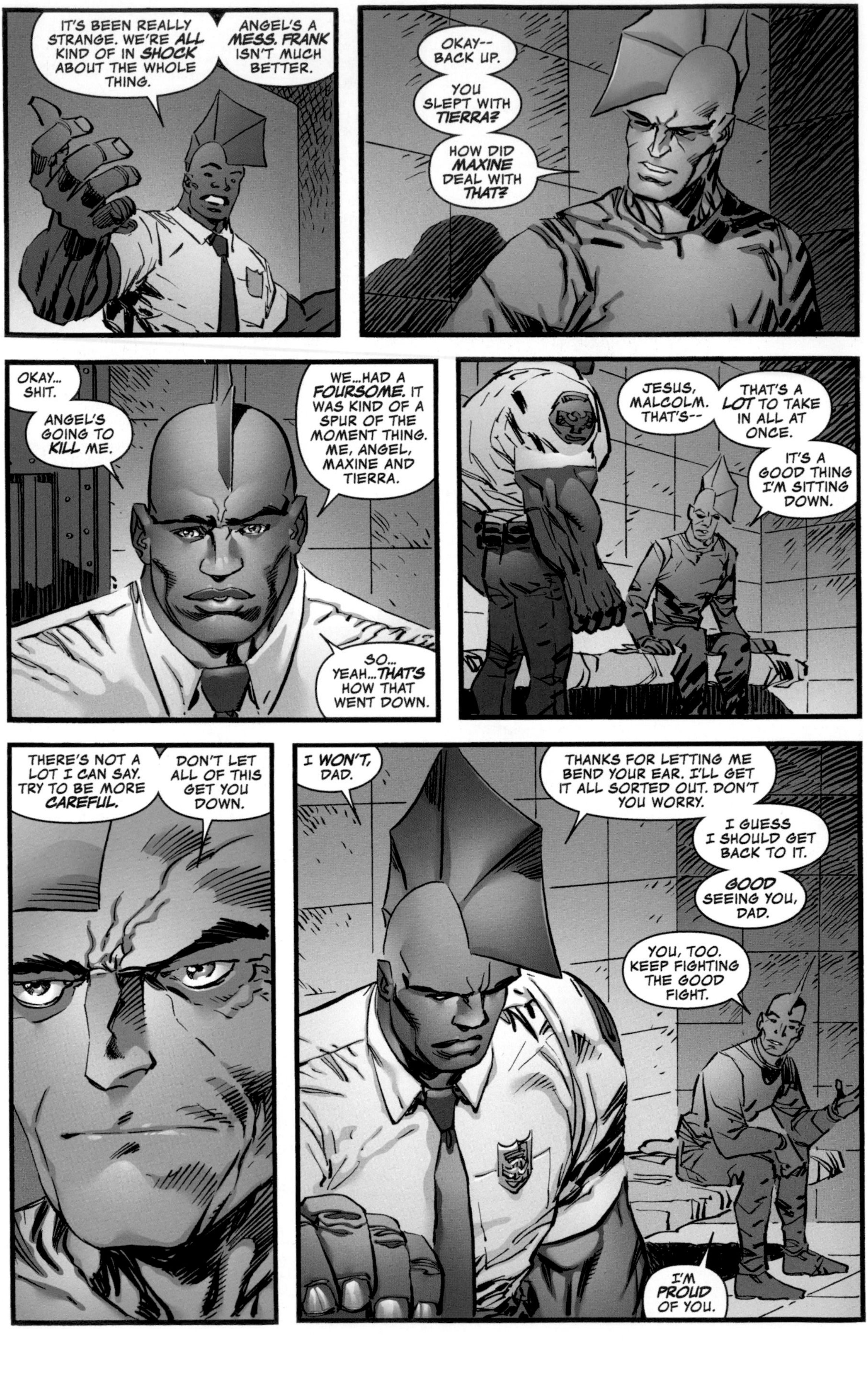
IT'S BEEN REALLY STRANGE. WE'RE ALL KIND OF IN SHOCK ABOUT THE WHOLE THING.
ANGEL'S A MESS. FRANK ISN'T MUCH BETTER.
OKAY-- BACK UP.
YOU SLEPT WITH TIERRA?
HOW DID MAXINE DEAL WITH THAT?
OKAY... SHIT.
ANGEL'S GOING TO KILL ME.
WE...HAD A FOURSOME. IT WAS KIND OF A SPUR OF THE MOMENT THING. ME, ANGEL, MAXINE AND TIERRA.
SO... YEAH...THAT'S HOW THAT WENT DOWN.
JESUS, MALCOLM. THAT'S--
THAT'S A LOT TO TAKE IN ALL AT ONCE.
IT'S A GOOD THING I'M SITTING DOWN.
THERE'S NOT A LOT I CAN SAY. TRY TO BE MORE CAREFUL.
DON'T LET ALL OF THIS GET YOU DOWN.
I WON'T, DAD.
THANKS FOR LETTING ME BEND YOUR EAR. I'LL GET IT ALL SORTED OUT. DON'T YOU WORRY.
I GUESS I SHOULD GET BACK TO IT.
GOOD SEEING YOU, DAD.
YOU, TOO. KEEP FIGHTING THE GOOD FIGHT.
I'M PROUD OF YOU.

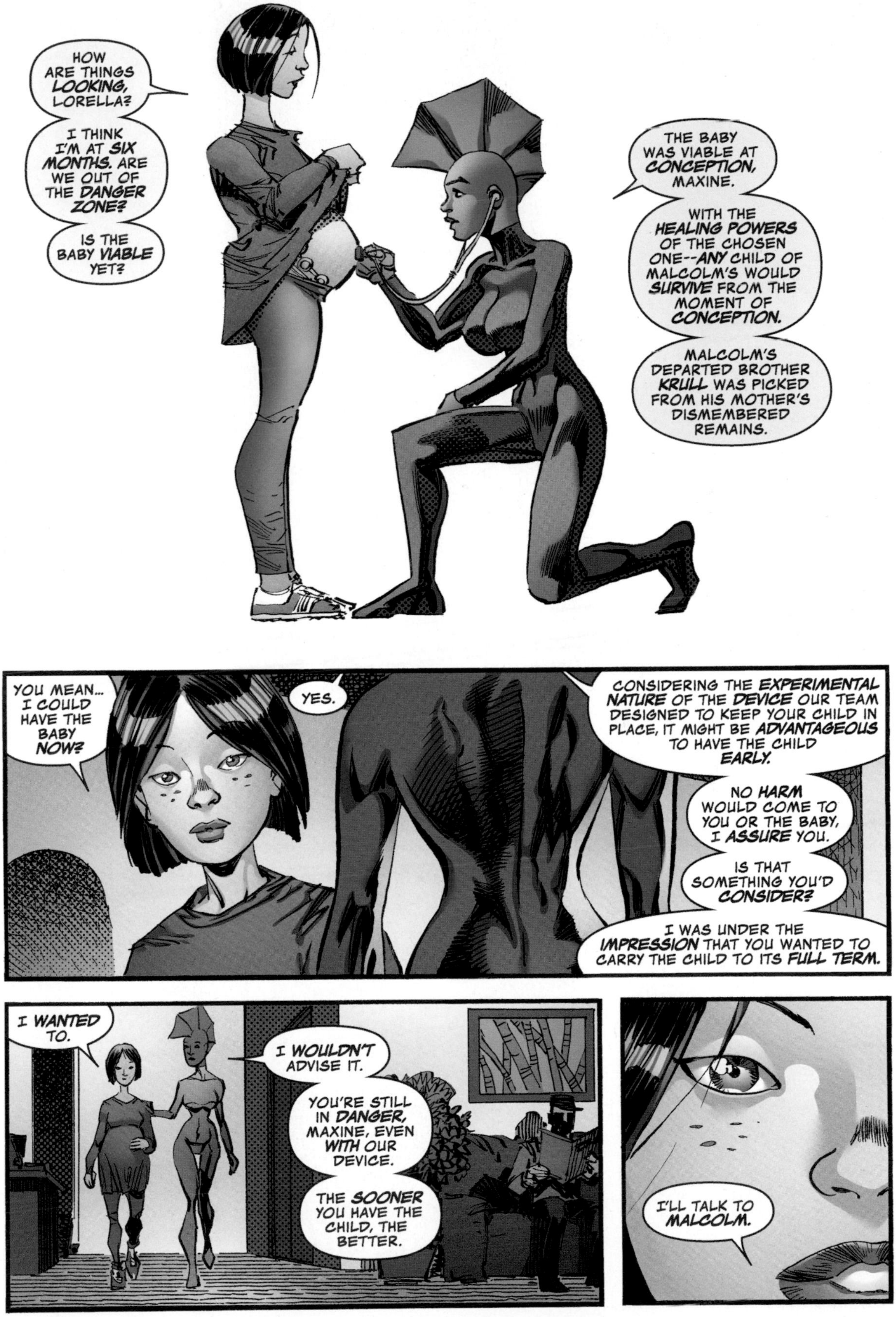
HOW ARE THINGS LOOKING, LORELLA?
I THINK I'M AT SIX MONTHS. ARE WE OUT OF THE DANGER ZONE?
IS THE BABY VIABLE YET?
THE BABY WAS VIABLE AT CONCEPTION, MAXINE.
WITH THE HEALING POWERS OF THE CHOSEN ONE--ANY CHILD OF MALCOLM'S WOULD SURVIVE FROM THE MOMENT OF CONCEPTION.
MALCOLM'S DEPARTED BROTHER KRULL WAS PICKED FROM HIS MOTHER'S DISMEMBERED REMAINS.
YOU MEAN... I COULD HAVE THE BABY NOW?
YES.
CONSIDERING THE EXPERIMENTAL NATURE OF THE DEVICE OUR TEAM DESIGNED TO KEEP YOUR CHILD IN PLACE, IT MIGHT BE ADVANTAGEOUS TO HAVE THE CHILD EARLY.
NO HARM WOULD COME TO YOU OR THE BABY, I ASSURE YOU.
IS THAT SOMETHING YOU'D CONSIDER?
I WAS UNDER THE IMPRESSION THAT YOU WANTED TO CARRY THE CHILD TO ITS FULL TERM.
I WANTED TO.
I WOULDN'T ADVISE IT.
YOU'RE STILL IN DANGER, MAXINE, EVEN WITH OUR DEVICE.
THE SOONER YOU HAVE THE CHILD, THE BETTER.
I'LL TALK TO MALCOLM.

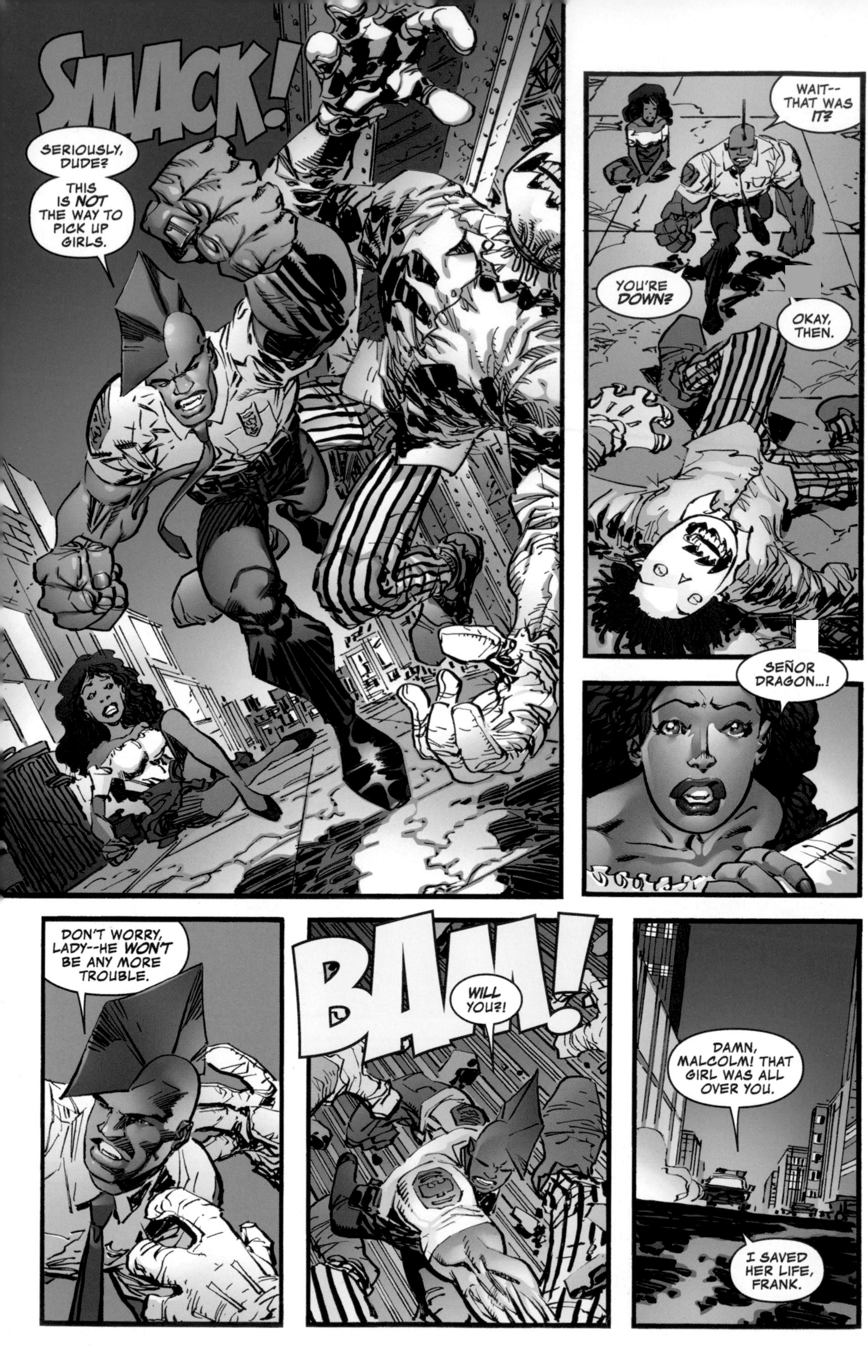
SMACK!
SERIOUSLY, DUDE?
THIS IS NOT THE WAY TO PICK UP GIRLS.
WAIT-- THAT WAS IT?
YOU'RE DOWN?
OKAY, THEN.
SEÑOR DRAGON...!
DON'T WORRY, LADY--HE WON'T BE ANY MORE TROUBLE.
BAM!
WILL YOU?!
DAMN, MALCOLM! THAT GIRL WAS ALL OVER YOU.
I SAVED HER LIFE, FRANK.

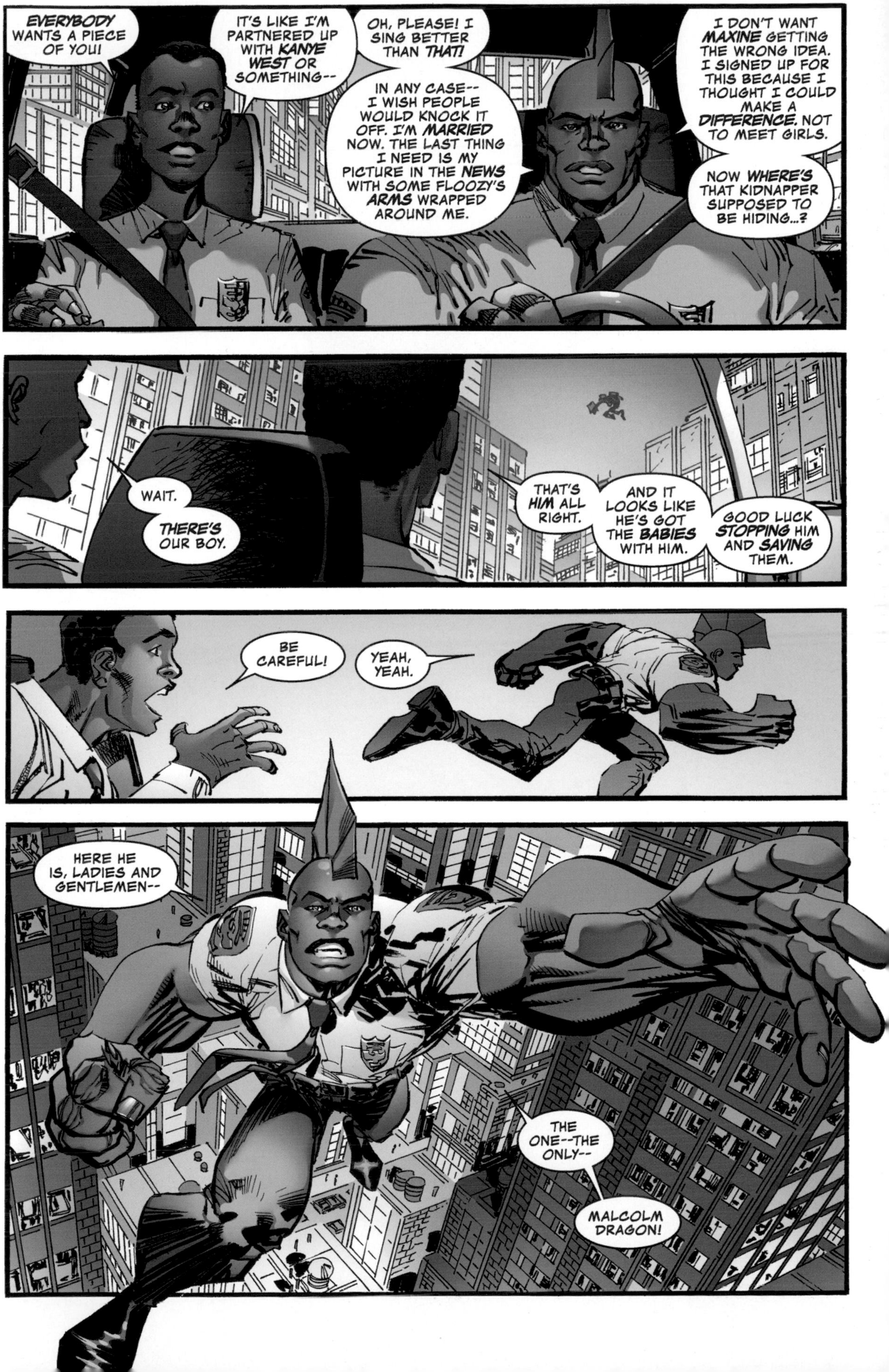
EVERYBODY WANTS A PIECE OF YOU!
IT'S LIKE I'M PARTNERED UP WITH KANYE WEST OR SOMETHING--
OH, PLEASE! I SING BETTER THAN THAT!
IN ANY CASE-- I WISH PEOPLE WOULD KNOCK IT OFF. I'M MARRIED NOW. THE LAST THING I NEED IS MY PICTURE IN THE NEWS WITH SOME FLOOZY'S ARMS WRAPPED AROUND ME.
I DON'T WANT MAXINE GETTING THE WRONG IDEA. I SIGNED UP FOR THIS BECAUSE I THOUGHT I COULD MAKE A DIFFERENCE. NOT TO MEET GIRLS.
NOW WHERE'S THAT KIDNAPPER SUPPOSED TO BE HIDING...?
WAIT.
THERE'S OUR BOY.
THAT'S HIM ALL RIGHT.
AND IT LOOKS LIKE HE'S GOT THE BABIES WITH HIM.
GOOD LUCK STOPPING HIM AND SAVING THEM.
BE CAREFUL!
YEAH, YEAH.
HERE HE IS, LADIES AND GENTLEMEN--
THE ONE--THE ONLY--
MALCOLM DRAGON!

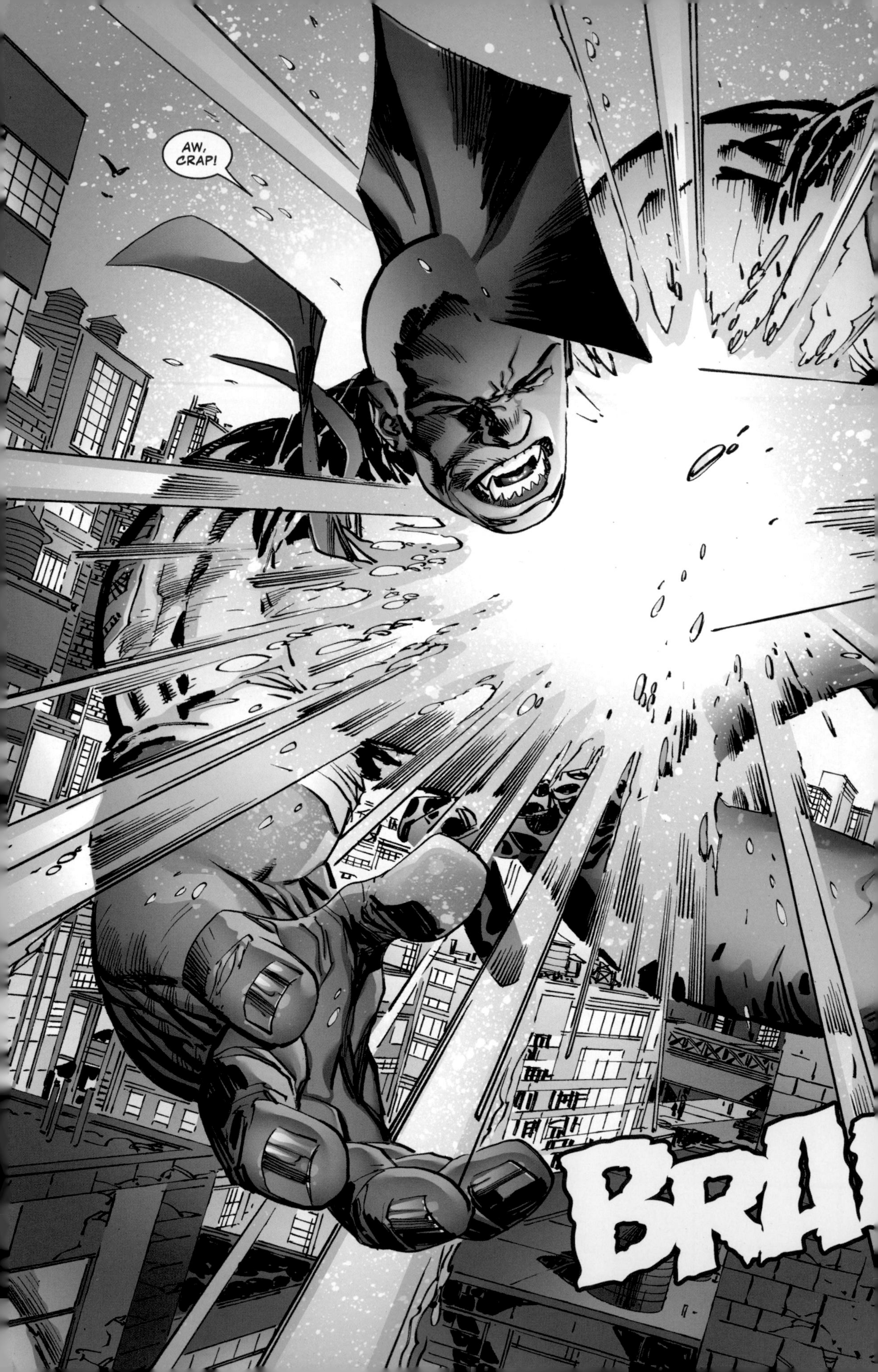
AW, CRAP!
BRA

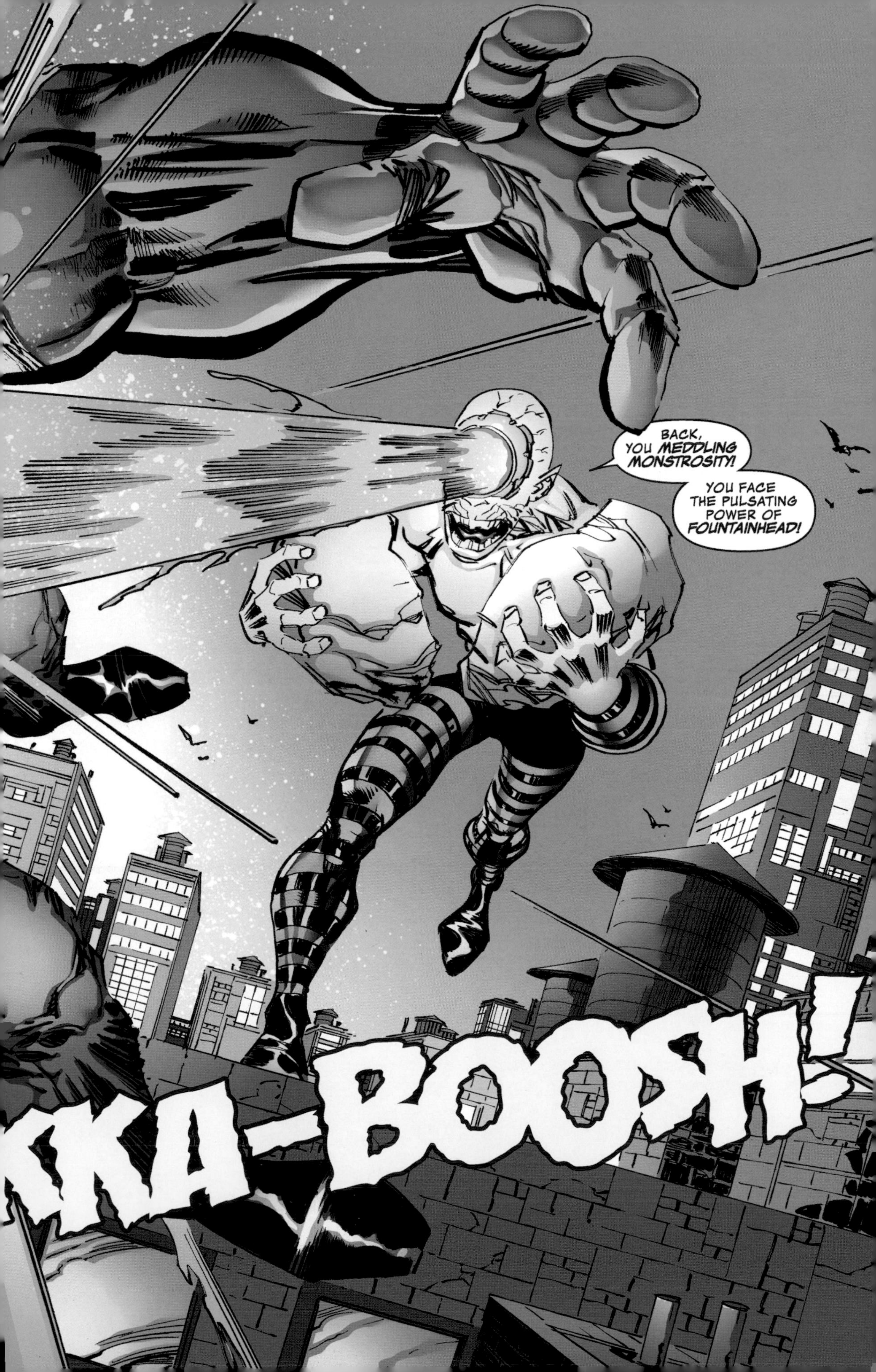
BACK, YOU MEDDLING MONSTROSITY!
YOU FACE THE PULSATING POWER OF FOUNTAINHEAD!
KA-BOOSH!

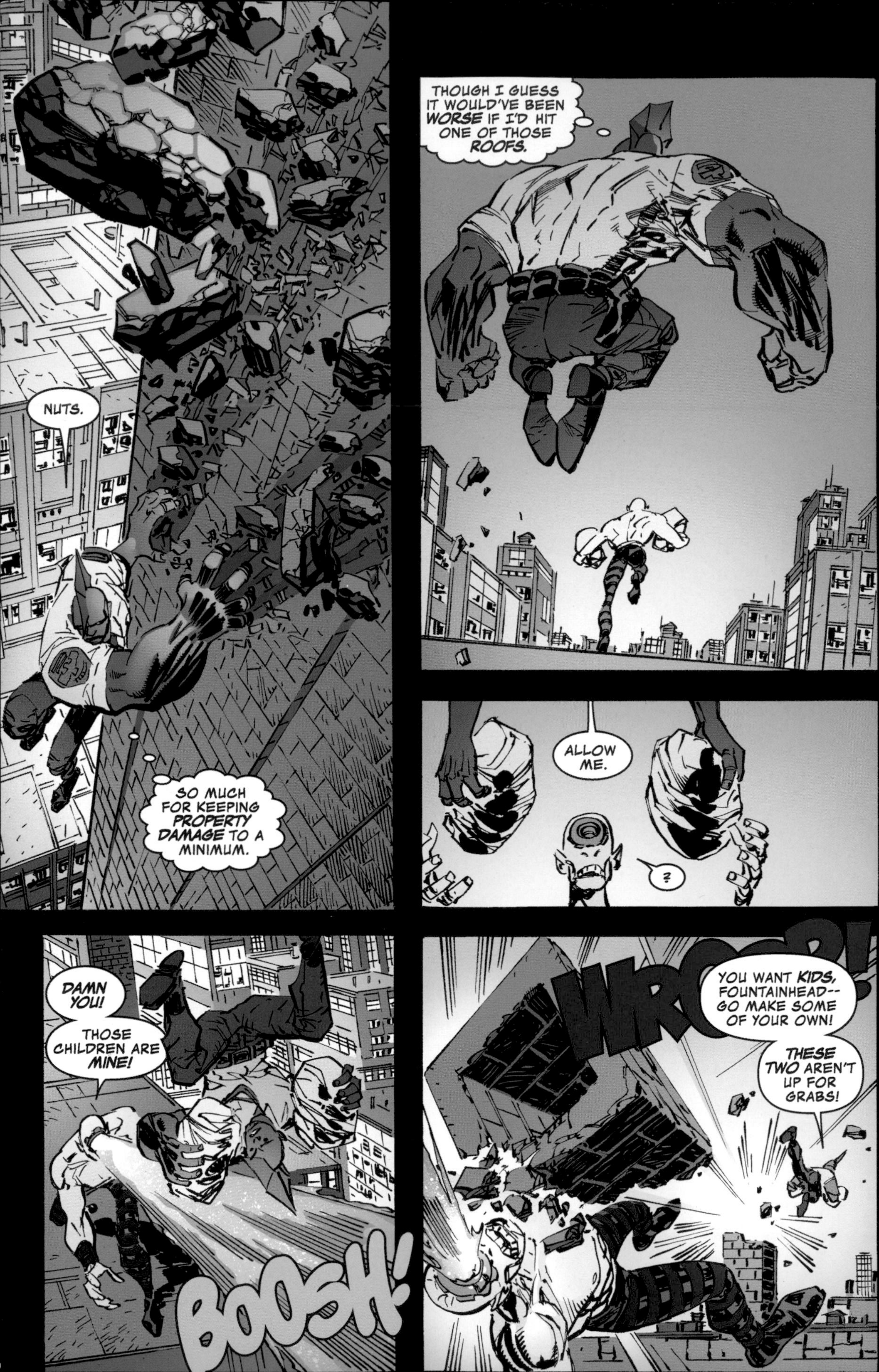
NUTS.
SO MUCH FOR KEEPING PROPERTY DAMAGE TO A MINIMUM.
THOUGH I GUESS IT WOULD'VE BEEN WORSE IF I'D HIT ONE OF THOSE ROOFS.
ALLOW ME.
?
DAMN YOU!
THOSE CHILDREN ARE MINE!
BOOSH!
WROOP!
YOU WANT KIDS, FOUNTAINHEAD-- GO MAKE SOME OF YOUR OWN!
THESE TWO AREN'T UP FOR GRABS!

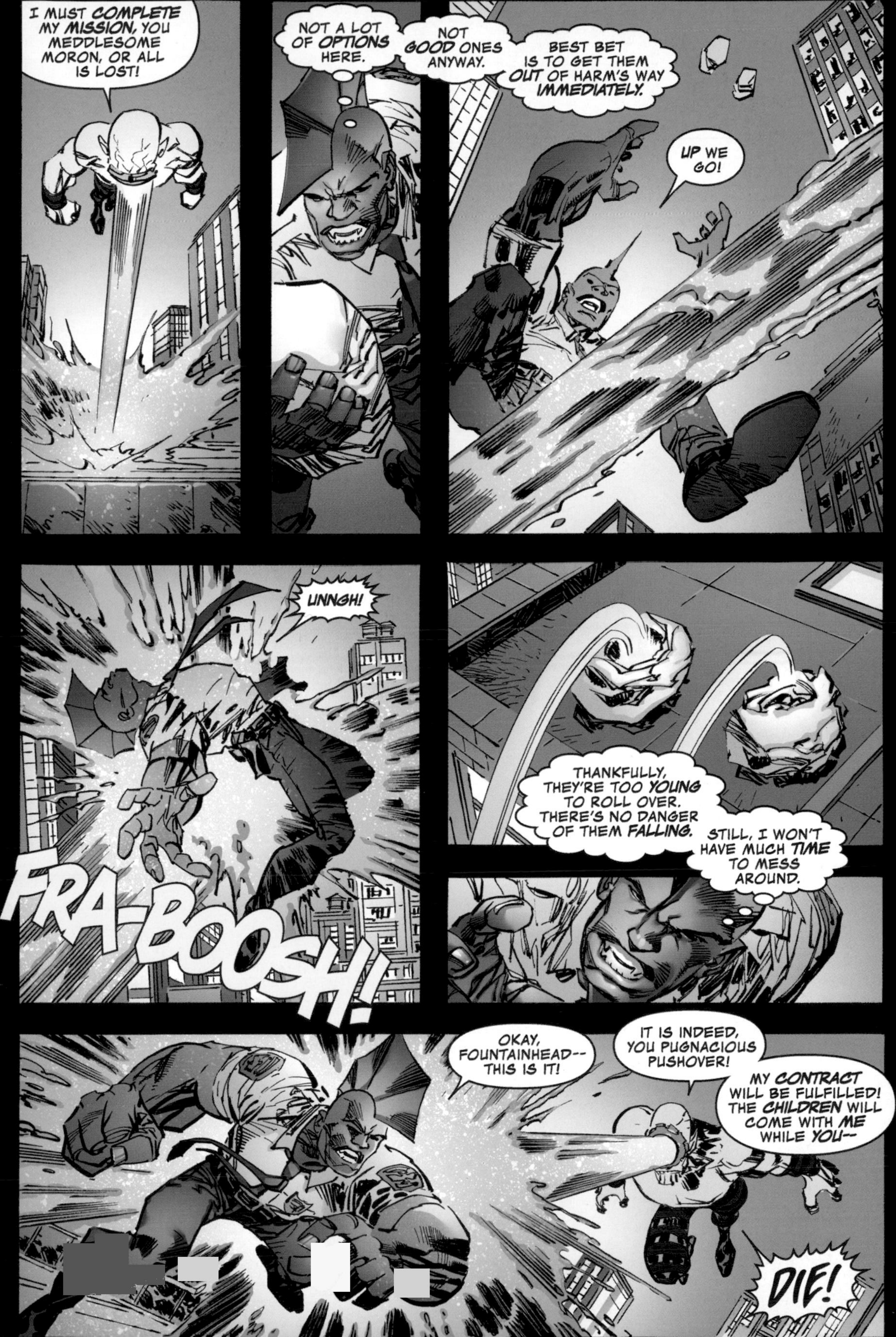

I MUST COMPLETE MY MISSION, YOU MEDDLESOME MORON, OR ALL IS LOST!
NOT A LOT OF OPTIONS HERE.
NOT GOOD ONES ANYWAY.
BEST BET IS TO GET THEM OUT OF HARM'S WAY IMMEDIATELY.
UP WE GO!
UNNGH!
FRA-BOOSH!
THANKFULLY, THEY'RE TOO YOUNG TO ROLL OVER. THERE'S NO DANGER OF THEM FALLING.
STILL, I WON'T HAVE MUCH TIME TO MESS AROUND.
OKAY, FOUNTAINHEAD-- THIS IS IT!
IT IS INDEED, YOU PUGNACIOUS PUSHOVER!
MY CONTRACT WILL BE FULFILLED! THE CHILDREN WILL COME WITH ME WHILE YOU--
DIE!

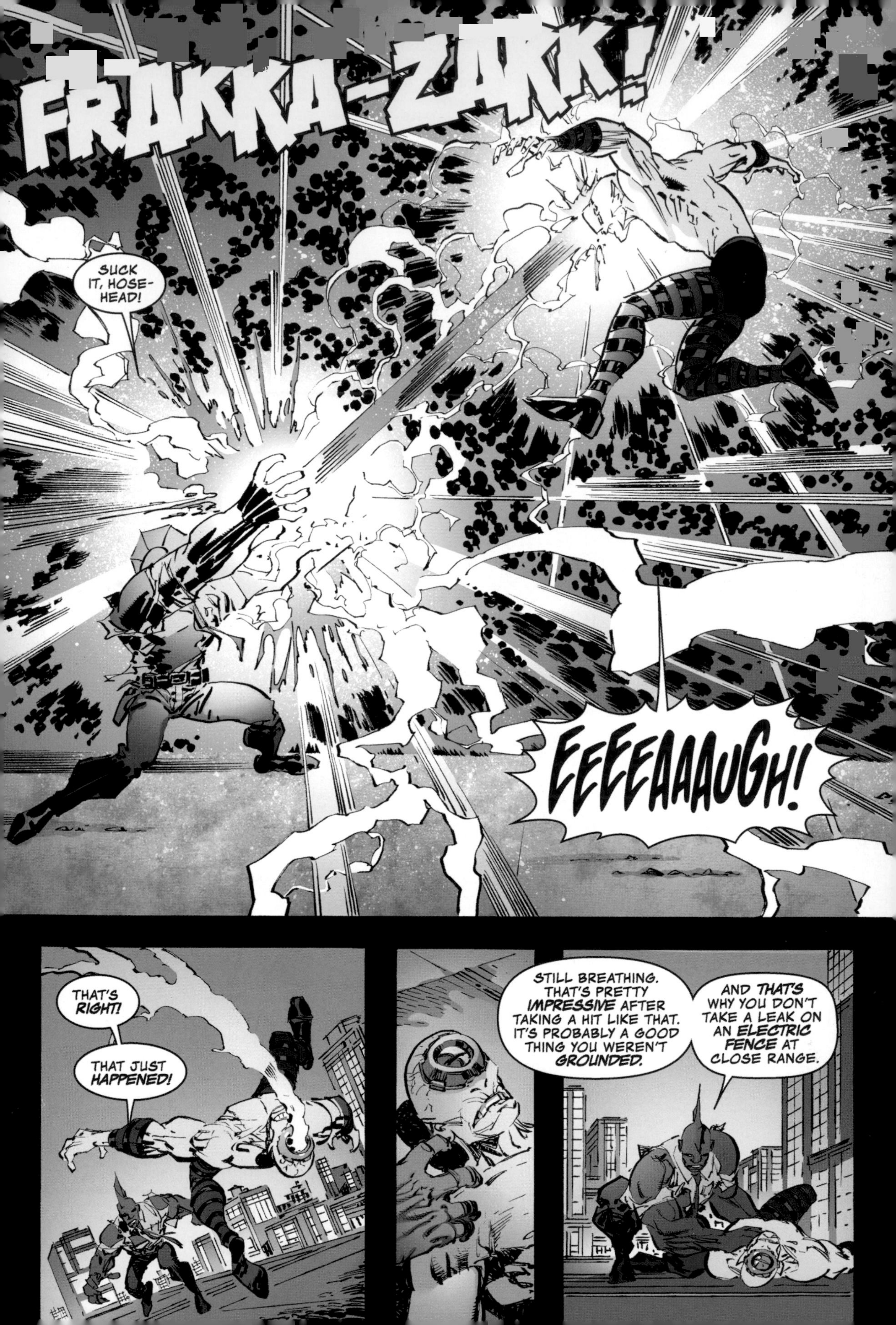

FRAKKA-ZARK!
SUCK IT, HOSE-HEAD!
EEEEAAAUGH!
THAT'S RIGHT!
THAT JUST HAPPENED!
STILL BREATHING. THAT'S PRETTY IMPRESSIVE AFTER TAKING A HIT LIKE THAT. IT'S PROBABLY A GOOD THING YOU WEREN'T GROUNDED.
AND THAT'S WHY YOU DON'T TAKE A LEAK ON AN ELECTRIC FENCE AT CLOSE RANGE.

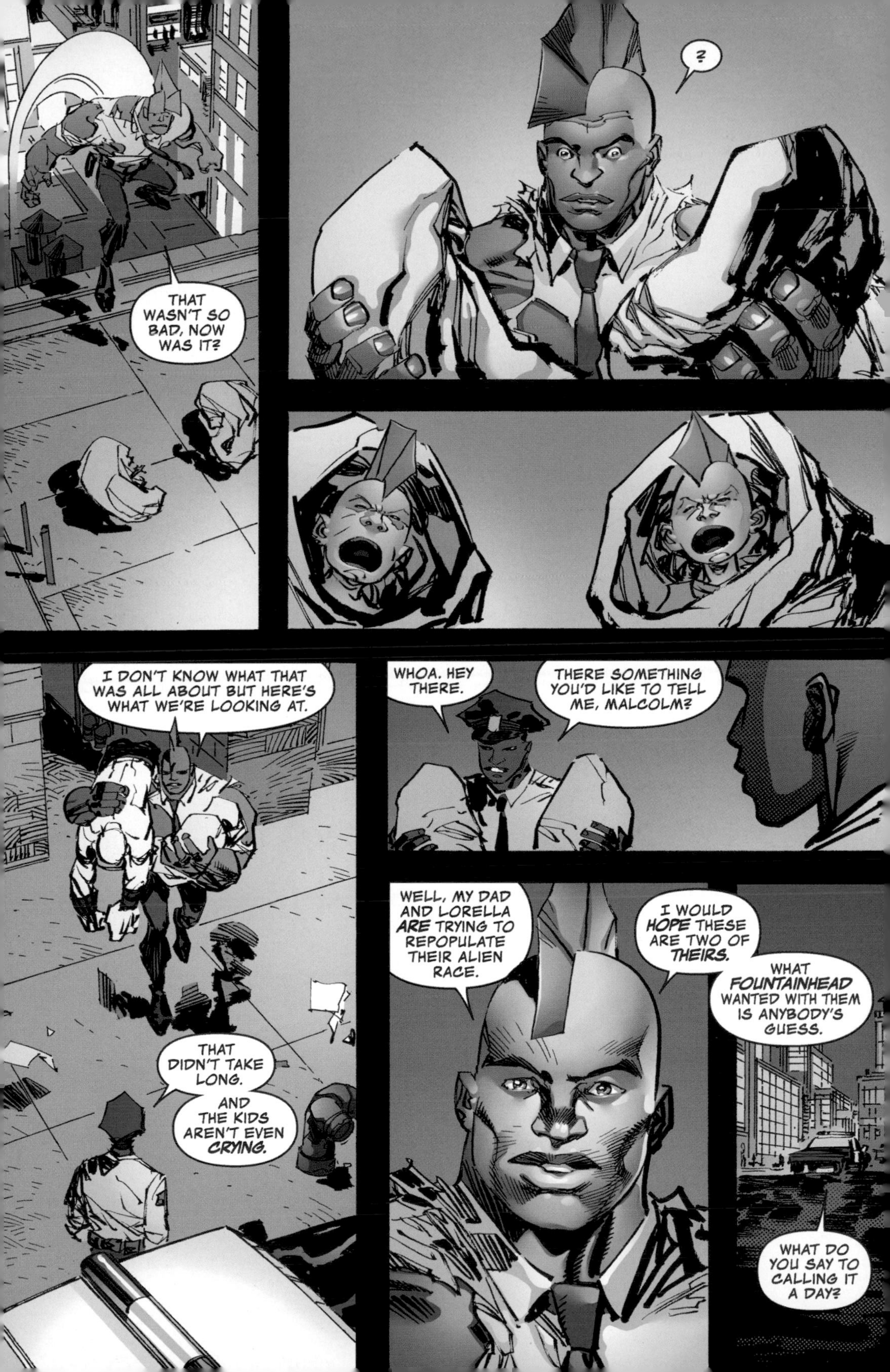
THAT WASN'T SO BAD, NOW WAS IT?
?
I DON'T KNOW WHAT THAT WAS ALL ABOUT BUT HERE'S WHAT WE'RE LOOKING AT.
THAT DIDN'T TAKE LONG.
AND THE KIDS AREN'T EVEN CRYING.
WHOA. HEY THERE.
THERE SOMETHING YOU'D LIKE TO TELL ME, MALCOLM?
WELL, MY DAD AND LORELLA ARE TRYING TO REPOPULATE THEIR ALIEN RACE.
I WOULD HOPE THESE ARE TWO OF THEIRS.
WHAT FOUNTAINHEAD WANTED WITH THEM IS ANYBODY'S GUESS.
WHAT DO YOU SAY TO CALLING IT A DAY?

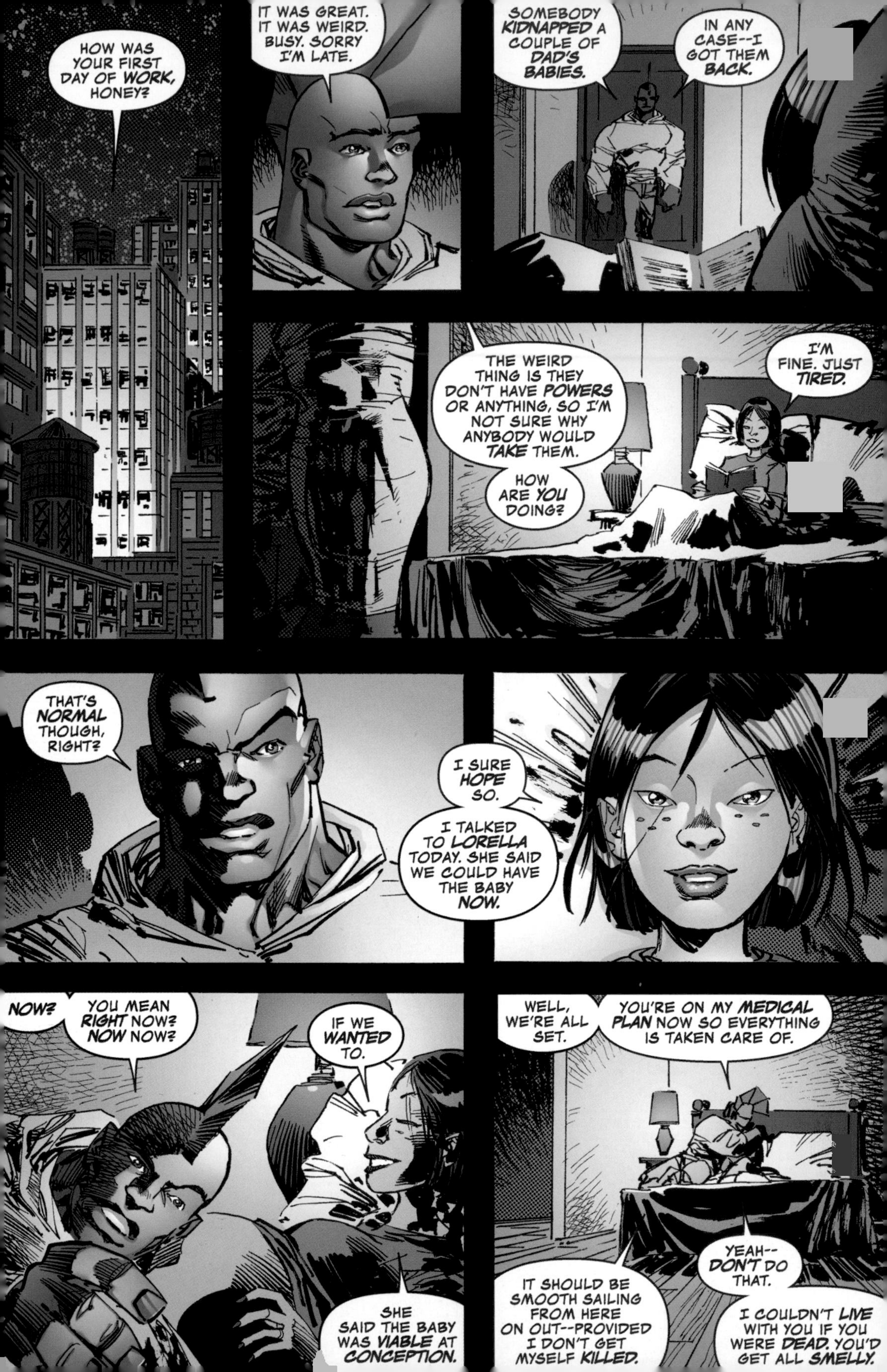
HOW WAS YOUR FIRST DAY OF WORK, HONEY?
IT WAS GREAT. IT WAS WEIRD. BUSY. SORRY I'M LATE.
SOMEBODY KIDNAPPED A COUPLE OF DAD'S BABIES.
IN ANY CASE--I GOT THEM BACK.
THE WEIRD THING IS THEY DON'T HAVE POWERS OR ANYTHING, SO I'M NOT SURE WHY ANYBODY WOULD TAKE THEM.
HOW ARE YOU DOING?
I'M FINE. JUST TIRED.
THAT'S NORMAL THOUGH, RIGHT?
I SURE HOPE SO.
I TALKED TO LORELLA TODAY. SHE SAID WE COULD HAVE THE BABY NOW.
NOW?
YOU MEAN RIGHT NOW? NOW NOW?
IF WE WANTED TO.
SHE SAID THE BABY WAS VIABLE AT CONCEPTION.
WELL, WE'RE ALL SET.
YOU'RE ON MY MEDICAL PLAN NOW SO EVERYTHING IS TAKEN CARE OF.
IT SHOULD BE SMOOTH SAILING FROM HERE ON OUT--PROVIDED I DON'T GET MYSELF KILLED.
YEAH-- DON'T DO THAT.
I COULDN'T LIVE WITH YOU IF YOU WERE DEAD. YOU'D GET ALL SMELLY.

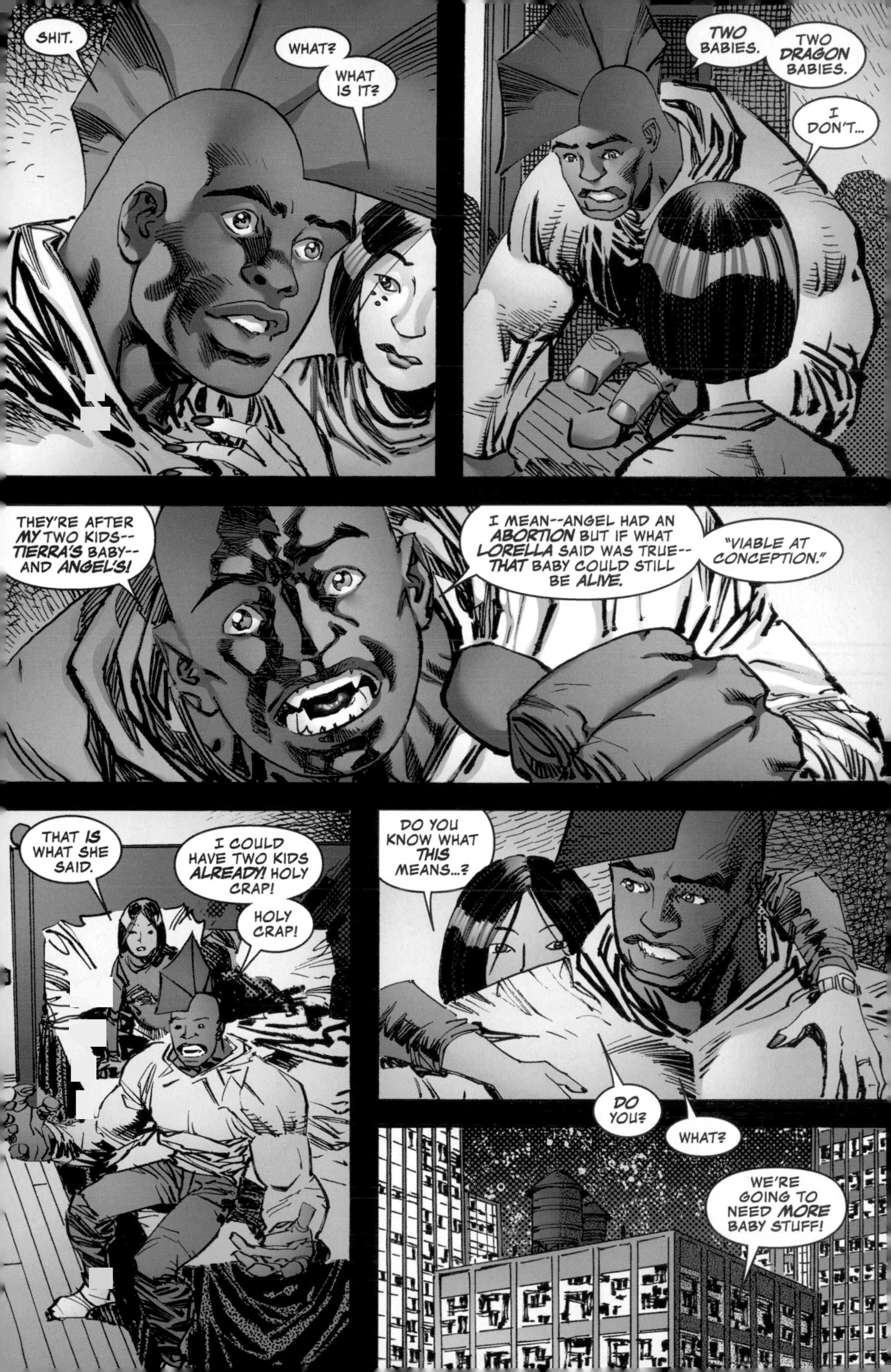
SHIT.
WHAT?
WHAT IS IT?
TWO BABIES.
TWO DRAGON BABIES.
I DON'T...
THEY'RE AFTER MY TWO KIDS-- TIERRA'S BABY-- AND ANGEL'S!
I MEAN--ANGEL HAD AN ABORTION BUT IF WHAT LORELLA SAID WAS TRUE-- THAT BABY COULD STILL BE ALIVE.
"VIABLE AT CONCEPTION."
THAT IS WHAT SHE SAID.
I COULD HAVE TWO KIDS ALREADY! HOLY CRAP!
HOLY CRAP!
DO YOU KNOW WHAT THIS MEANS...?
DO YOU?
WHAT?
WE'RE GOING TO NEED MORE BABY STUFF!

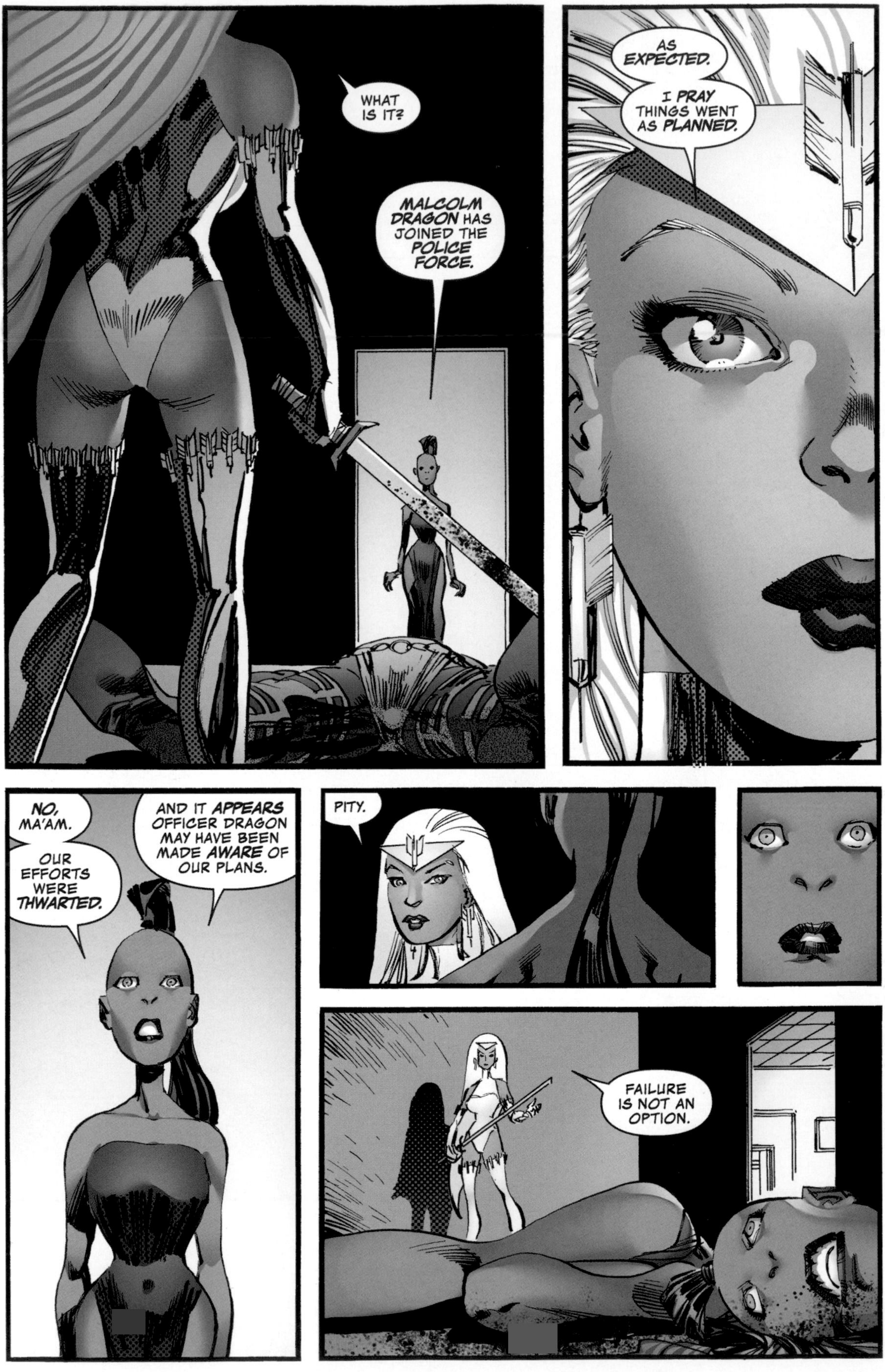
WHAT IS IT?
MALCOLM DRAGON HAS JOINED THE POLICE FORCE.
AS EXPECTED.
I PRAY THINGS WENT AS PLANNED.
NO, MA'AM.
OUR EFFORTS WERE THWARTED.
AND IT APPEARS OFFICER DRAGON MAY HAVE BEEN MADE AWARE OF OUR PLANS.
PITY.
FAILURE IS NOT AN OPTION.

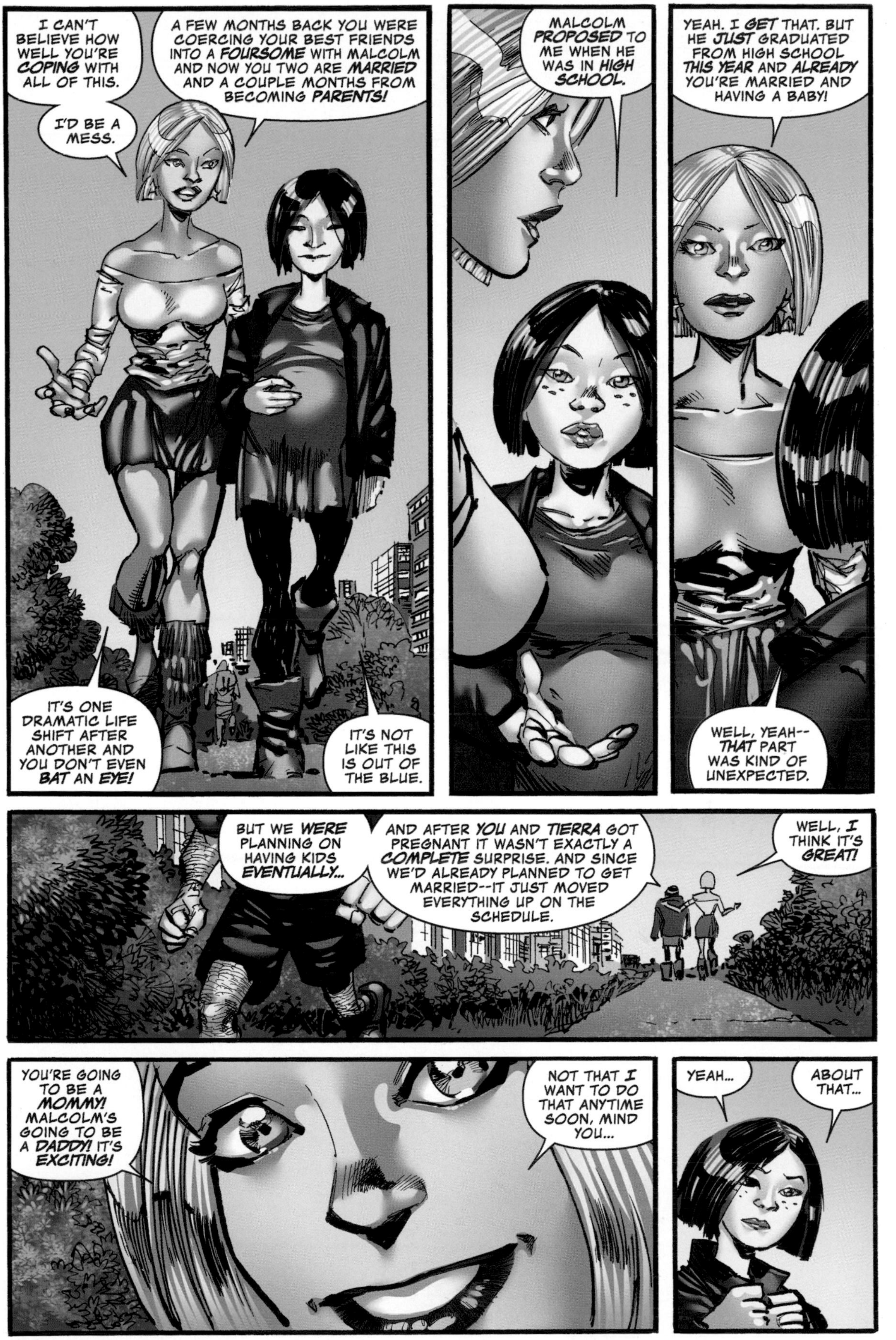
I CAN'T BELIEVE HOW WELL YOU'RE COPING WITH ALL OF THIS.
I'D BE A MESS.
A FEW MONTHS BACK YOU WERE COERCING YOUR BEST FRIENDS INTO A FOURSOME WITH MALCOLM AND NOW YOU TWO ARE MARRIED AND A COUPLE MONTHS FROM BECOMING PARENTS!
IT'S ONE DRAMATIC LIFE SHIFT AFTER ANOTHER AND YOU DON'T EVEN BAT AN EYE!
IT'S NOT LIKE THIS IS OUT OF THE BLUE.
MALCOLM PROPOSED TO ME WHEN HE WAS IN HIGH SCHOOL.
YEAH. I GET THAT. BUT HE JUST GRADUATED FROM HIGH SCHOOL THIS YEAR AND ALREADY YOU'RE MARRIED AND HAVING A BABY!
WELL, YEAH-- THAT PART WAS KIND OF UNEXPECTED.
BUT WE WERE PLANNING ON HAVING KIDS EVENTUALLY...
AND AFTER YOU AND TIERRA GOT PREGNANT IT WASN'T EXACTLY A COMPLETE SURPRISE. AND SINCE WE'D ALREADY PLANNED TO GET MARRIED--IT JUST MOVED EVERYTHING UP ON THE SCHEDULE.
WELL, I THINK IT'S GREAT!
YOU'RE GOING TO BE A MOMMY! MALCOLM'S GOING TO BE A DADDY! IT'S EXCITING!
NOT THAT I WANT TO DO THAT ANYTIME SOON, MIND YOU...
YEAH...
ABOUT THAT...

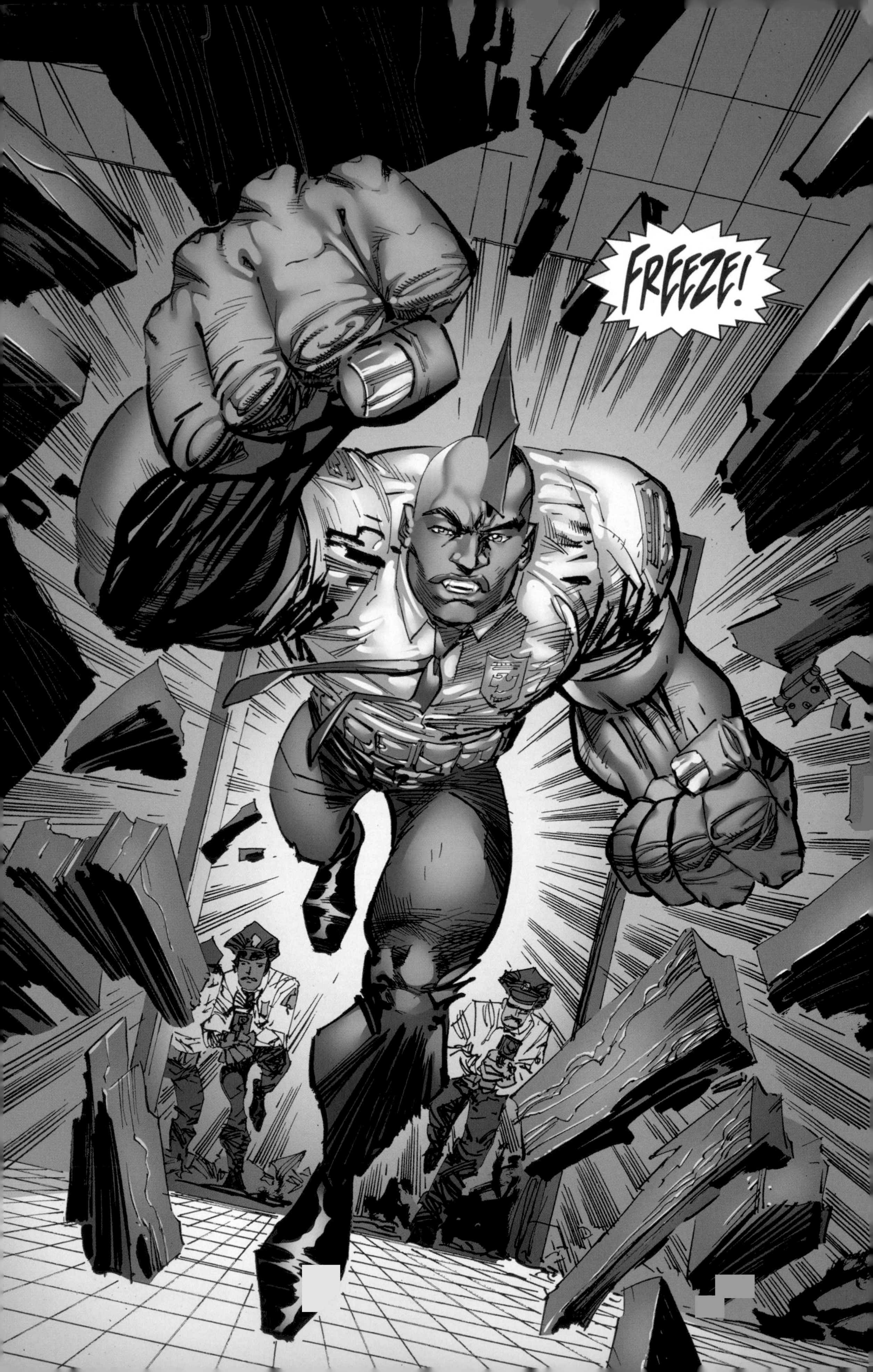
FREEZE!

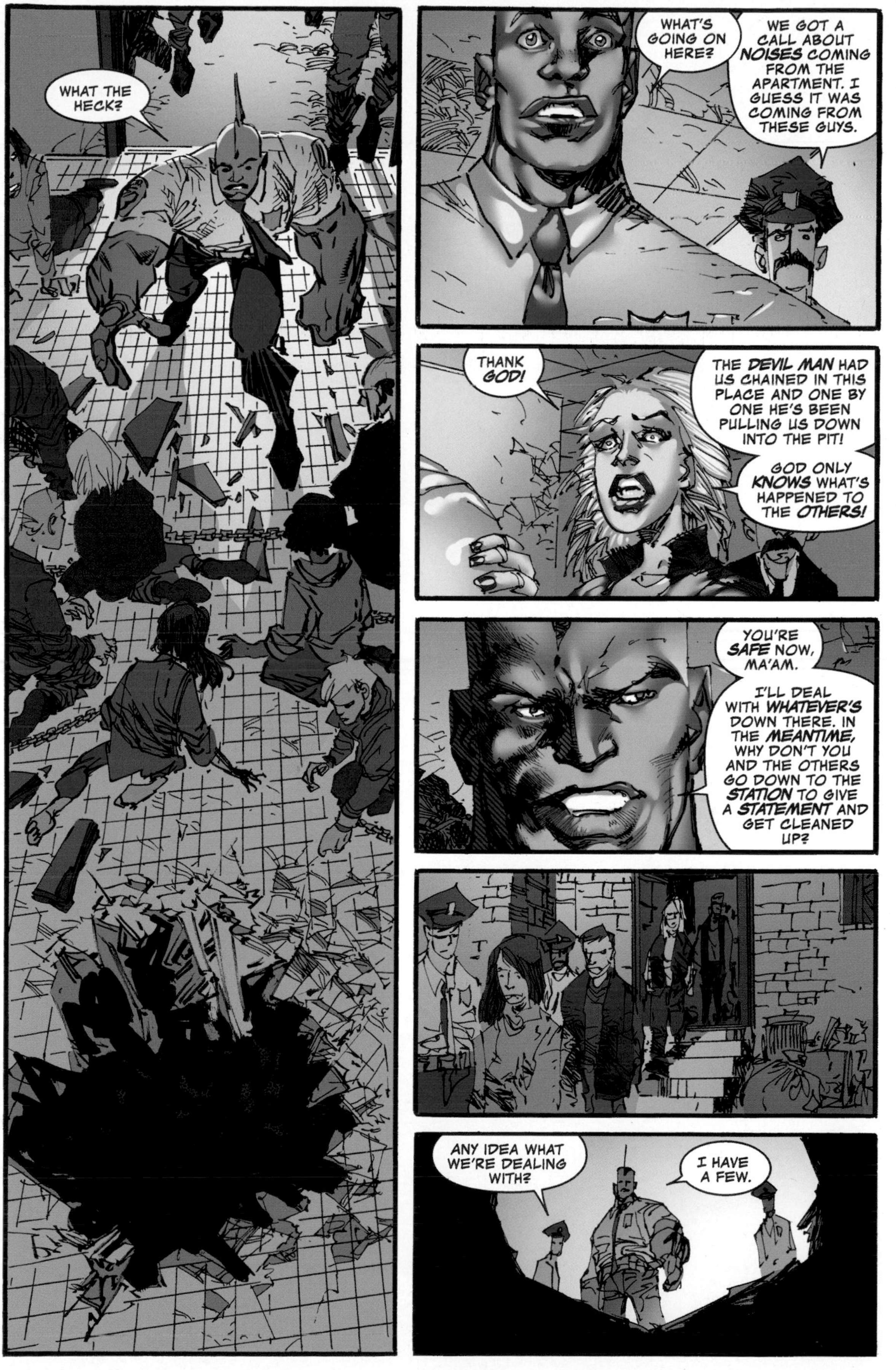

WHAT THE HECK?
WHAT'S GOING ON HERE?
WE GOT A CALL ABOUT NOISES COMING FROM THE APARTMENT. I GUESS IT WAS COMING FROM THESE GUYS.
THANK GOD!
THE DEVIL MAN HAD US CHAINED IN THIS PLACE AND ONE BY ONE HE'S BEEN PULLING US DOWN INTO THE PIT!
GOD ONLY KNOWS WHAT'S HAPPENED TO THE OTHERS!
YOU'RE SAFE NOW, MA'AM.
I'LL DEAL WITH WHATEVER'S DOWN THERE. IN THE MEANTIME, WHY DON'T YOU AND THE OTHERS GO DOWN TO THE STATION TO GIVE A STATEMENT AND GET CLEANED UP?
ANY IDEA WHAT WE'RE DEALING WITH?
I HAVE A FEW.

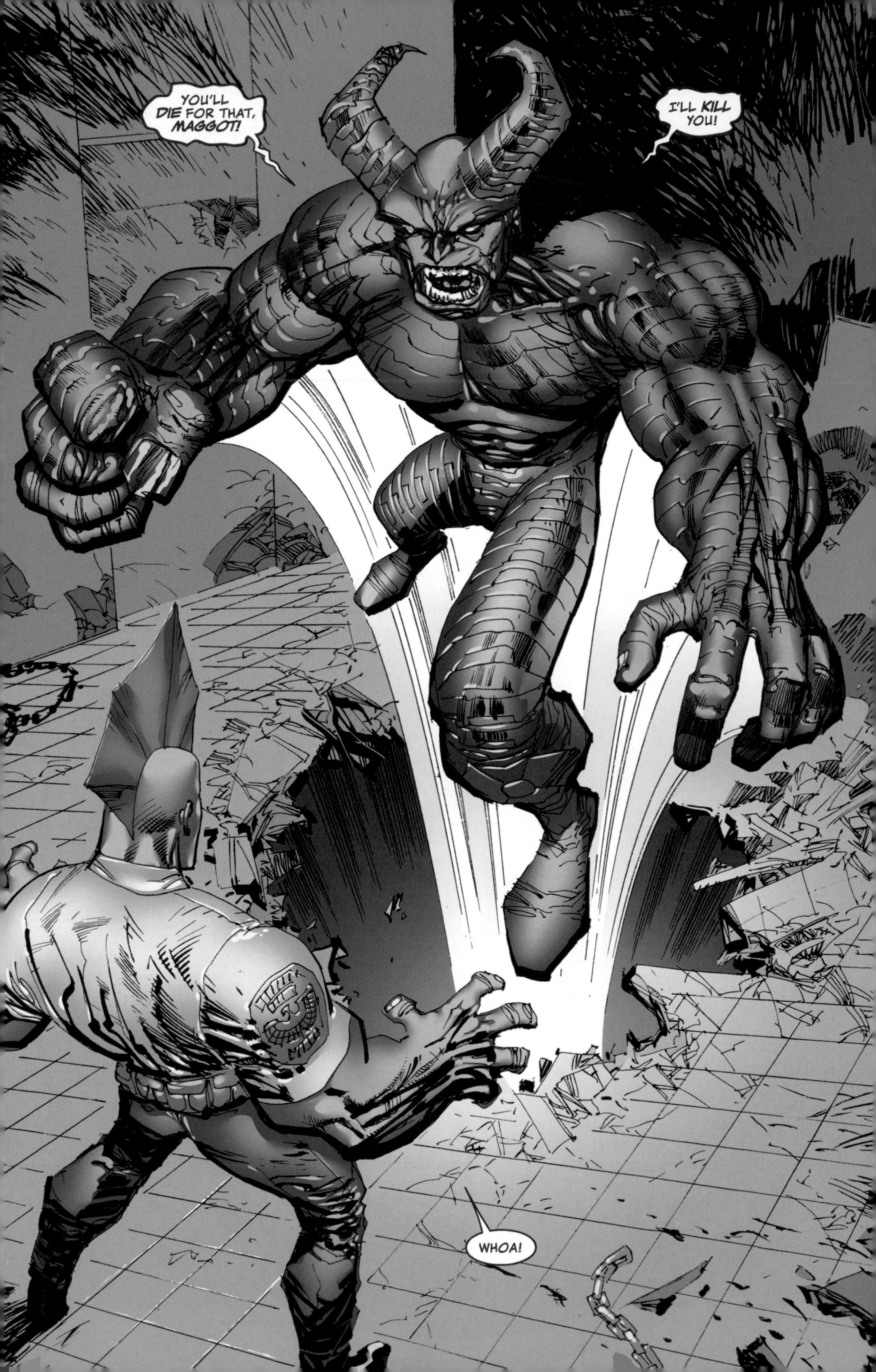
YOU'LL DIE FOR THAT, MAGGOT!
I'LL KILL YOU!
WHOA!

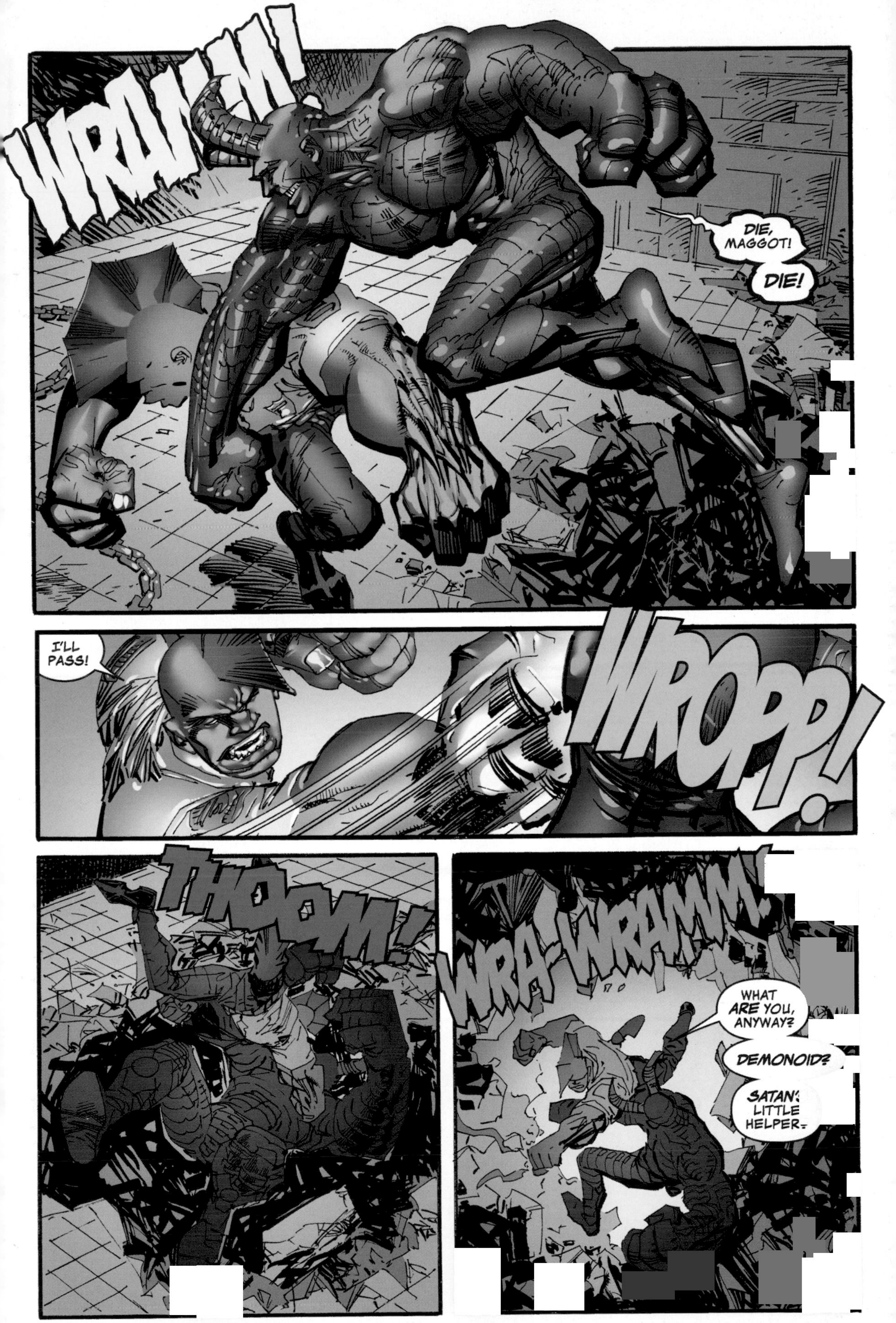
DIE, MAGGOT!
DIE!
I'LL PASS!
WROPP!
THOOM!
WRA-WRAMM!
WHAT ARE YOU, ANYWAY?
DEMONOID?
SATAN'S LITTLE HELPER?

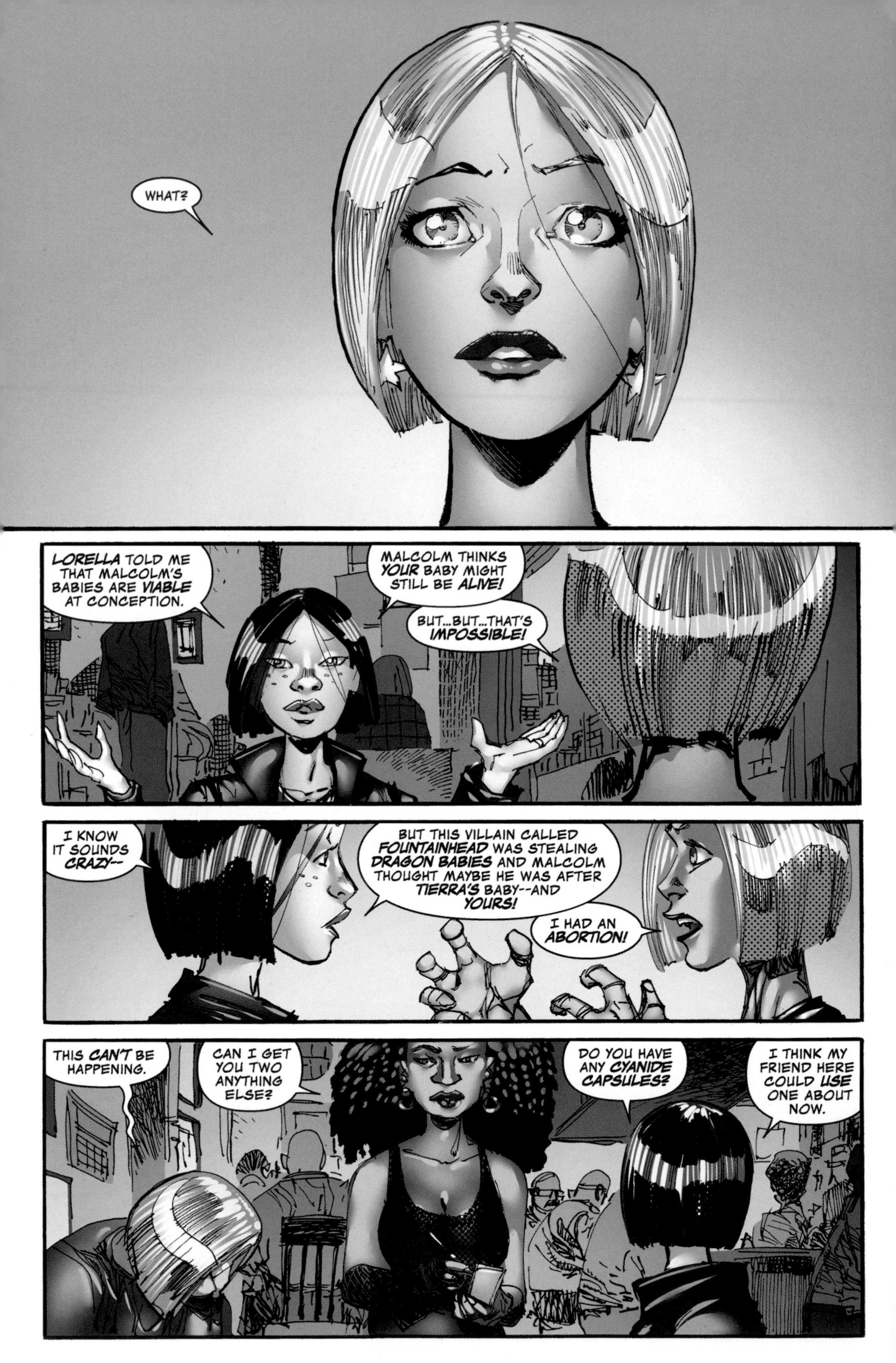
WHAT?
LORELLA TOLD ME THAT MALCOLM'S BABIES ARE VIABLE AT CONCEPTION.
MALCOLM THINKS YOUR BABY MIGHT STILL BE ALIVE!
BUT...BUT...THAT'S IMPOSSIBLE!
I KNOW IT SOUNDS CRAZY--
BUT THIS VILLAIN CALLED FOUNTAINHEAD WAS STEALING DRAGON BABIES AND MALCOLM THOUGHT MAYBE HE WAS AFTER TIERRA'S BABY--AND YOURS!
I HAD AN ABORTION!
THIS CAN'T BE HAPPENING.
CAN I GET YOU TWO ANYTHING ELSE?
DO YOU HAVE ANY CYANIDE CAPSULES?
I THINK MY FRIEND HERE COULD USE ONE ABOUT NOW.

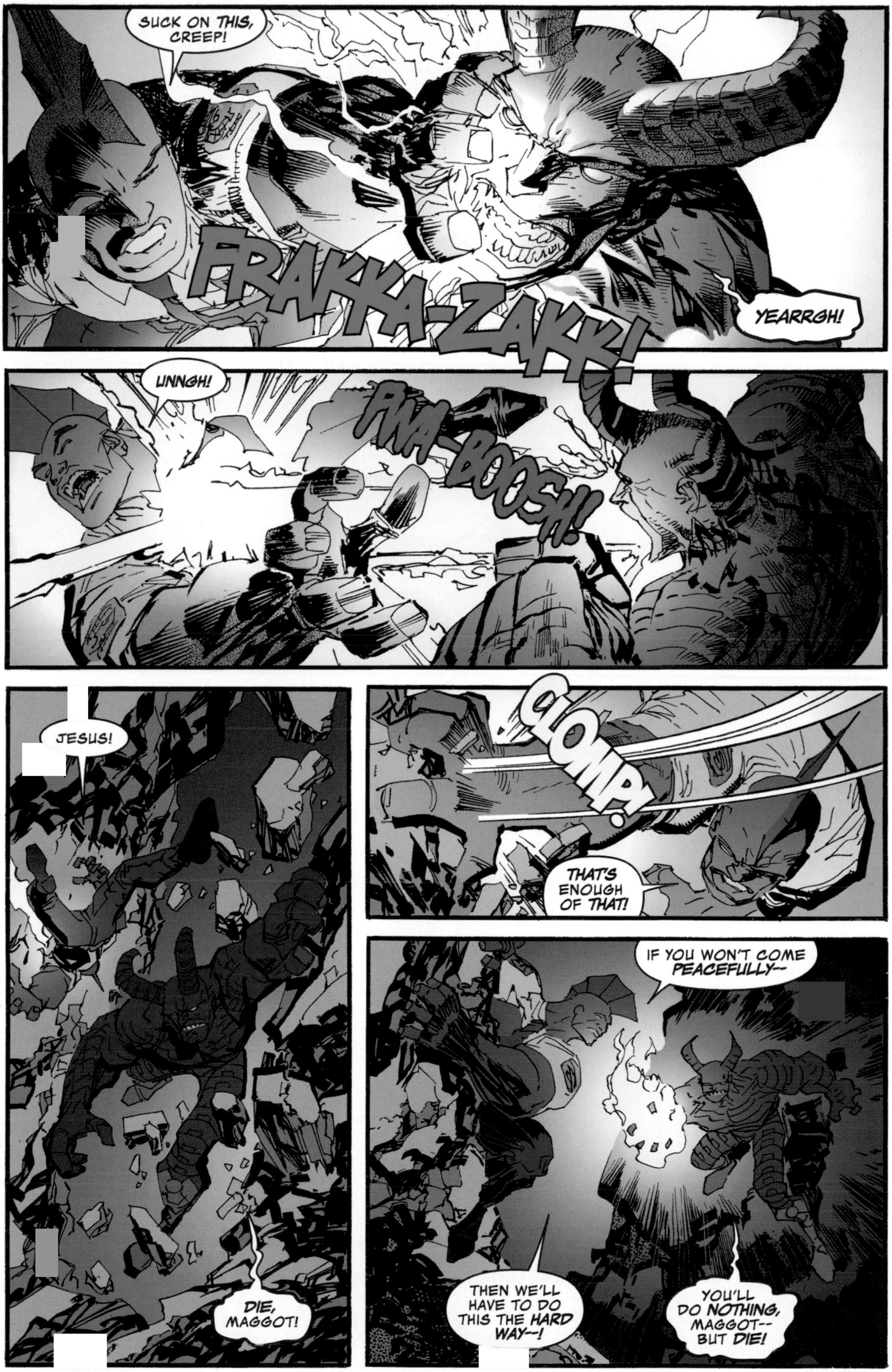
SUCK ON THIS, CREEP!
FRAKKA-ZAKK!
YEARRGH!
UNNGH!
FWA-BOOSH!
JESUS!
DIE, MAGGOT!
CLOMP!
THAT'S ENOUGH OF THAT!
IF YOU WON'T COME PEACEFULLY--
THEN WE'LL HAVE TO DO THIS THE HARD WAY--!
YOU'LL DO NOTHING, MAGGOT-- BUT DIE!

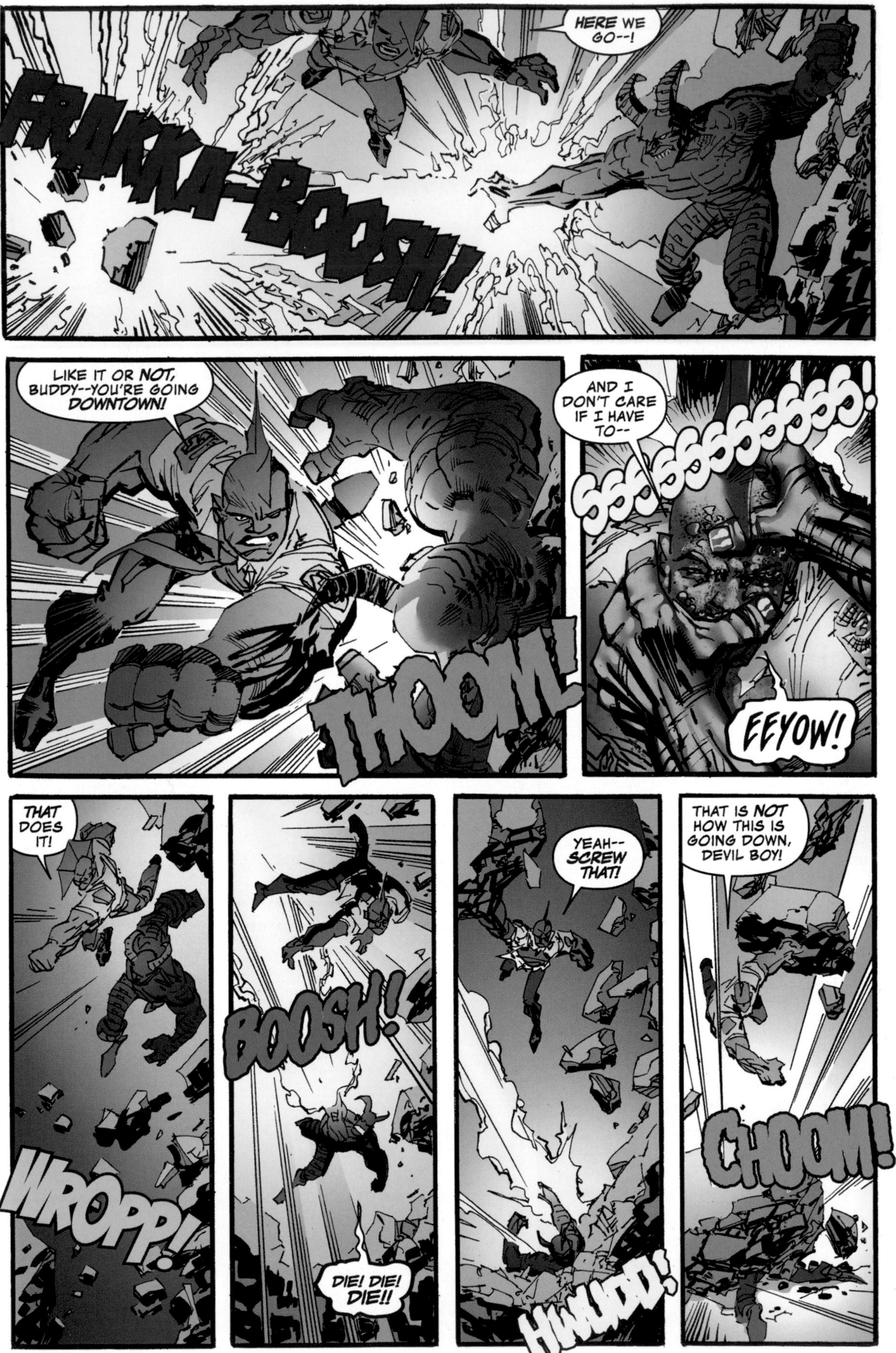
HERE WE GO--!
FRAKKA-BOOSH!
LIKE IT OR NOT, BUDDY--YOU'RE GOING DOWNTOWN!
THOOM!
AND I DON'T CARE IF I HAVE TO--
SSSSSSSSSSSSSSS!
EEYOW!
THAT DOES IT!
WROPP!
BOOSH!
DIE! DIE! DIE!!
YEAH--SCREW THAT!
HWUDD!
THAT IS NOT HOW THIS IS GOING DOWN, DEVIL BOY!
CHOOM!

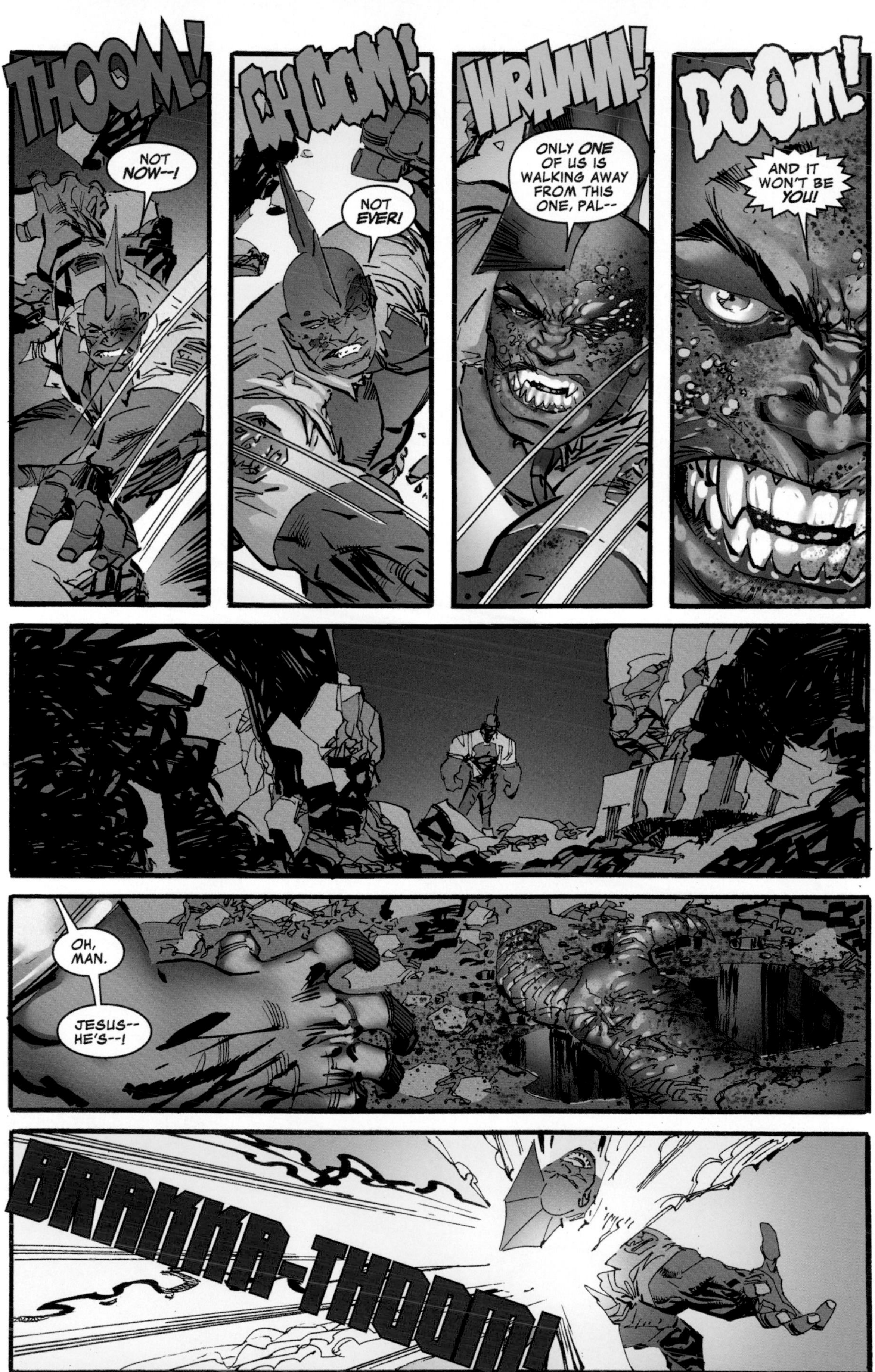
THOOM!
NOT NOW--!
CHOOM!
NOT EVER!
WRAMM!
ONLY ONE OF US IS WALKING AWAY FROM THIS ONE, PAL--
DOOM!
AND IT WON'T BE YOU!
OH, MAN.
JESUS-- HE'S--!
BRAKKA-THOOM!

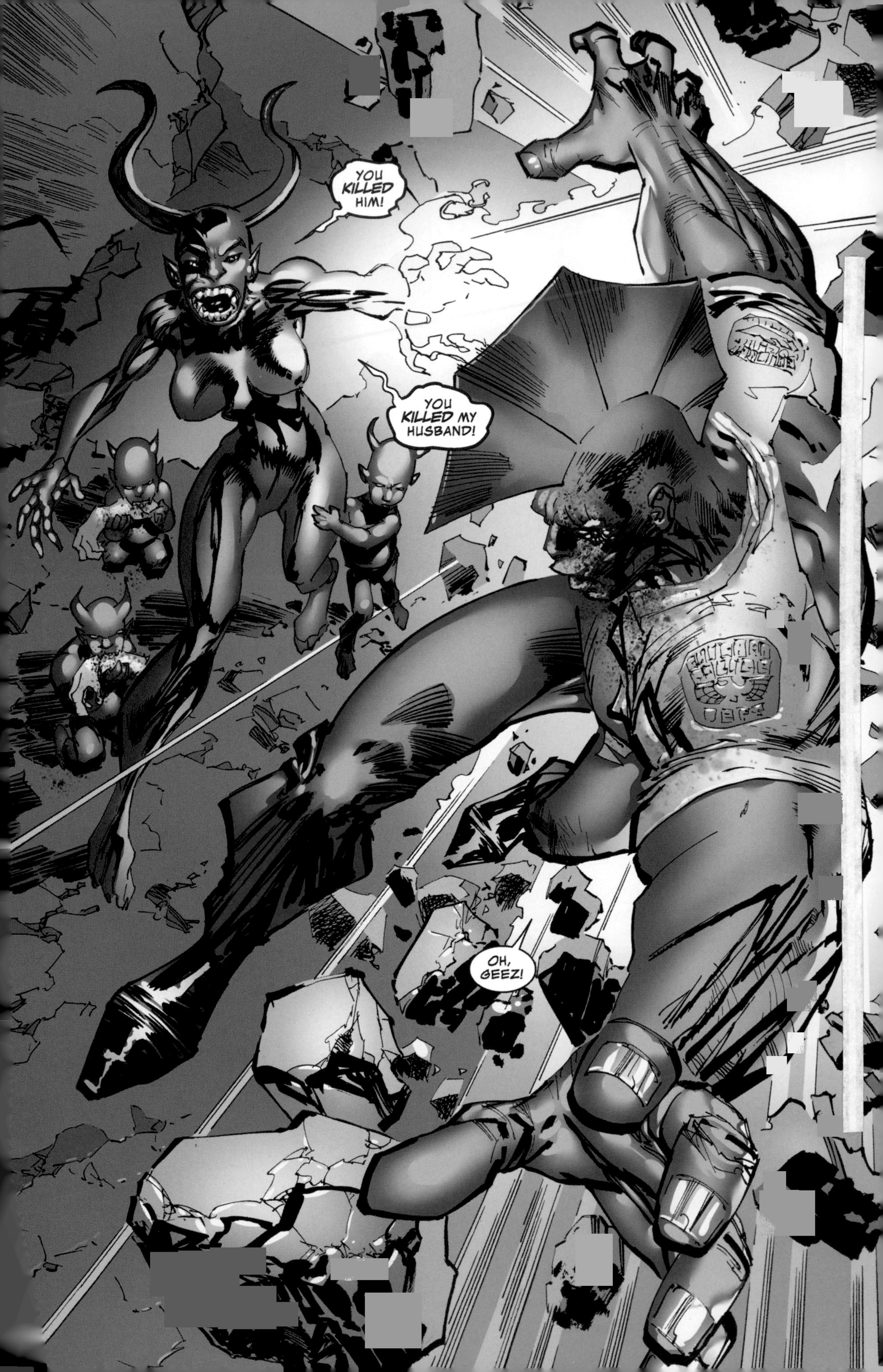
YOU KILLED HIM!
YOU KILLED MY HUSBAND!
OH, GEEZ!

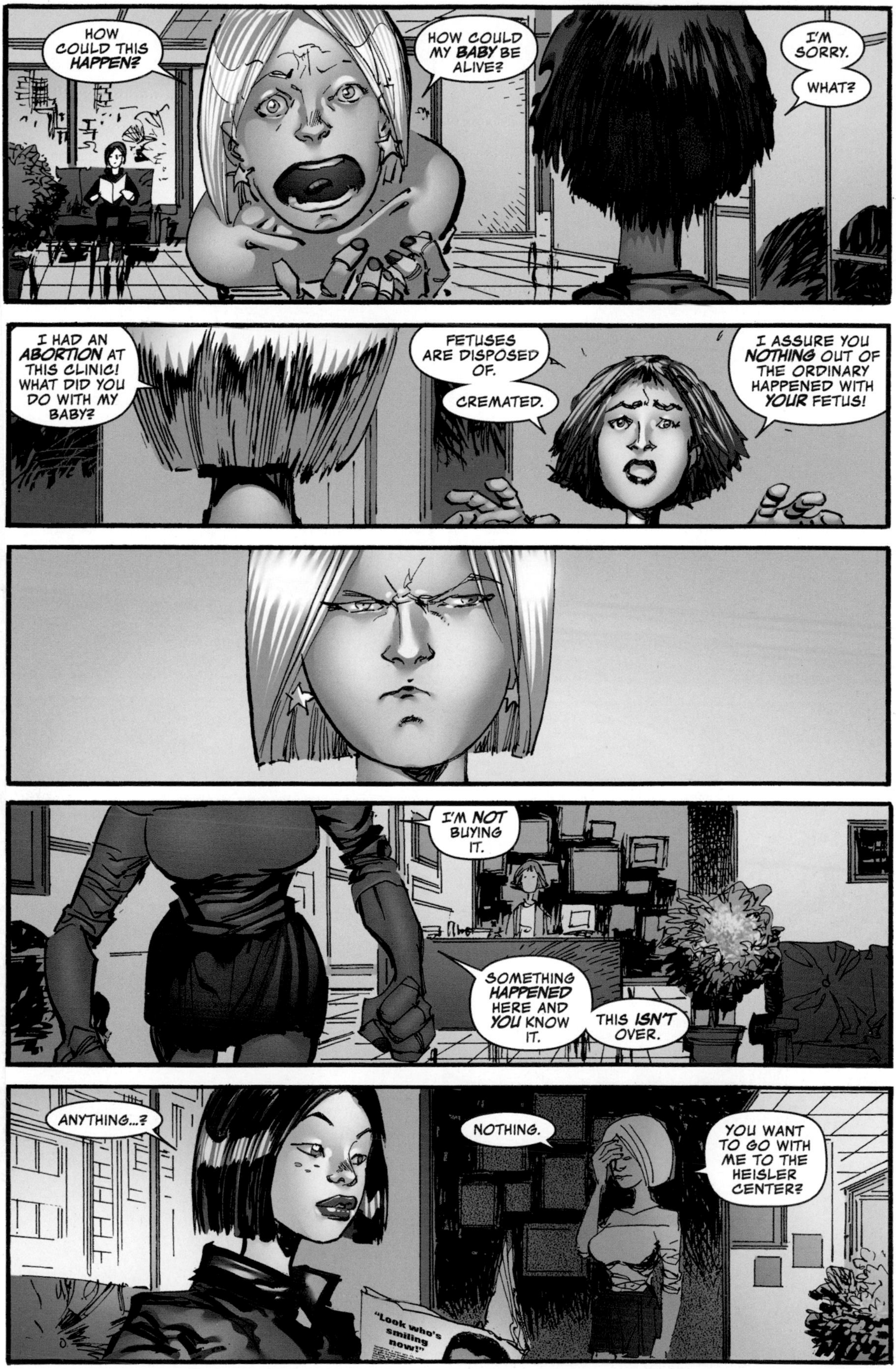
HOW COULD THIS HAPPEN?
HOW COULD MY BABY BE ALIVE?
I'M SORRY.
WHAT?
I HAD AN ABORTION AT THIS CLINIC! WHAT DID YOU DO WITH MY BABY?
FETUSES ARE DISPOSED OF.
CREMATED.
I ASSURE YOU NOTHING OUT OF THE ORDINARY HAPPENED WITH YOUR FETUS!
I'M NOT BUYING IT.
SOMETHING HAPPENED HERE AND YOU KNOW IT.
THIS ISN'T OVER.
ANYTHING...?
NOTHING.
YOU WANT TO GO WITH ME TO THE HEISLER CENTER?
"Look who's smiling now!"

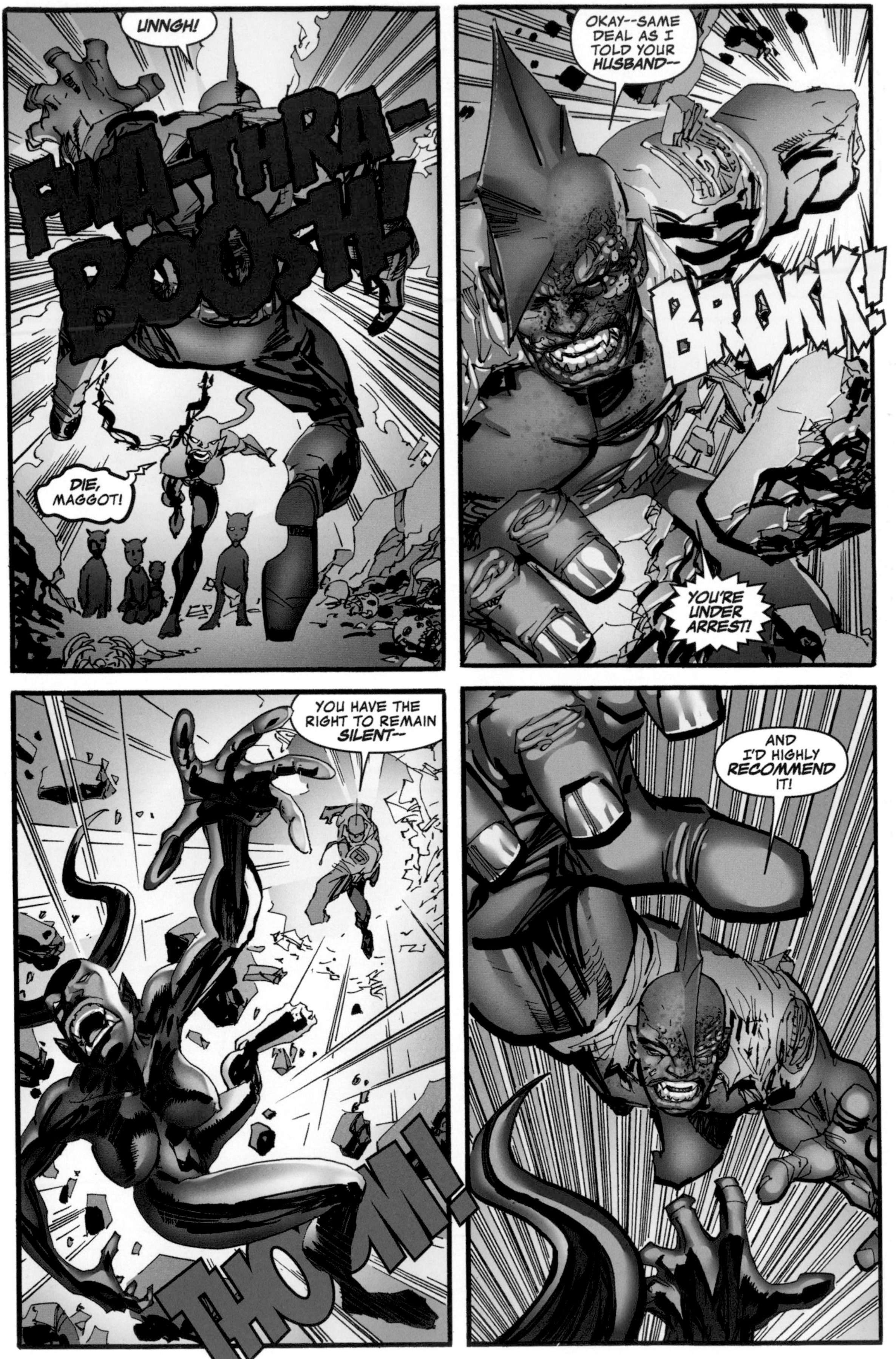
UNNGH!
PWA-THRA-BOOSH!
DIE, MAGGOT!
OKAY--SAME DEAL AS I TOLD YOUR HUSBAND--
BROKK!
YOU'RE UNDER ARREST!
YOU HAVE THE RIGHT TO REMAIN SILENT--
THOOM!!
AND I'D HIGHLY RECOMMEND IT!

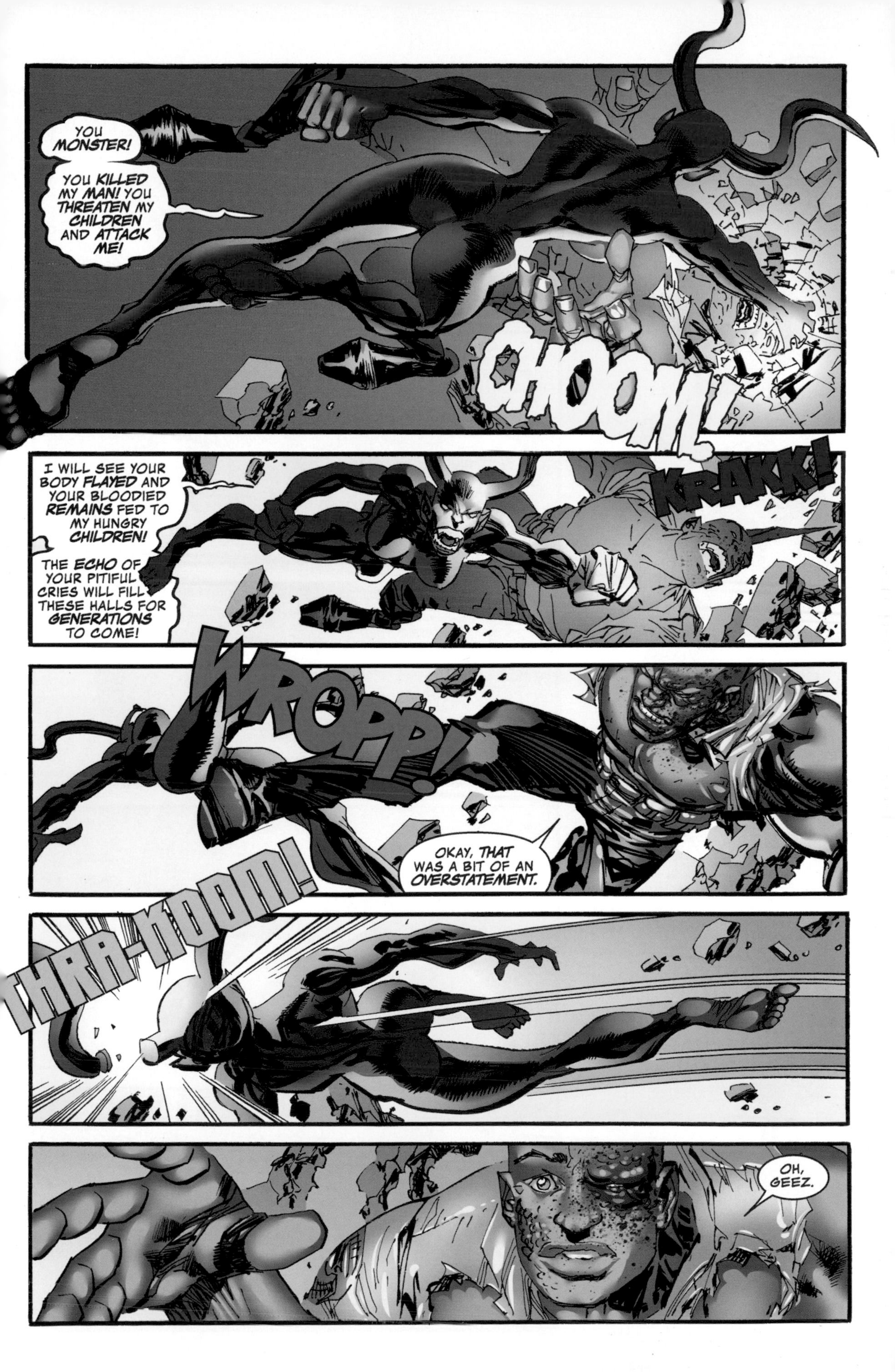
YOU MONSTER!
YOU KILLED MY MAN! YOU THREATEN MY CHILDREN AND ATTACK ME!
CHOOM!
I WILL SEE YOUR BODY FLAYED AND YOUR BLOODIED REMAINS FED TO MY HUNGRY CHILDREN!
THE ECHO OF YOUR PITIFUL CRIES WILL FILL THESE HALLS FOR GENERATIONS TO COME!
KRAKK!
WROPP!
OKAY, THAT WAS A BIT OF AN OVERSTATEMENT.
THRA-KOOM!
OH, GEEZ.

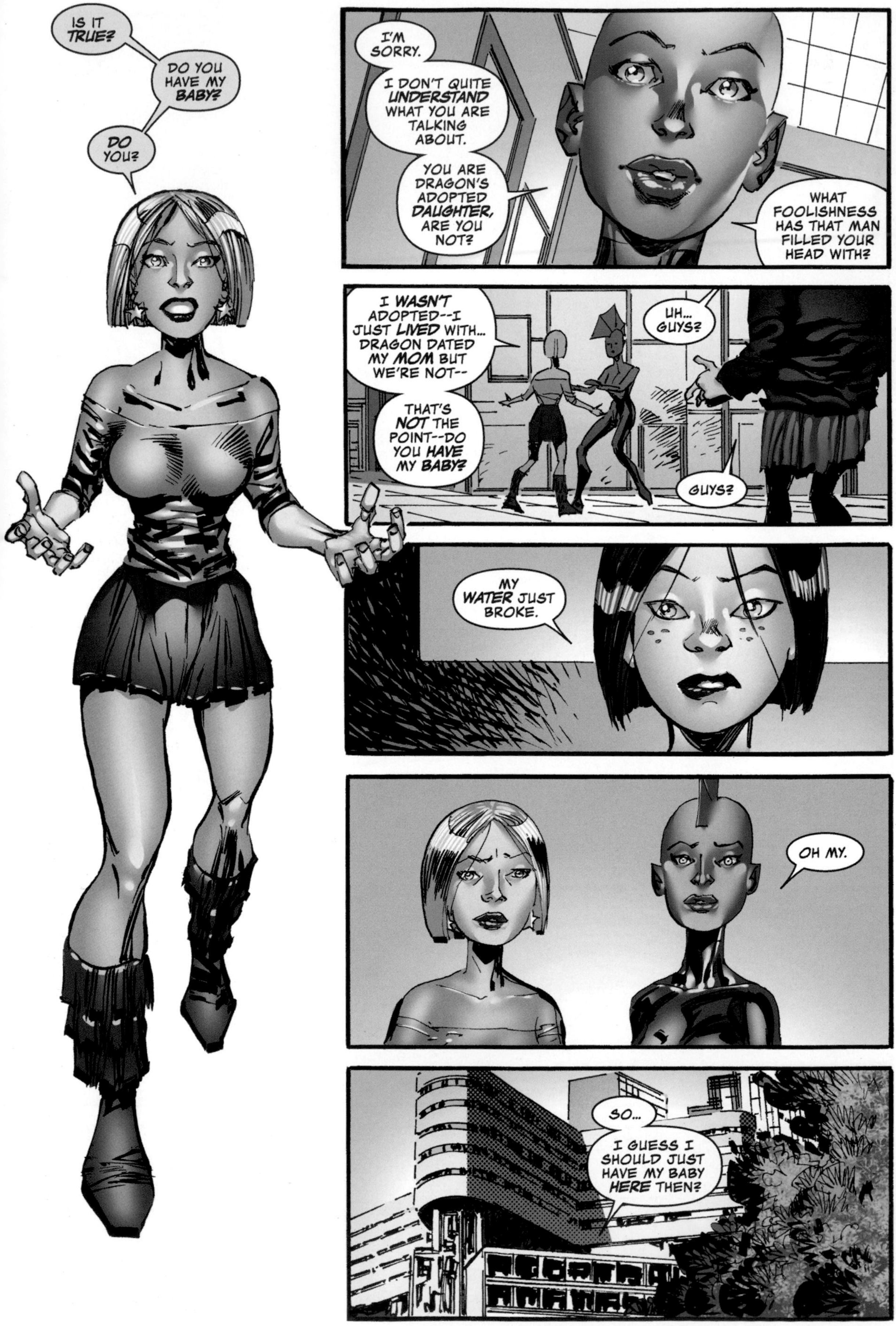
IS IT TRUE?
DO YOU HAVE MY BABY?
DO YOU?
I'M SORRY.
I DON'T QUITE UNDERSTAND WHAT YOU ARE TALKING ABOUT.
YOU ARE DRAGON'S ADOPTED DAUGHTER, ARE YOU NOT?
WHAT FOOLISHNESS HAS THAT MAN FILLED YOUR HEAD WITH?
I WASN'T ADOPTED--I JUST LIVED WITH... DRAGON DATED MY MOM BUT WE'RE NOT--
UH... GUYS?
THAT'S NOT THE POINT--DO YOU HAVE MY BABY?
GUYS?
MY WATER JUST BROKE.
OH MY.
SO...
I GUESS I SHOULD JUST HAVE MY BABY HERE THEN?

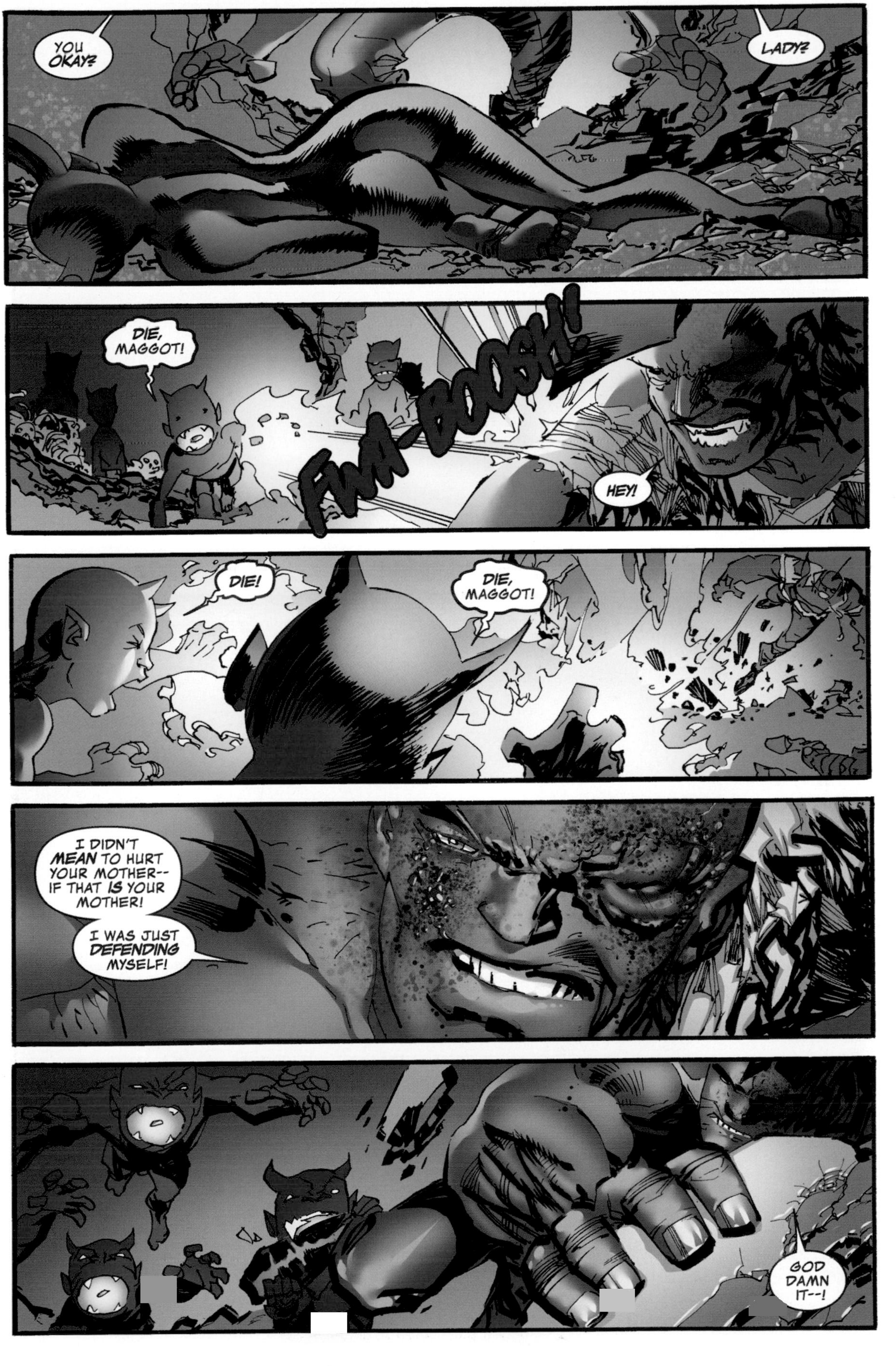
YOU OKAY?
LADY?
DIE, MAGGOT!
FWA-BOOSH!
HEY!
DIE!
DIE, MAGGOT!
I DIDN'T MEAN TO HURT YOUR MOTHER-- IF THAT IS YOUR MOTHER!
I WAS JUST DEFENDING MYSELF!
GOD DAMN IT--!

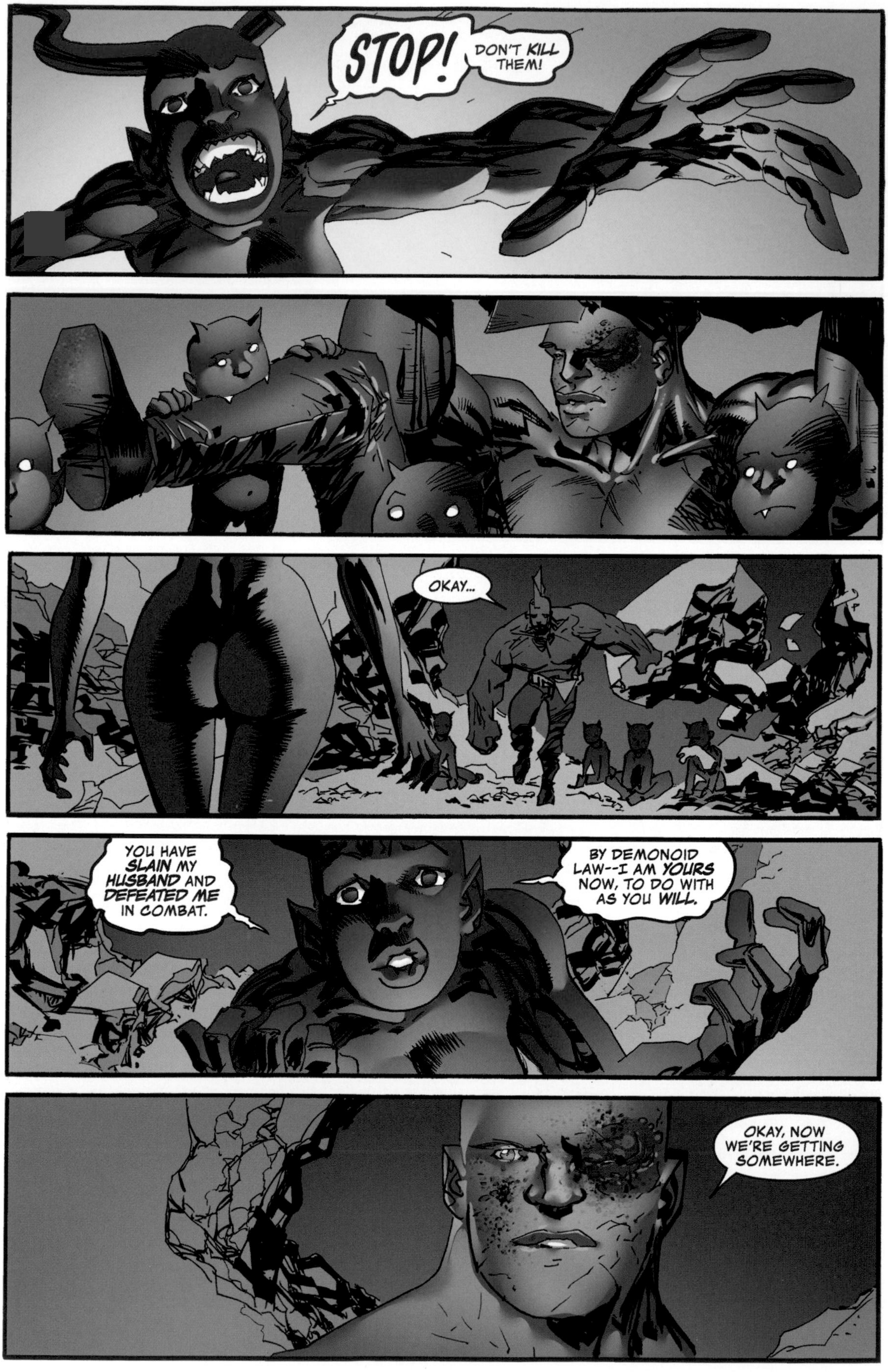
STOP!
DON'T KILL THEM!
OKAY...
YOU HAVE SLAIN MY HUSBAND AND DEFEATED ME IN COMBAT.
BY DEMONOID LAW--I AM YOURS NOW, TO DO WITH AS YOU WILL.
OKAY, NOW WE'RE GETTING SOMEWHERE.

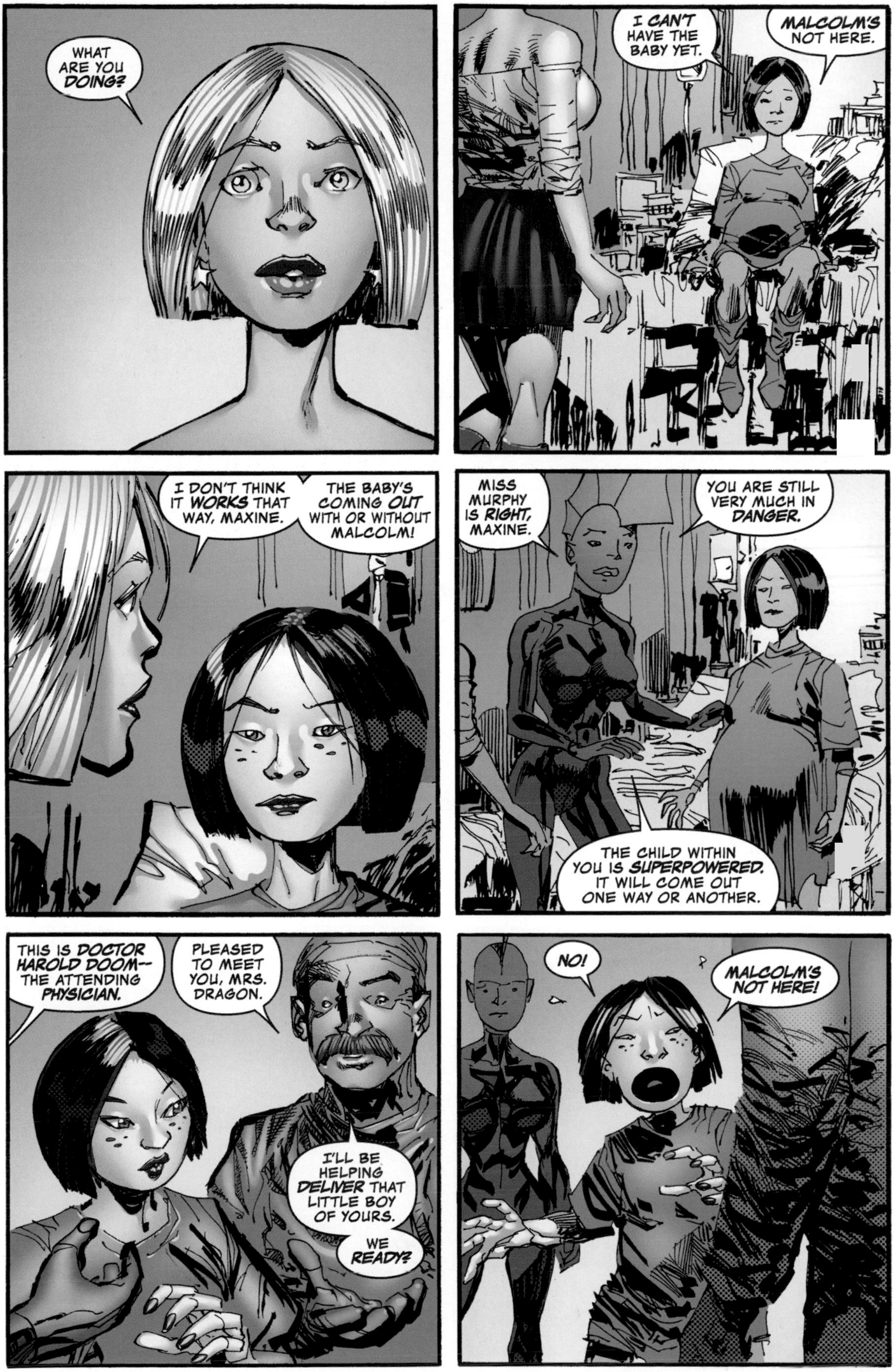
WHAT ARE YOU DOING?
I CAN'T HAVE THE BABY YET.
MALCOLM'S NOT HERE.
I DON'T THINK IT WORKS THAT WAY, MAXINE.
THE BABY'S COMING OUT WITH OR WITHOUT MALCOLM!
MISS MURPHY IS RIGHT, MAXINE.
YOU ARE STILL VERY MUCH IN DANGER.
THE CHILD WITHIN YOU IS SUPERPOWERED. IT WILL COME OUT ONE WAY OR ANOTHER.
THIS IS DOCTOR HAROLD DOOM-- THE ATTENDING PHYSICIAN.
PLEASED TO MEET YOU, MRS. DRAGON.
I'LL BE HELPING DELIVER THAT LITTLE BOY OF YOURS.
WE READY?
NO!
MALCOLM'S NOT HERE!

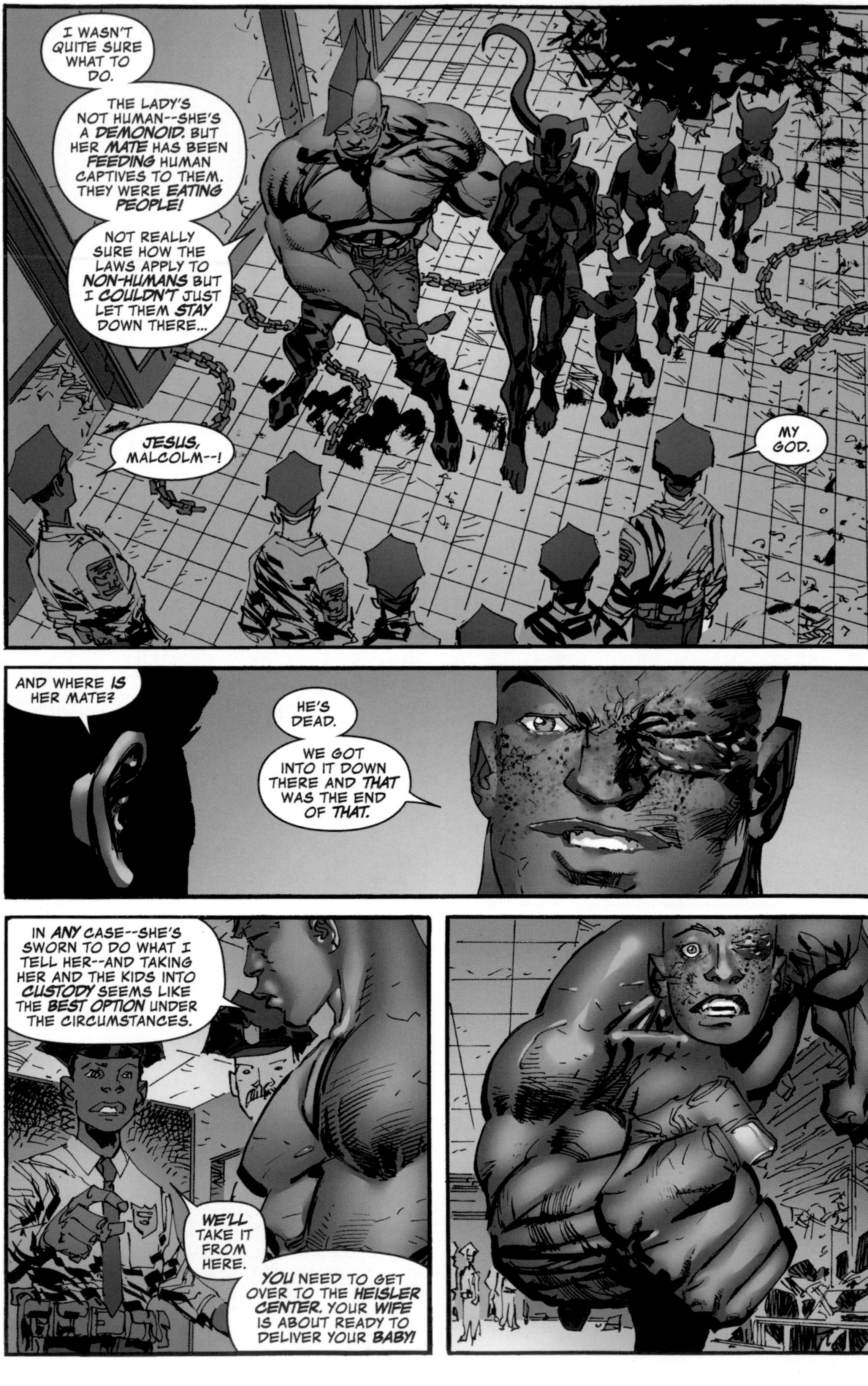
I WASN'T QUITE SURE WHAT TO DO.
THE LADY'S NOT HUMAN--SHE'S A DEMONOID. BUT HER MATE HAS BEEN FEEDING HUMAN CAPTIVES TO THEM. THEY WERE EATING PEOPLE!
NOT REALLY SURE HOW THE LAWS APPLY TO NON-HUMANS BUT I COULDN'T JUST LET THEM STAY DOWN THERE...
JESUS, MALCOLM--!
MY GOD.
AND WHERE IS HER MATE?
HE'S DEAD.
WE GOT INTO IT DOWN THERE AND THAT WAS THE END OF THAT.
IN ANY CASE--SHE'S SWORN TO DO WHAT I TELL HER--AND TAKING HER AND THE KIDS INTO CUSTODY SEEMS LIKE THE BEST OPTION UNDER THE CIRCUMSTANCES.
WE'LL TAKE IT FROM HERE.
YOU NEED TO GET OVER TO THE HEISLER CENTER. YOUR WIFE IS ABOUT READY TO DELIVER YOUR BABY!

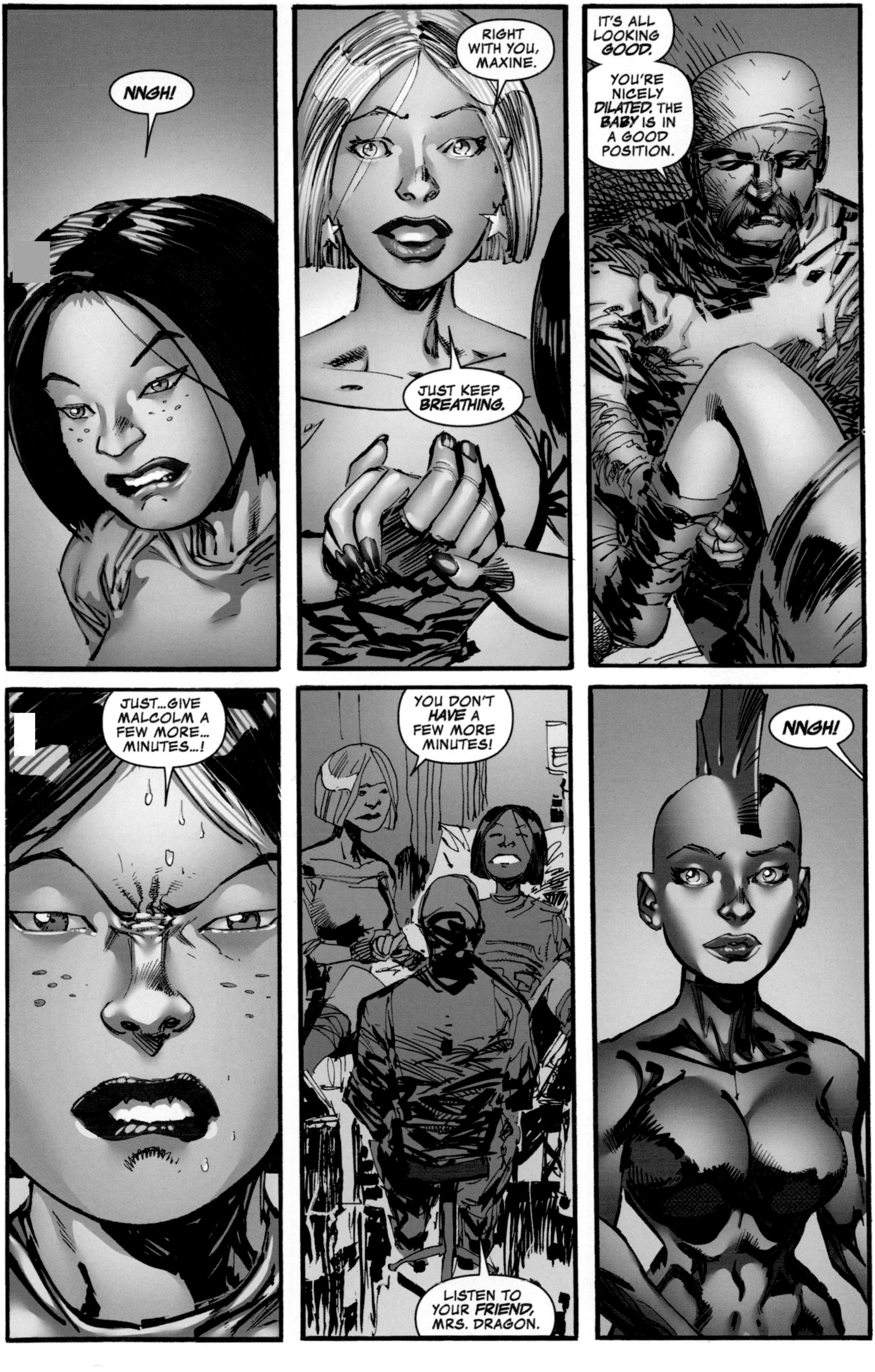
NNGH!
RIGHT WITH YOU, MAXINE.
JUST KEEP BREATHING.
IT'S ALL LOOKING GOOD.
YOU'RE NICELY DILATED. THE BABY IS IN A GOOD POSITION.
JUST...GIVE MALCOLM A FEW MORE... MINUTES...!
YOU DON'T HAVE A FEW MORE MINUTES!
LISTEN TO YOUR FRIEND, MRS. DRAGON.
NNGH!

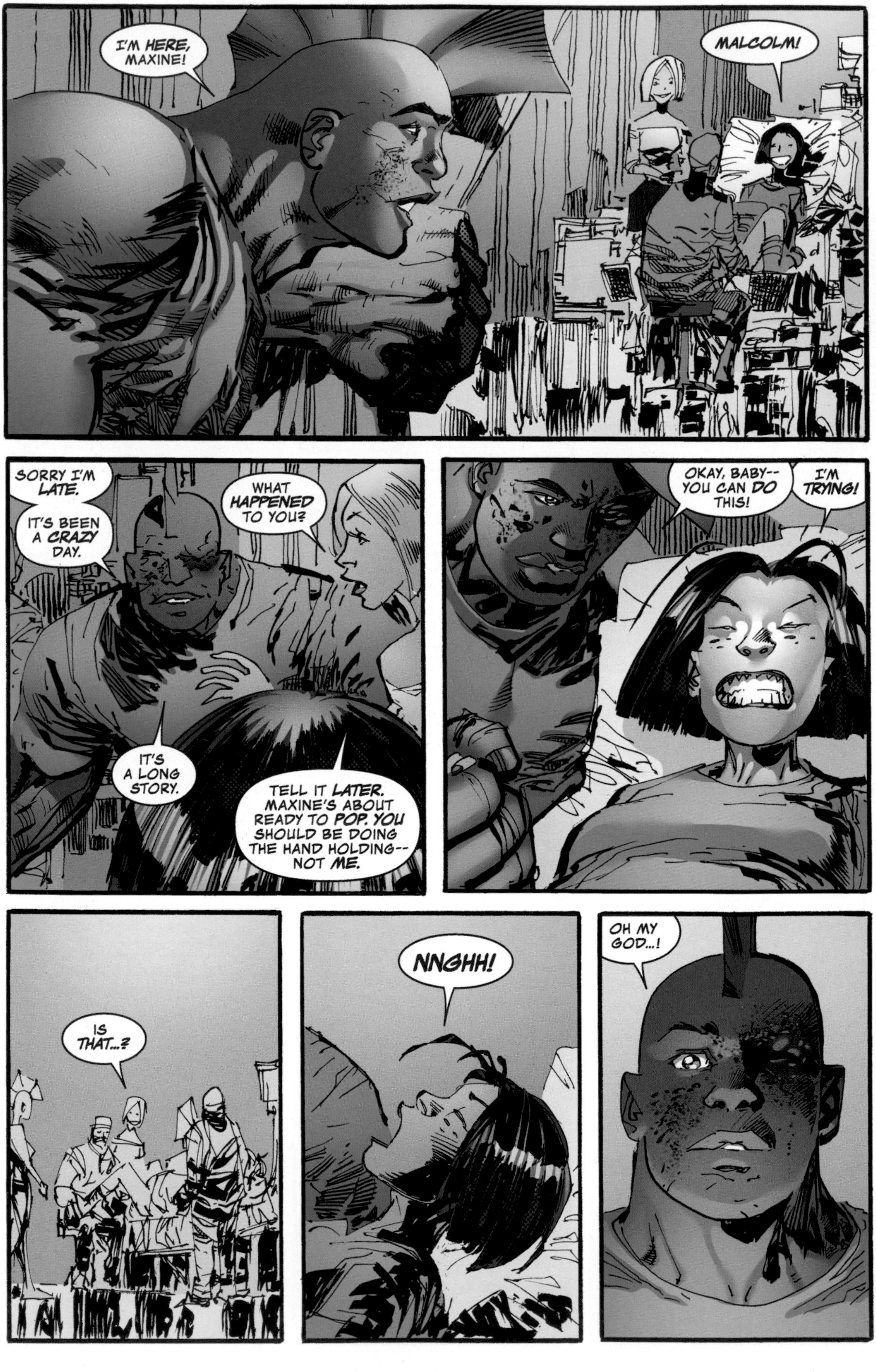
I'M HERE, MAXINE!
MALCOLM!
SORRY I'M LATE.
IT'S BEEN A CRAZY DAY.
WHAT HAPPENED TO YOU?
IT'S A LONG STORY.
TELL IT LATER. MAXINE'S ABOUT READY TO POP. YOU SHOULD BE DOING THE HAND HOLDING-- NOT ME.
OKAY, BABY-- YOU CAN DO THIS!
I'M TRYING!
IS THAT...?
NNGHH!
OH MY GOD...!

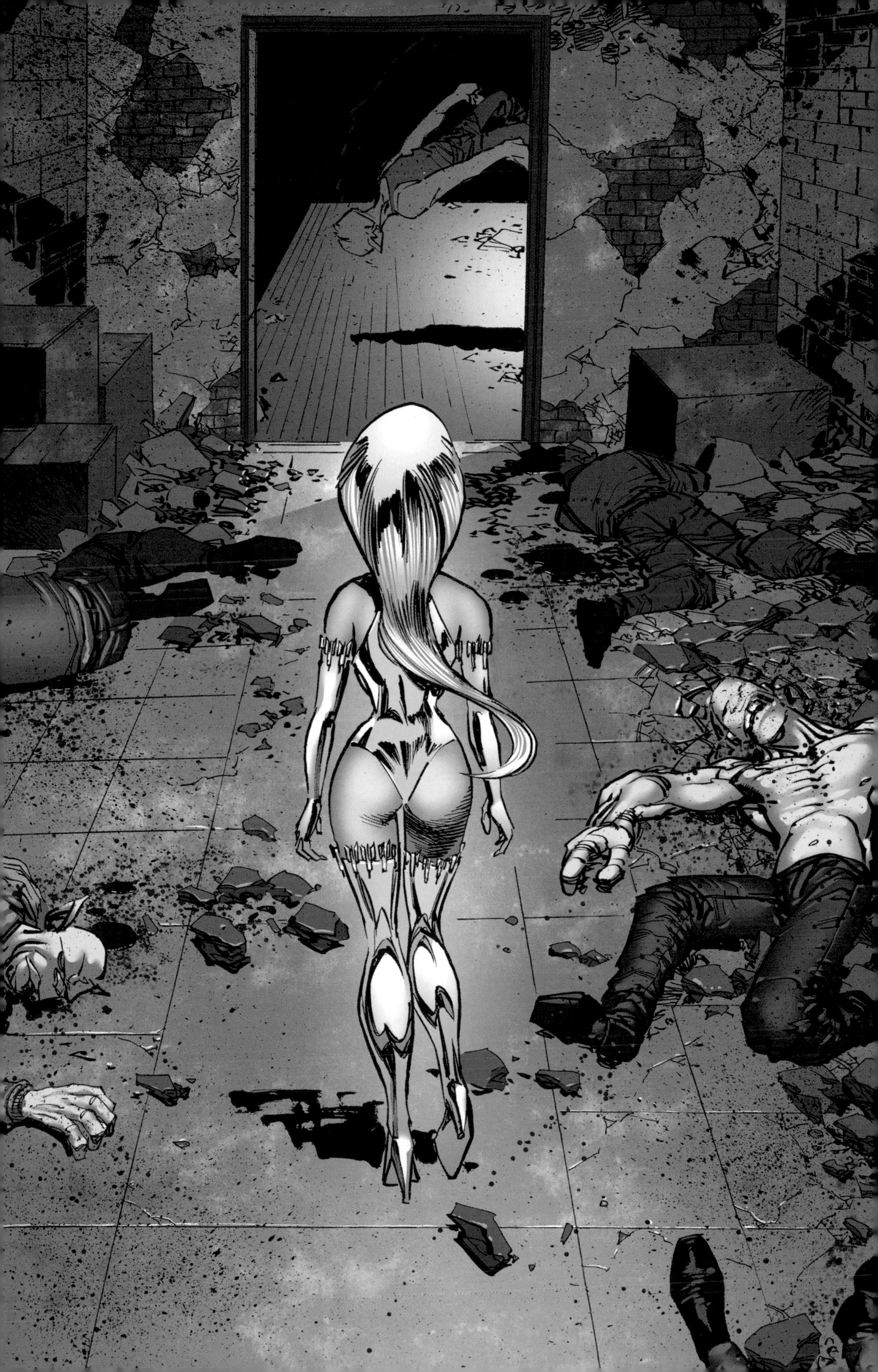

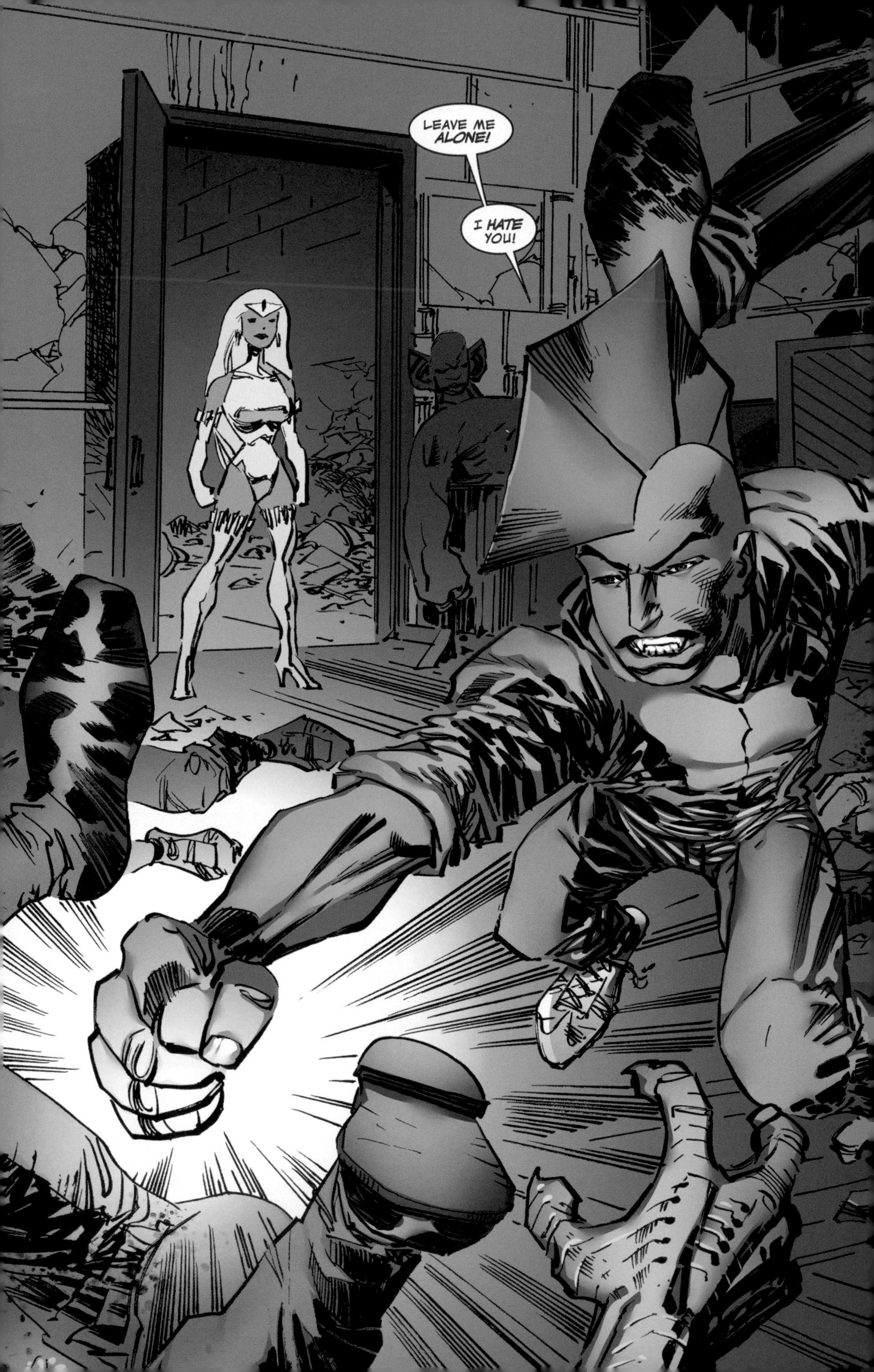
LEAVE ME ALONE!
I HATE YOU!

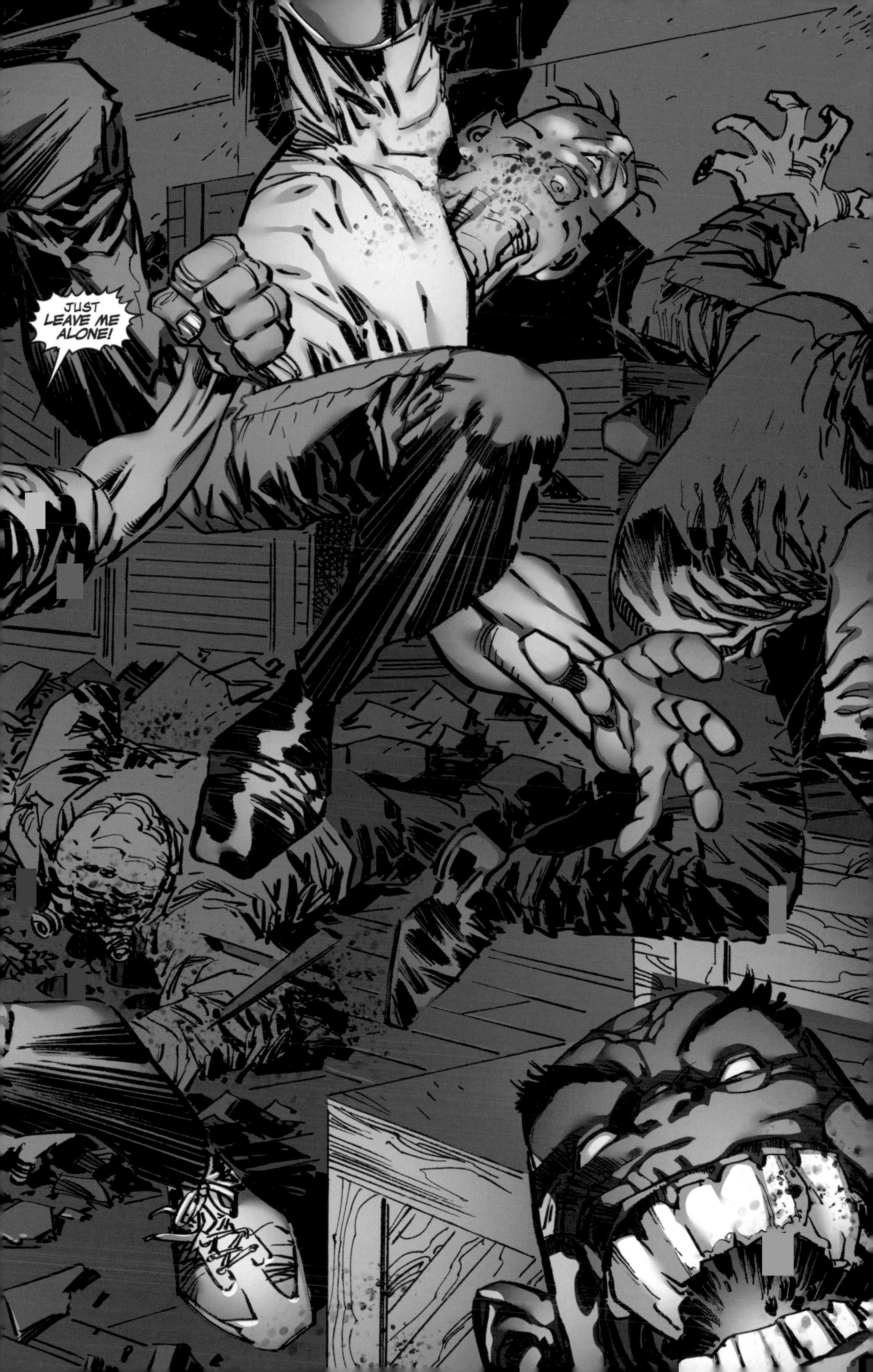
JUST LEAVE ME ALONE!

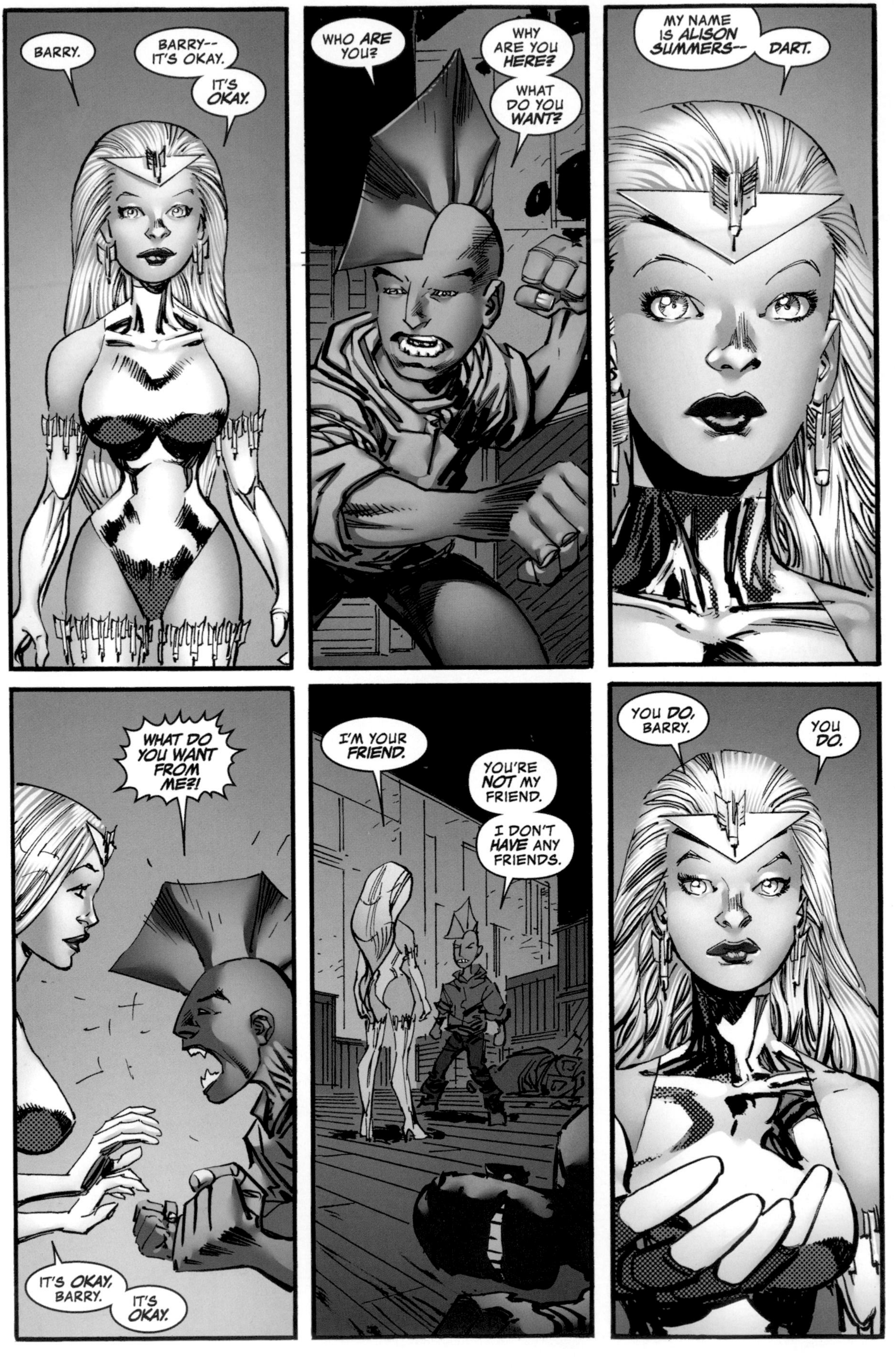
BARRY.
BARRY-- IT'S OKAY.
IT'S OKAY.
WHO ARE YOU?
WHY ARE YOU HERE?
WHAT DO YOU WANT?
MY NAME IS ALISON SUMMERS--
DART.
WHAT DO YOU WANT FROM ME?!
IT'S OKAY, BARRY.
IT'S OKAY.
I'M YOUR FRIEND.
YOU'RE NOT MY FRIEND.
I DON'T HAVE ANY FRIENDS.
YOU DO, BARRY.
YOU DO.

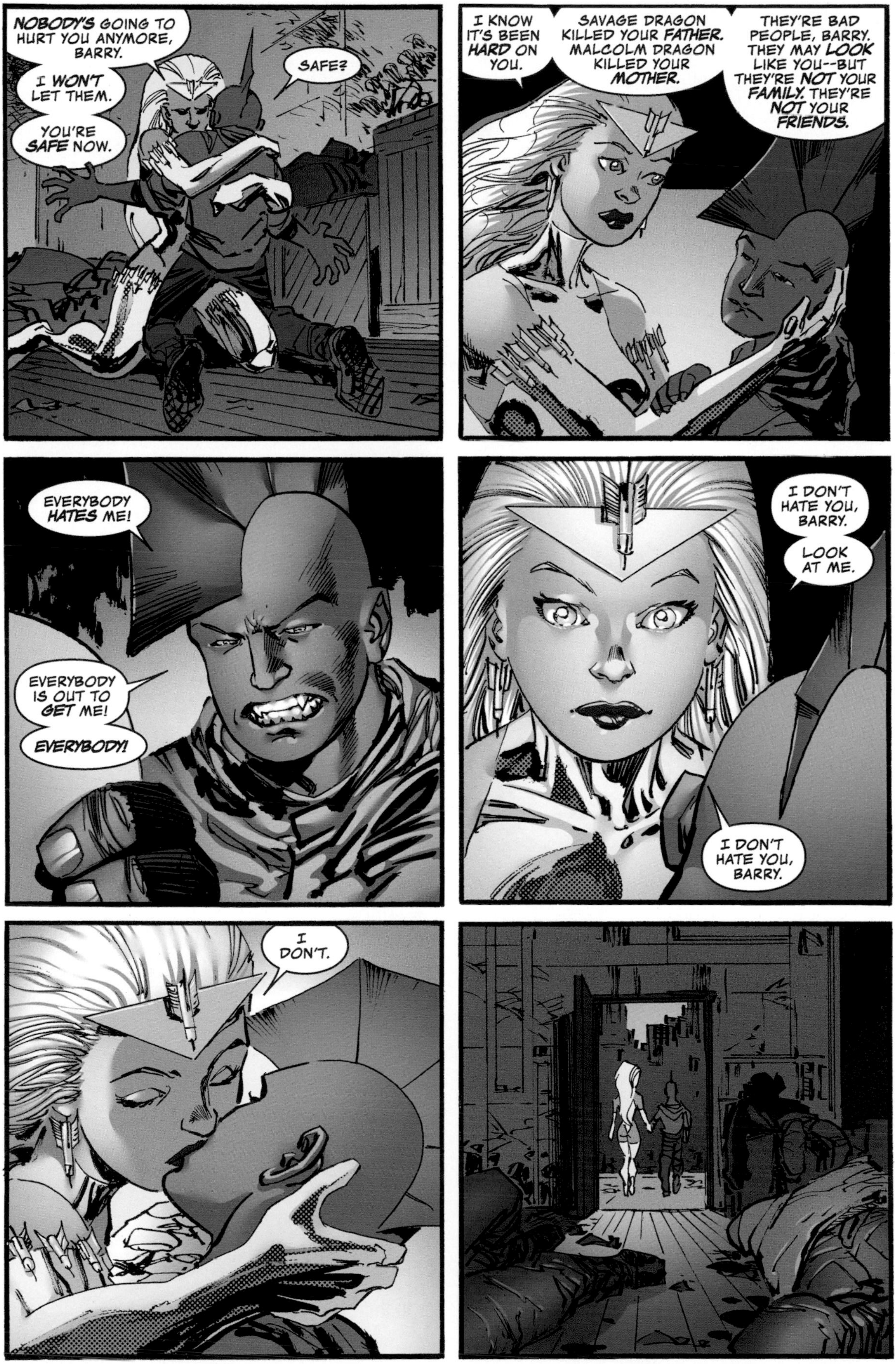
NOBODY'S GOING TO HURT YOU ANYMORE, BARRY.
I WON'T LET THEM.
YOU'RE SAFE NOW.
SAFE?
I KNOW IT'S BEEN HARD ON YOU.
SAVAGE DRAGON KILLED YOUR FATHER. MALCOLM DRAGON KILLED YOUR MOTHER.
THEY'RE BAD PEOPLE, BARRY. THEY MAY LOOK LIKE YOU--BUT THEY'RE NOT YOUR FAMILY. THEY'RE NOT YOUR FRIENDS.
EVERYBODY HATES ME!
EVERYBODY IS OUT TO GET ME!
EVERYBODY!
I DON'T HATE YOU, BARRY.
LOOK AT ME.
I DON'T HATE YOU, BARRY.
I DON'T.

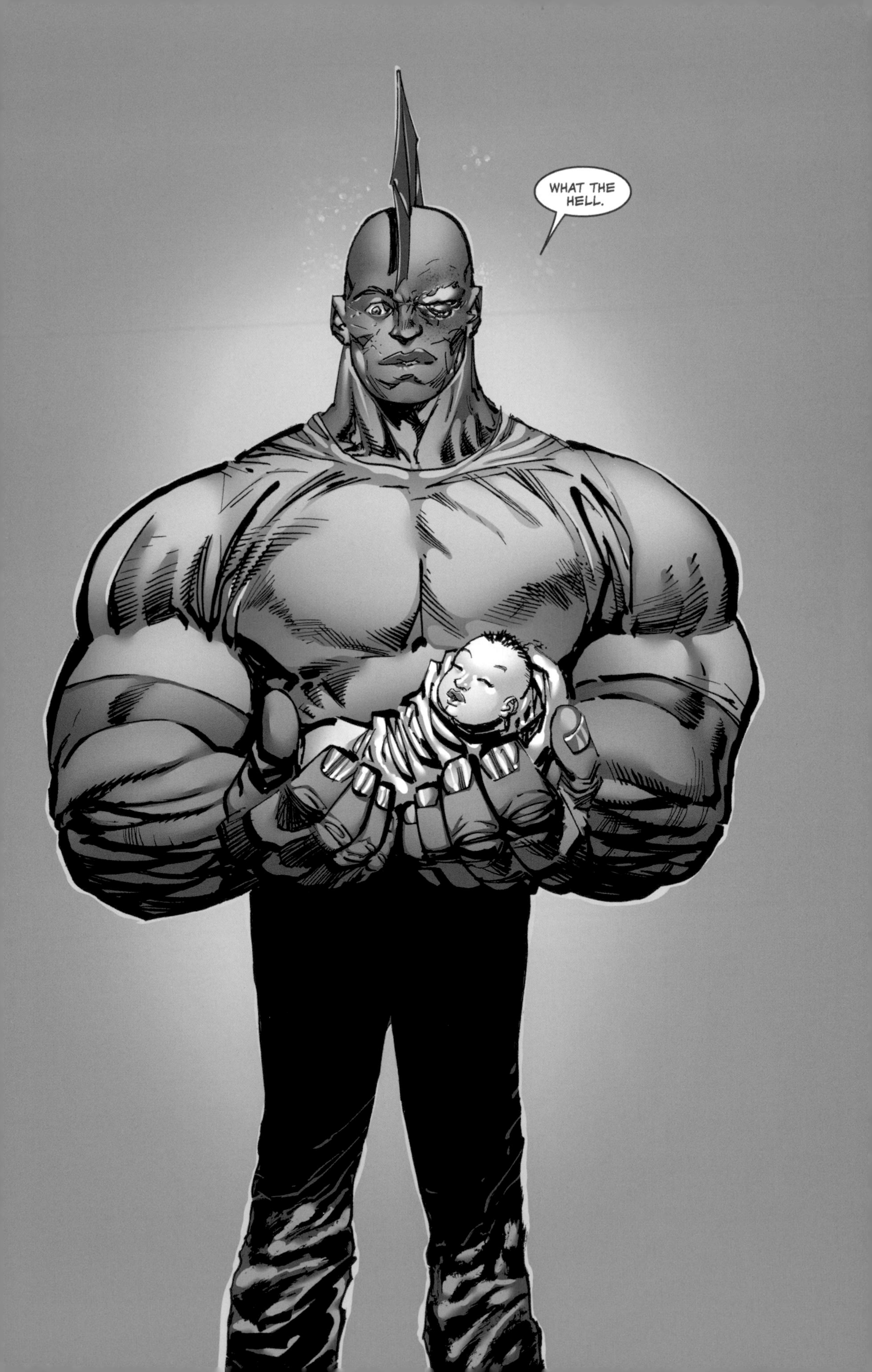
WHAT THE HELL.

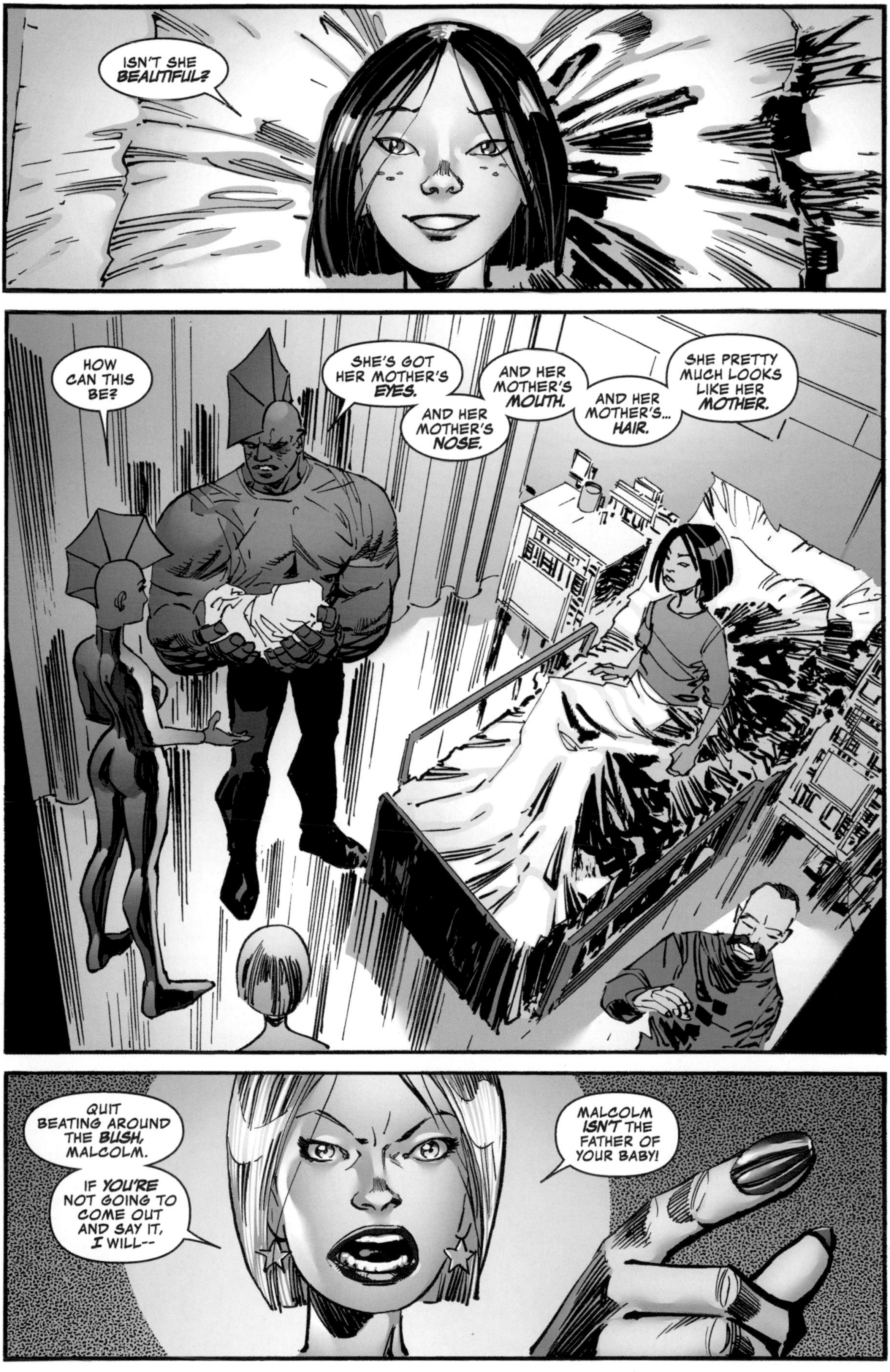
ISN'T SHE BEAUTIFUL?
HOW CAN THIS BE?
SHE'S GOT HER MOTHER'S EYES.
AND HER MOTHER'S NOSE.
AND HER MOTHER'S MOUTH.
AND HER MOTHER'S... HAIR.
SHE PRETTY MUCH LOOKS LIKE HER MOTHER.
QUIT BEATING AROUND THE BUSH, MALCOLM.
IF YOU'RE NOT GOING TO COME OUT AND SAY IT, I WILL--
MALCOLM ISN'T THE FATHER OF YOUR BABY!

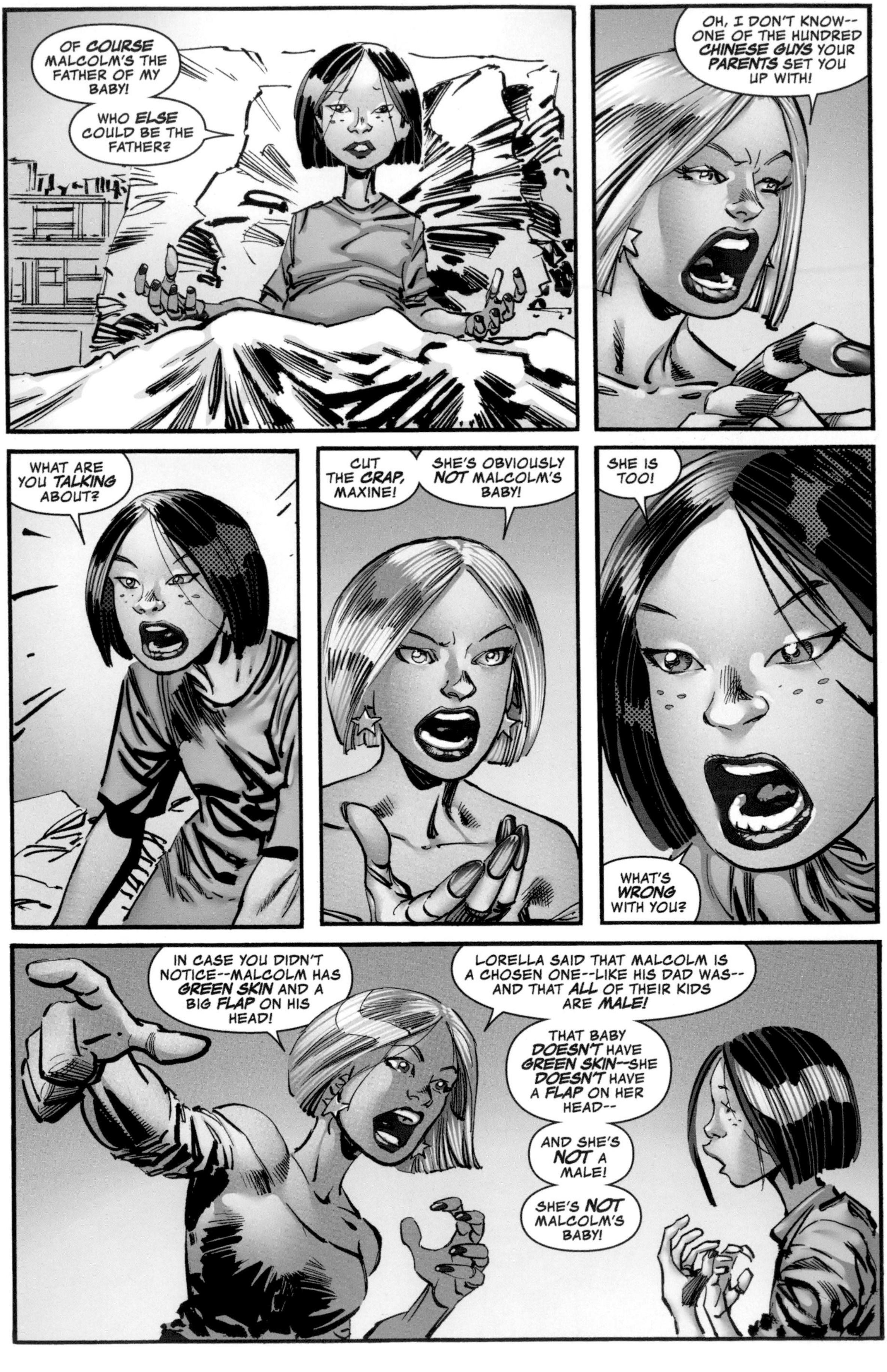
OF COURSE MALCOLM'S THE FATHER OF MY BABY!
WHO ELSE COULD BE THE FATHER?
OH, I DON'T KNOW-- ONE OF THE HUNDRED CHINESE GUYS YOUR PARENTS SET YOU UP WITH!
WHAT ARE YOU TALKING ABOUT?
CUT THE CRAP, MAXINE!
SHE'S OBVIOUSLY NOT MALCOLM'S BABY!
SHE IS TOO!
WHAT'S WRONG WITH YOU?
IN CASE YOU DIDN'T NOTICE--MALCOLM HAS GREEN SKIN AND A BIG FLAP ON HIS HEAD!
LORELLA SAID THAT MALCOLM IS A CHOSEN ONE--LIKE HIS DAD WAS-- AND THAT ALL OF THEIR KIDS ARE MALE!
THAT BABY DOESN'T HAVE GREEN SKIN--SHE DOESN'T HAVE A FLAP ON HER HEAD--
AND SHE'S NOT A MALE!
SHE'S NOT MALCOLM'S BABY!

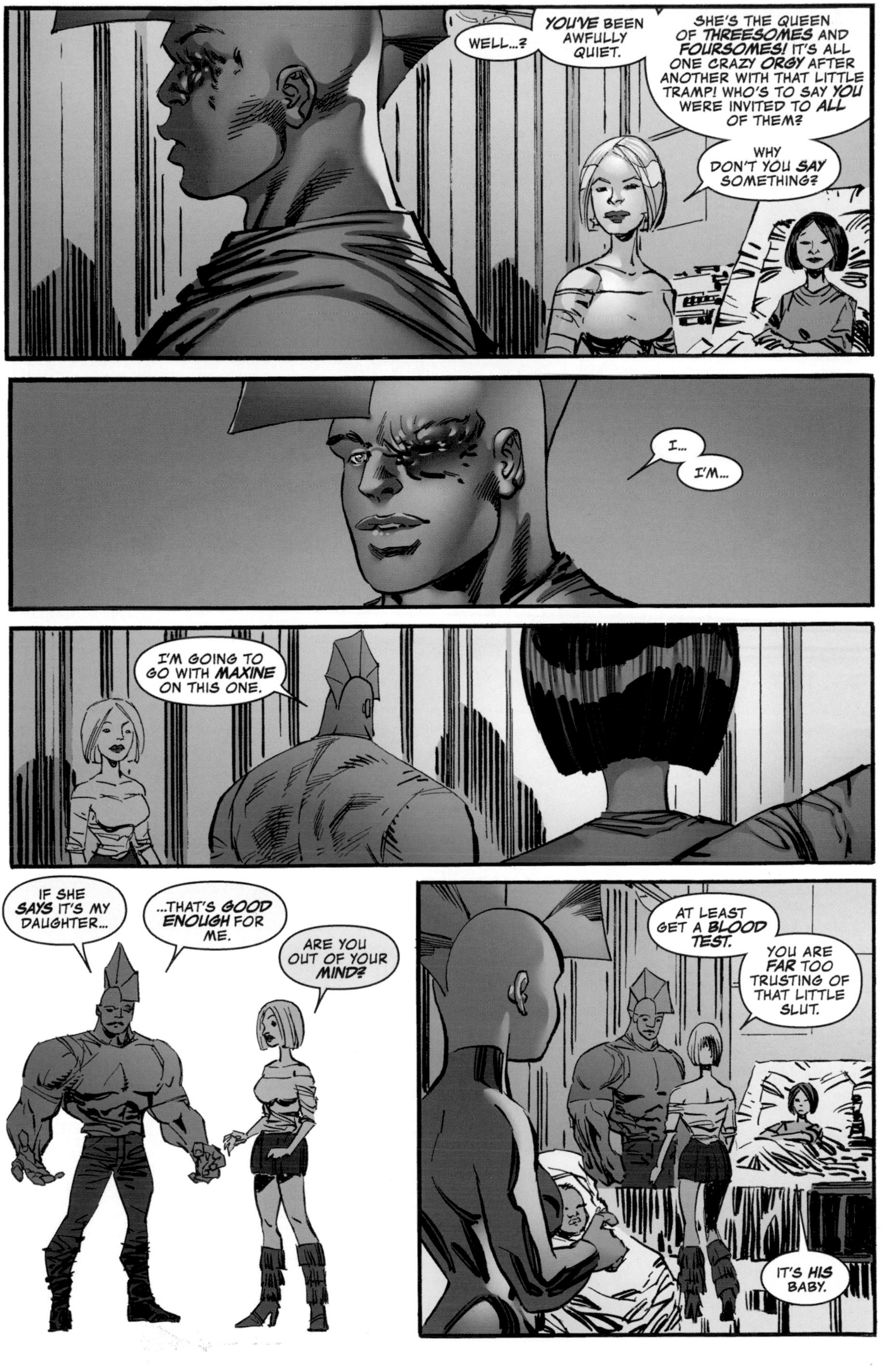
WELL...?
YOU'VE BEEN AWFULLY QUIET.
SHE'S THE QUEEN OF THREESOMES AND FOURSOMES! IT'S ALL ONE CRAZY ORGY AFTER ANOTHER WITH THAT LITTLE TRAMP! WHO'S TO SAY YOU WERE INVITED TO ALL OF THEM?
WHY DON'T YOU SAY SOMETHING?
I...
I'M...
I'M GOING TO GO WITH MAXINE ON THIS ONE.
IF SHE SAYS IT'S MY DAUGHTER...
...THAT'S GOOD ENOUGH FOR ME.
ARE YOU OUT OF YOUR MIND?
AT LEAST GET A BLOOD TEST.
YOU ARE FAR TOO TRUSTING OF THAT LITTLE SLUT.
IT'S HIS BABY.

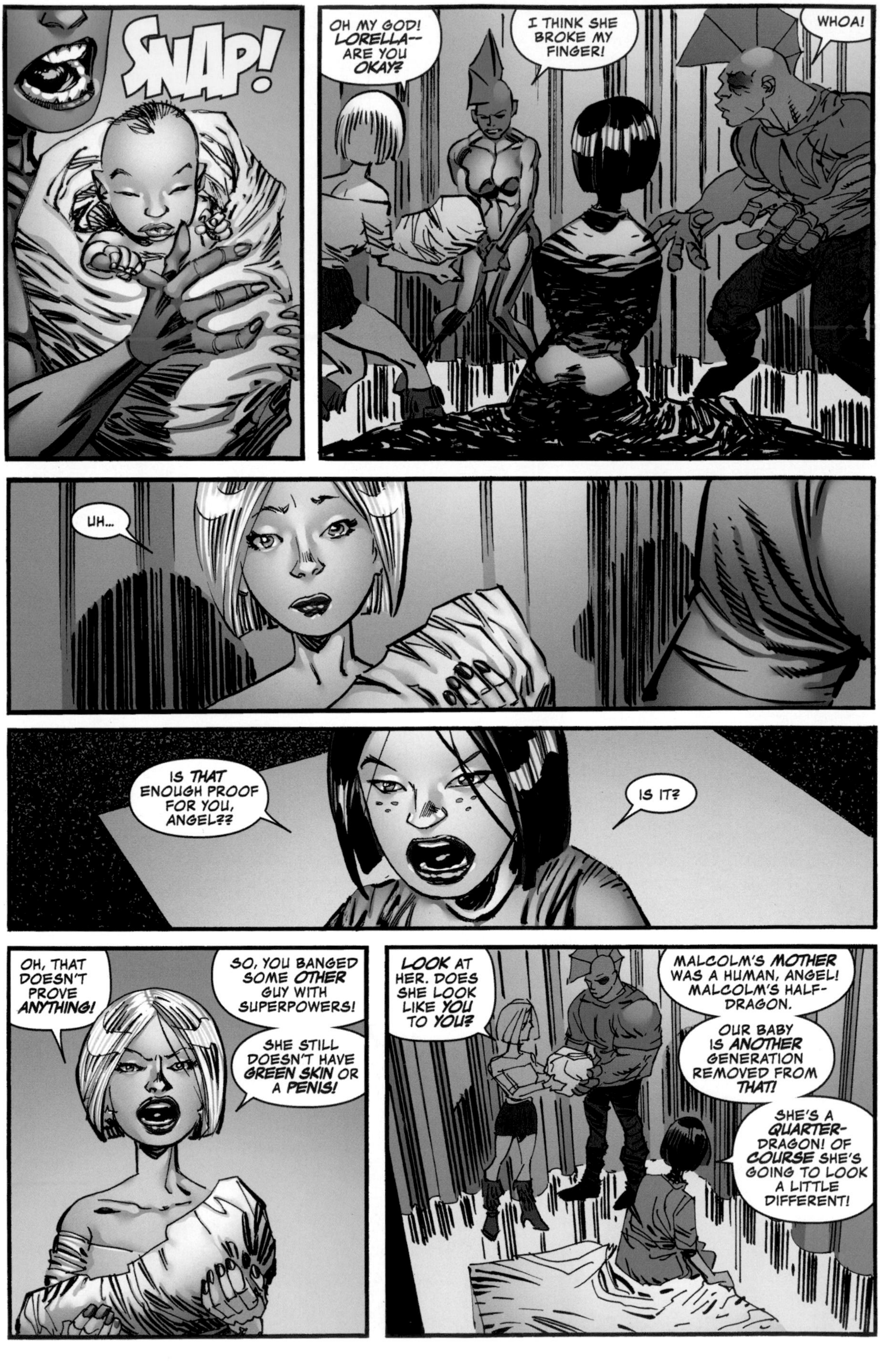
SNAP!
OH MY GOD! LORELLA-- ARE YOU OKAY?
I THINK SHE BROKE MY FINGER!
WHOA!
UH...
IS THAT ENOUGH PROOF FOR YOU, ANGEL??
IS IT?
OH, THAT DOESN'T PROVE ANYTHING!
SO, YOU BANGED SOME OTHER GUY WITH SUPERPOWERS!
SHE STILL DOESN'T HAVE GREEN SKIN OR A PENIS!
LOOK AT HER. DOES SHE LOOK LIKE YOU TO YOU?
MALCOLM'S MOTHER WAS A HUMAN, ANGEL! MALCOLM'S HALF-DRAGON.
OUR BABY IS ANOTHER GENERATION REMOVED FROM THAT!
SHE'S A QUARTER-DRAGON! OF COURSE SHE'S GOING TO LOOK A LITTLE DIFFERENT!

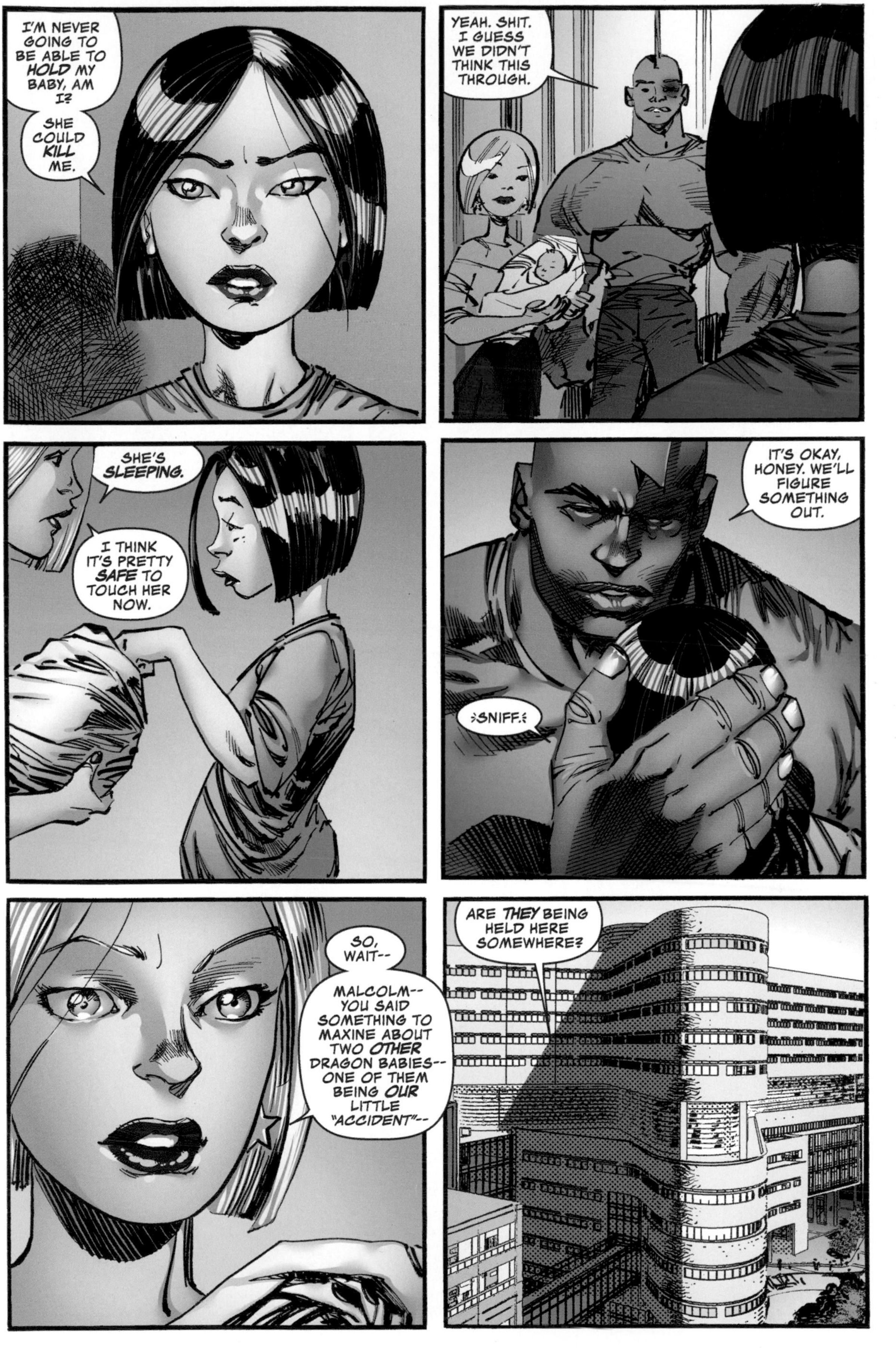
I'M NEVER GOING TO BE ABLE TO HOLD MY BABY, AM I?
SHE COULD KILL ME.
YEAH. SHIT. I GUESS WE DIDN'T THINK THIS THROUGH.
SHE'S SLEEPING.
I THINK IT'S PRETTY SAFE TO TOUCH HER NOW.
IT'S OKAY, HONEY. WE'LL FIGURE SOMETHING OUT.
SNIFF.
SO, WAIT--
MALCOLM-- YOU SAID SOMETHING TO MAXINE ABOUT TWO OTHER DRAGON BABIES-- ONE OF THEM BEING OUR LITTLE "ACCIDENT"--
ARE THEY BEING HELD HERE SOMEWHERE?

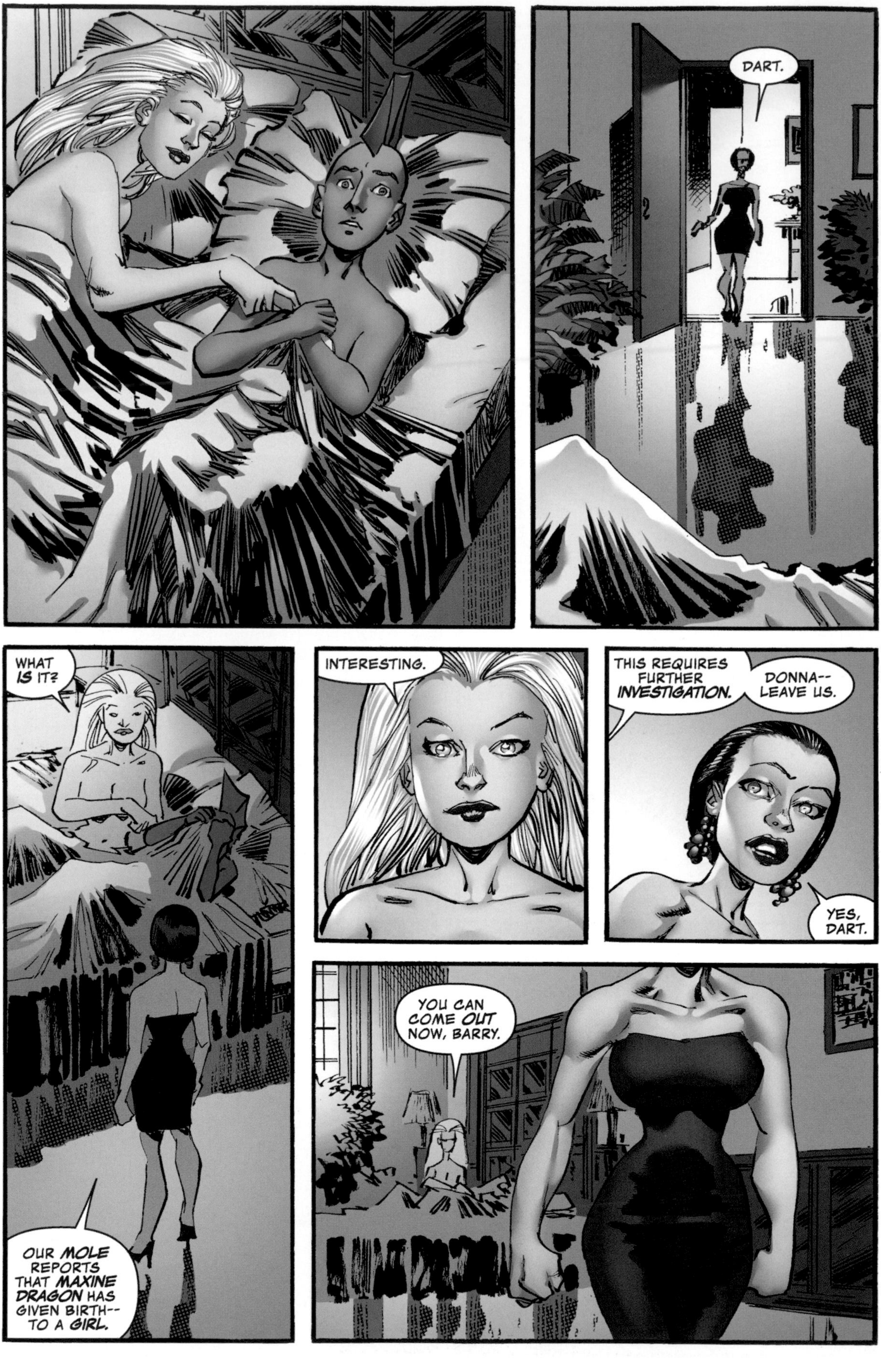
DART.
WHAT IS IT?
OUR MOLE REPORTS THAT MAXINE DRAGON HAS GIVEN BIRTH-- TO A GIRL.
INTERESTING.
THIS REQUIRES FURTHER INVESTIGATION.
DONNA-- LEAVE US.
YES, DART.
YOU CAN COME OUT NOW, BARRY.

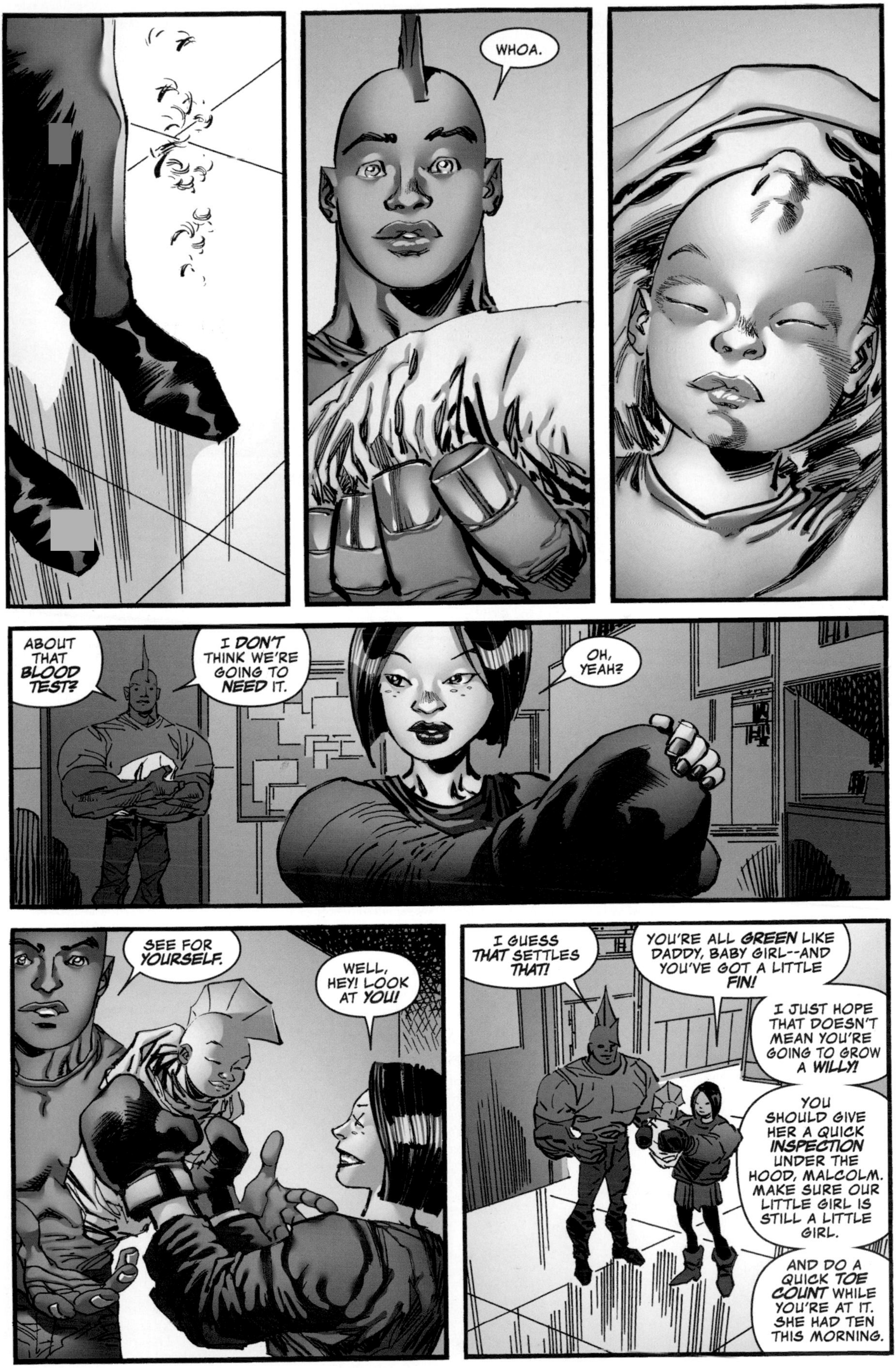
WHOA.
ABOUT THAT BLOOD TEST?
I DON'T THINK WE'RE GOING TO NEED IT.
OH, YEAH?
SEE FOR YOURSELF.
WELL, HEY! LOOK AT YOU!
I GUESS THAT SETTLES THAT!
YOU'RE ALL GREEN LIKE DADDY, BABY GIRL--AND YOU'VE GOT A LITTLE FIN!
I JUST HOPE THAT DOESN'T MEAN YOU'RE GOING TO GROW A WILLY!
YOU SHOULD GIVE HER A QUICK INSPECTION UNDER THE HOOD, MALCOLM. MAKE SURE OUR LITTLE GIRL IS STILL A LITTLE GIRL.
AND DO A QUICK TOE COUNT WHILE YOU'RE AT IT. SHE HAD TEN THIS MORNING.

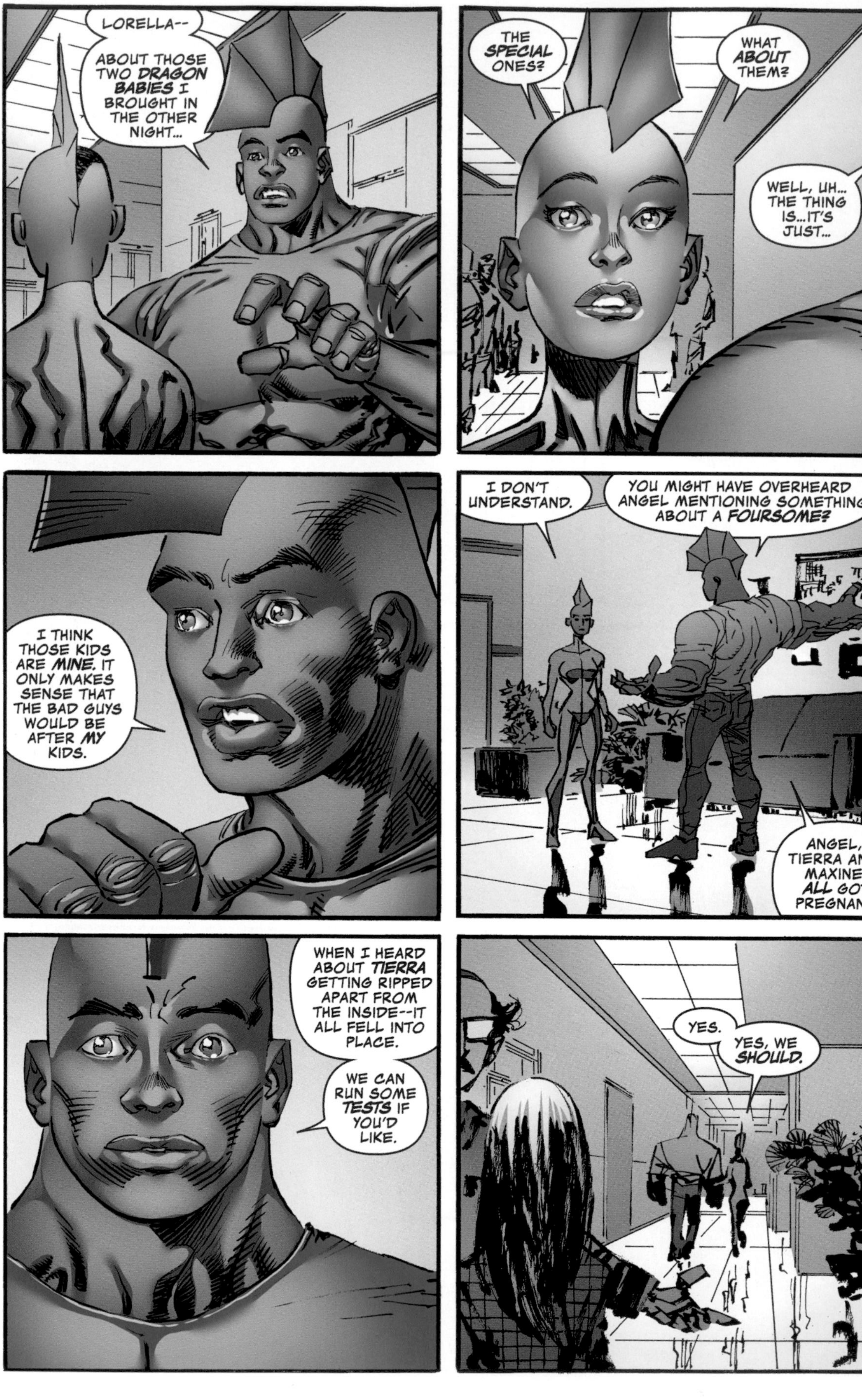
LORELLA--
ABOUT THOSE TWO DRAGON BABIES I BROUGHT IN THE OTHER NIGHT...
THE SPECIAL ONES?
WHAT ABOUT THEM?
WELL, UH... THE THING IS...IT'S JUST...
I THINK THOSE KIDS ARE MINE. IT ONLY MAKES SENSE THAT THE BAD GUYS WOULD BE AFTER MY KIDS.
I DON'T UNDERSTAND.
YOU MIGHT HAVE OVERHEARD ANGEL MENTIONING SOMETHING ABOUT A FOURSOME?
ANGEL, TIERRA AND MAXINE ALL GOT PREGNANT.
WHEN I HEARD ABOUT TIERRA GETTING RIPPED APART FROM THE INSIDE--IT ALL FELL INTO PLACE.
WE CAN RUN SOME TESTS IF YOU'D LIKE.
YES.
YES, WE SHOULD.

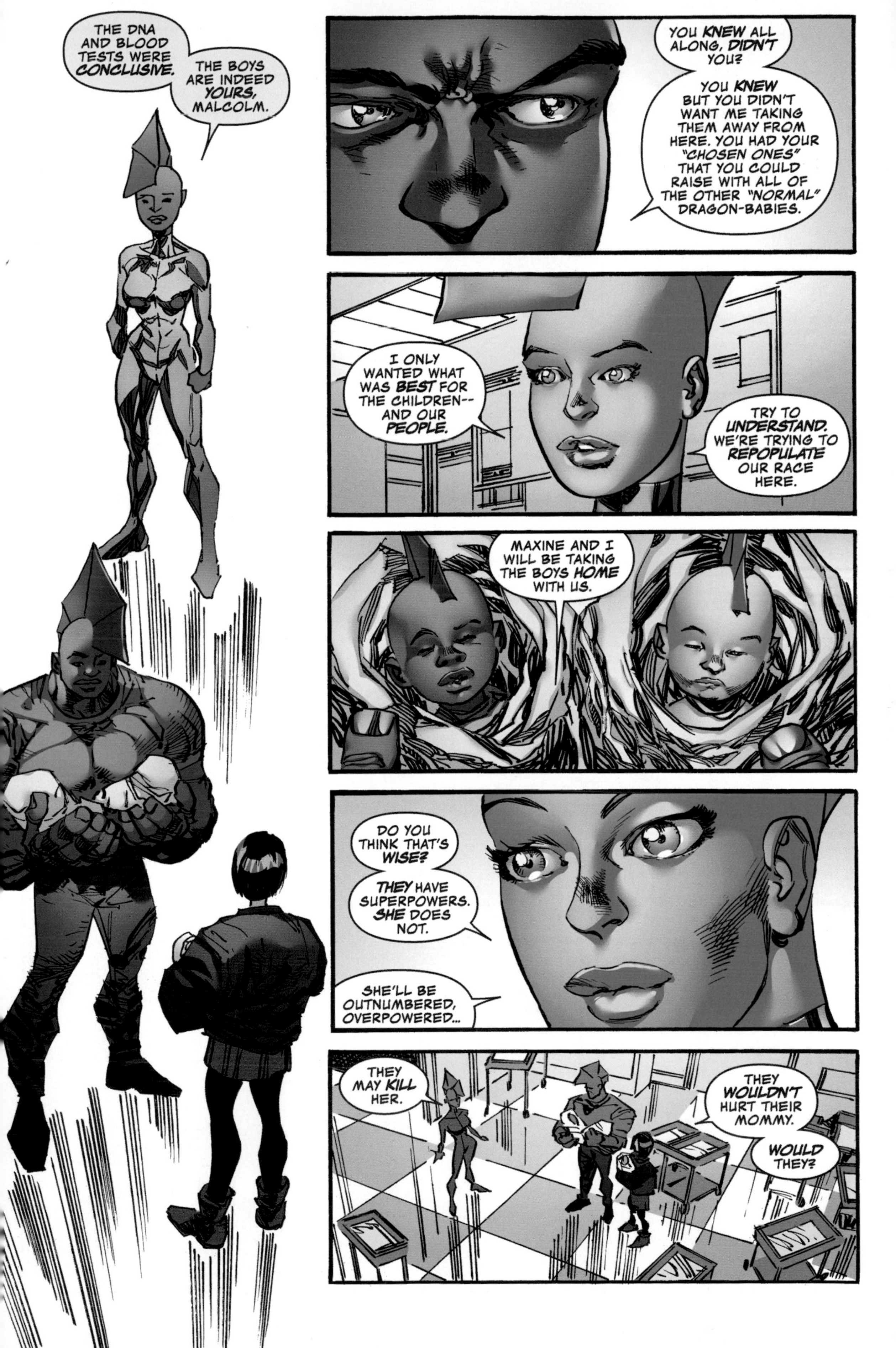
THE DNA AND BLOOD TESTS WERE CONCLUSIVE.
THE BOYS ARE INDEED YOURS, MALCOLM.
YOU KNEW ALL ALONG, DIDN'T YOU?
YOU KNEW BUT YOU DIDN'T WANT ME TAKING THEM AWAY FROM HERE. YOU HAD YOUR "CHOSEN ONES" THAT YOU COULD RAISE WITH ALL OF THE OTHER "NORMAL" DRAGON-BABIES.
I ONLY WANTED WHAT WAS BEST FOR THE CHILDREN-- AND OUR PEOPLE.
TRY TO UNDERSTAND. WE'RE TRYING TO REPOPULATE OUR RACE HERE.
MAXINE AND I WILL BE TAKING THE BOYS HOME WITH US.
DO YOU THINK THAT'S WISE?
THEY HAVE SUPERPOWERS. SHE DOES NOT.
SHE'LL BE OUTNUMBERED, OVERPOWERED...
THEY MAY KILL HER.
THEY WOULDN'T HURT THEIR MOMMY.
WOULD THEY?

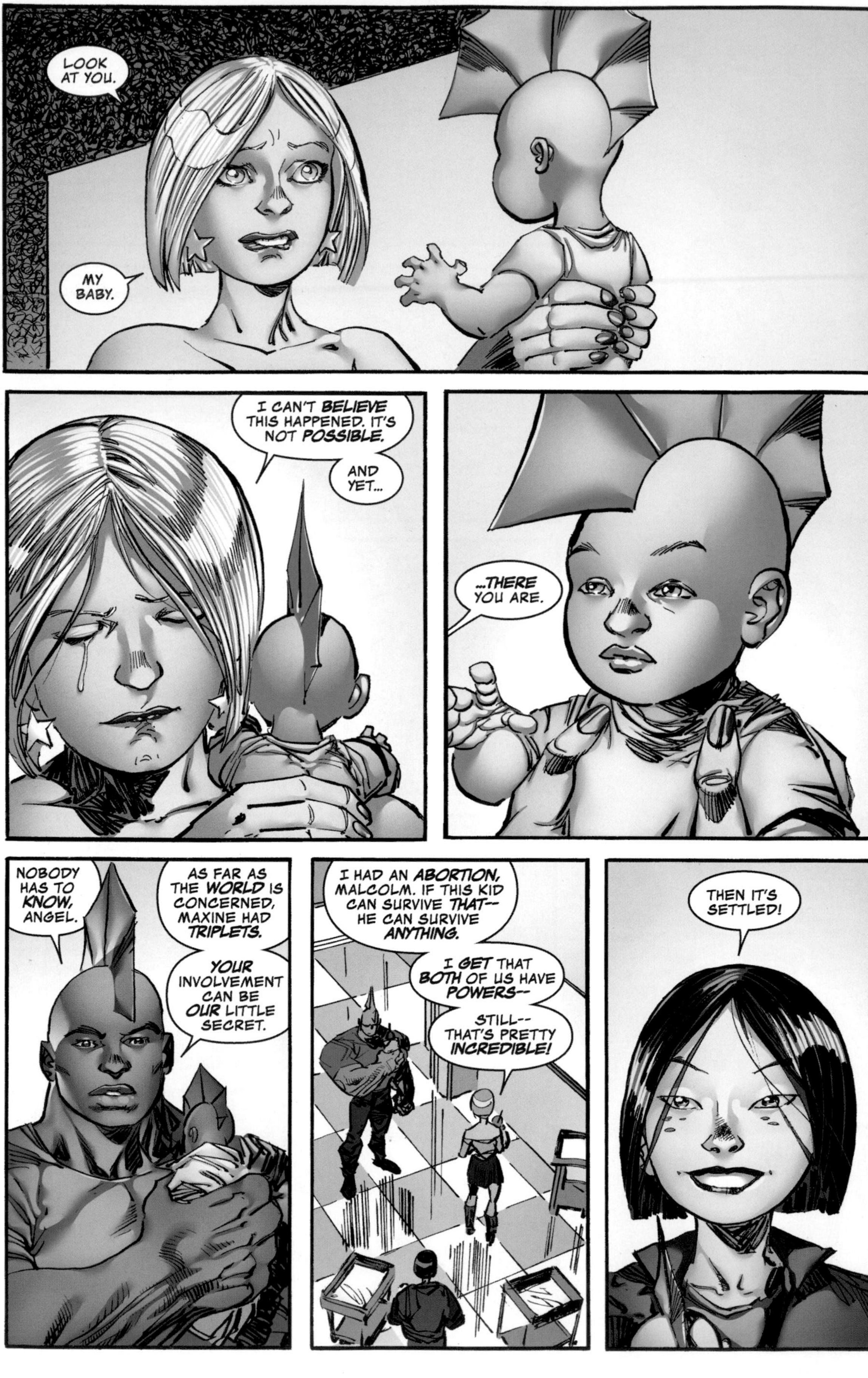
LOOK AT YOU.
MY BABY.
I CAN'T BELIEVE THIS HAPPENED. IT'S NOT POSSIBLE.
AND YET...
...THERE YOU ARE.
NOBODY HAS TO KNOW, ANGEL.
AS FAR AS THE WORLD IS CONCERNED, MAXINE HAD TRIPLETS.
YOUR INVOLVEMENT CAN BE OUR LITTLE SECRET.
I HAD AN ABORTION, MALCOLM. IF THIS KID CAN SURVIVE THAT-- HE CAN SURVIVE ANYTHING.
I GET THAT BOTH OF US HAVE POWERS--
STILL-- THAT'S PRETTY INCREDIBLE!
THEN IT'S SETTLED!

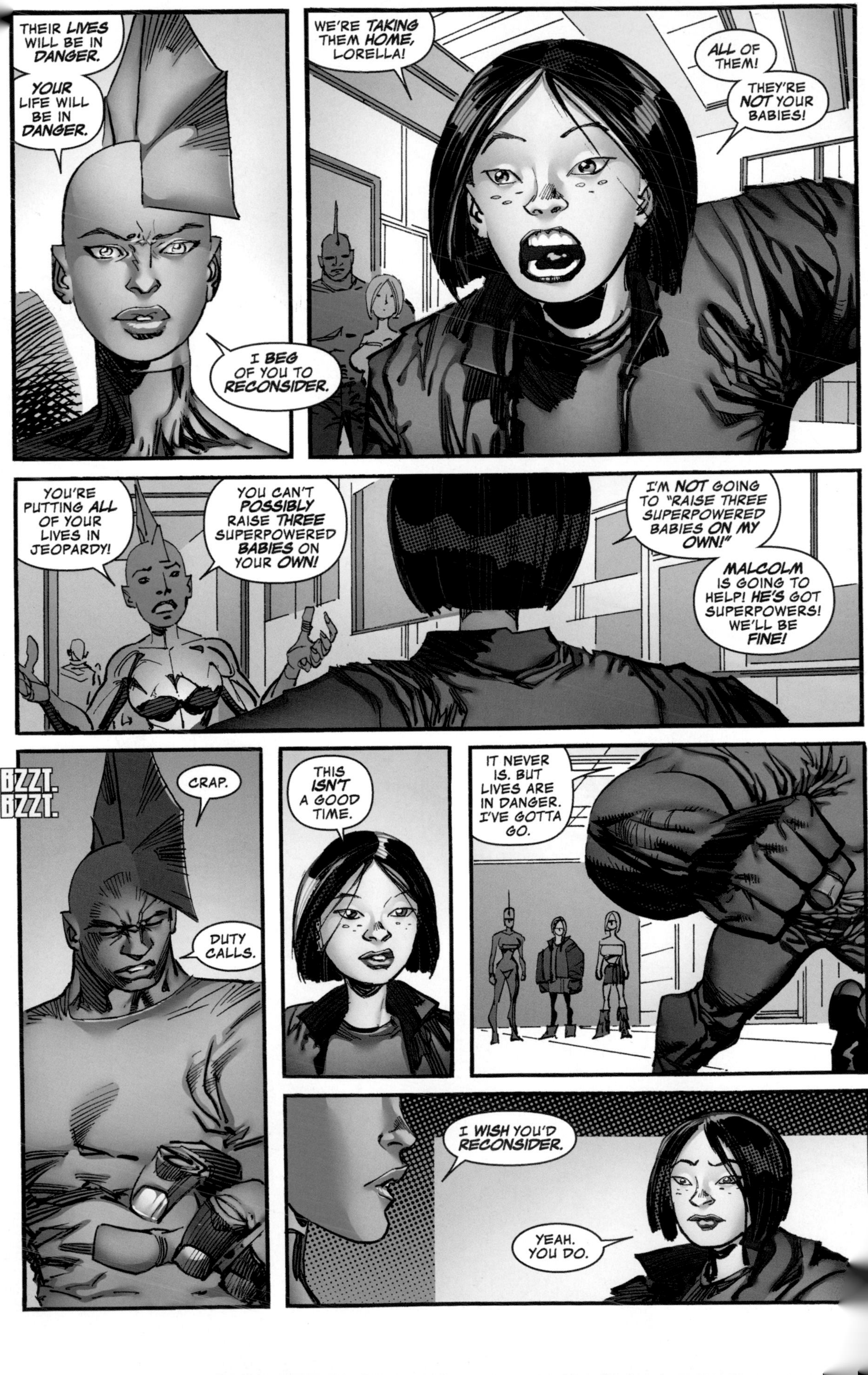

THEIR LIVES WILL BE IN DANGER.
YOUR LIFE WILL BE IN DANGER.
I BEG OF YOU TO RECONSIDER.
WE'RE TAKING THEM HOME, LORELLA!
ALL OF THEM!
THEY'RE NOT YOUR BABIES!
YOU'RE PUTTING ALL OF YOUR LIVES IN JEOPARDY!
YOU CAN'T POSSIBLY RAISE THREE SUPERPOWERED BABIES ON YOUR OWN!
I'M NOT GOING TO "RAISE THREE SUPERPOWERED BABIES ON MY OWN!"
MALCOLM IS GOING TO HELP! HE'S GOT SUPERPOWERS! WE'LL BE FINE!
BZZT. BZZT.
CRAP.
DUTY CALLS.
THIS ISN'T A GOOD TIME.
IT NEVER IS. BUT LIVES ARE IN DANGER. I'VE GOTTA GO.
I WISH YOU'D RECONSIDER.
YEAH. YOU DO.

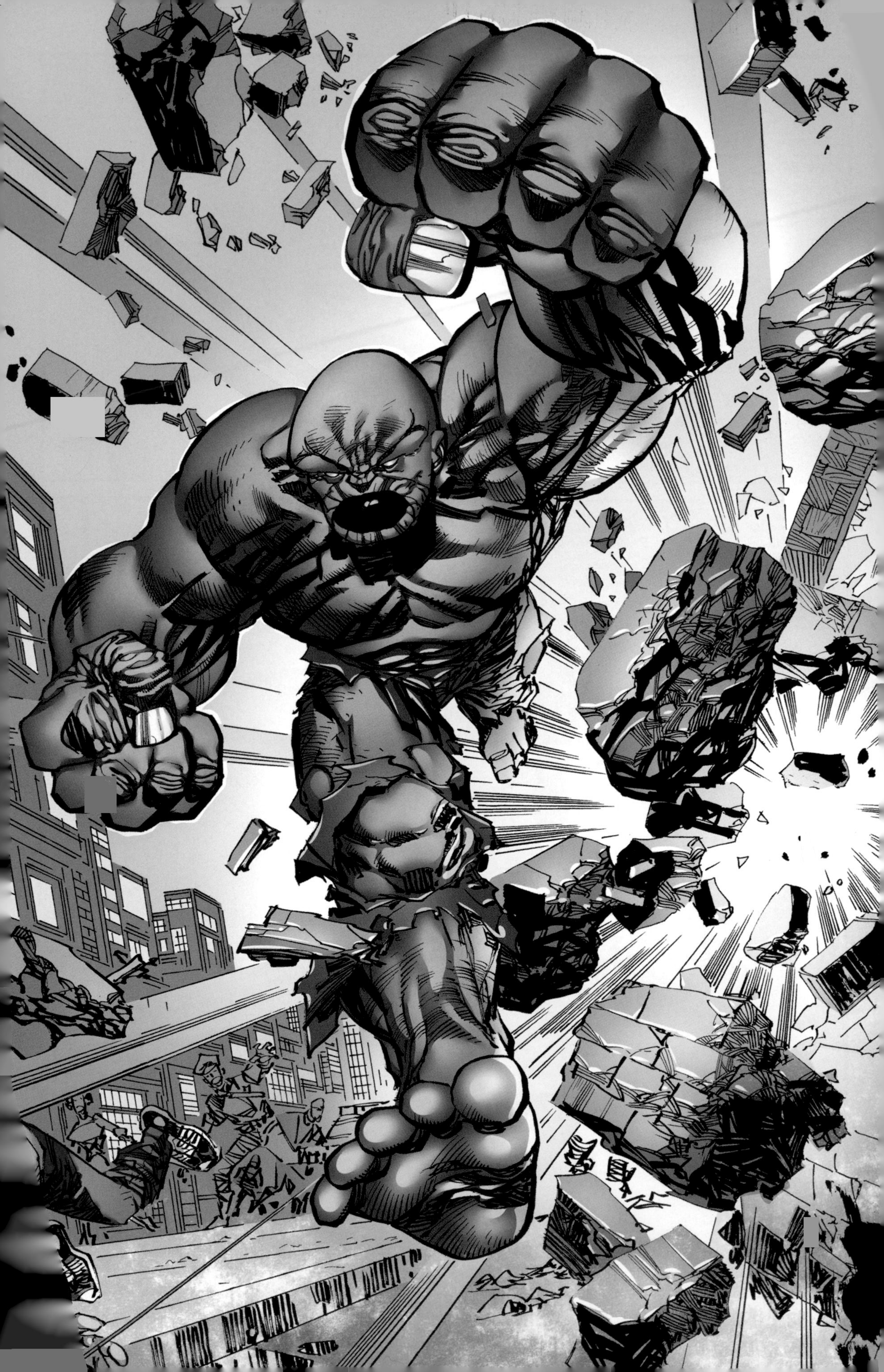

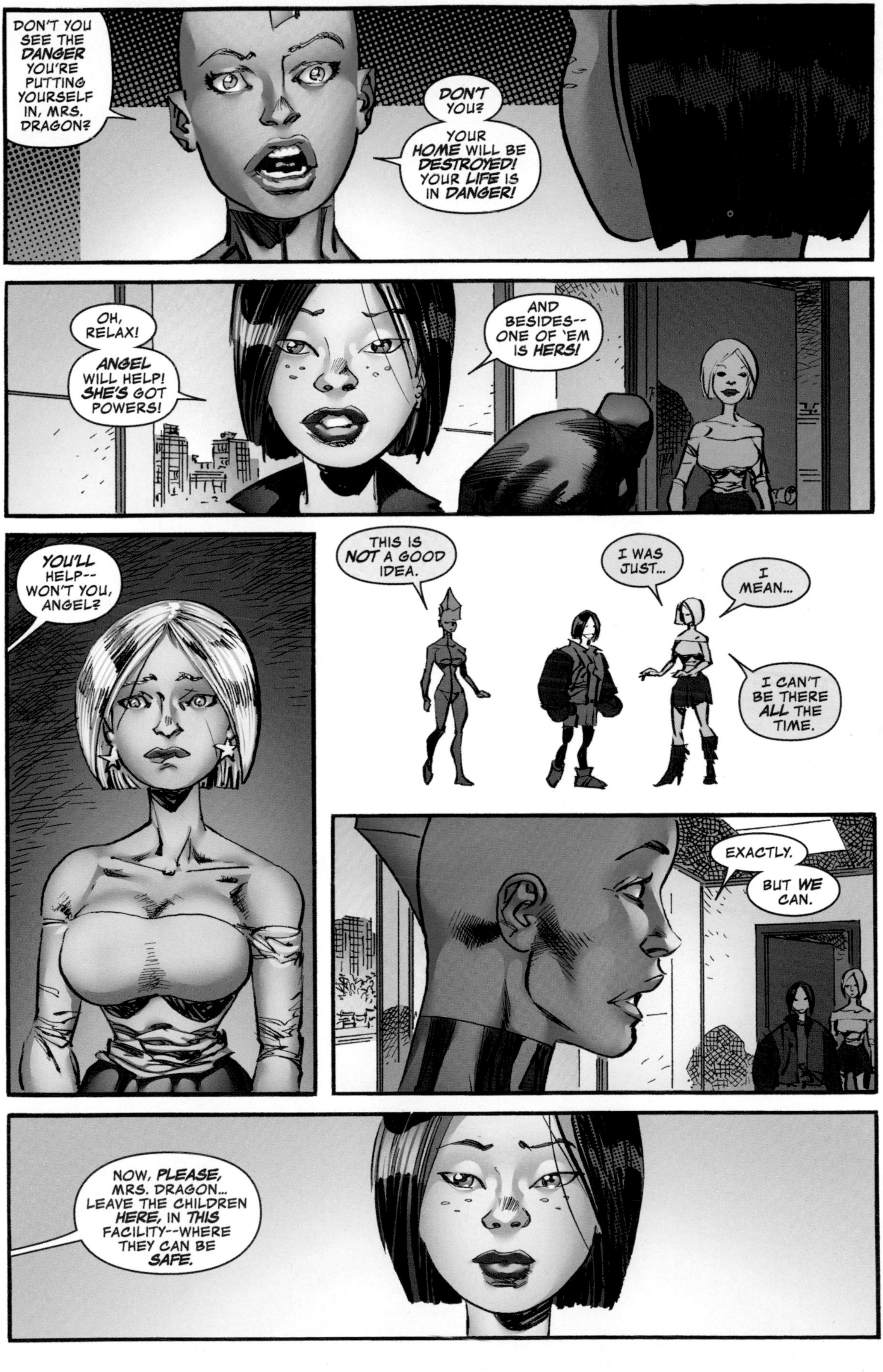

DON'T YOU SEE THE DANGER YOU'RE PUTTING YOURSELF IN, MRS. DRAGON?
DON'T YOU?
YOUR HOME WILL BE DESTROYED! YOUR LIFE IS IN DANGER!
OH, RELAX!
ANGEL WILL HELP! SHE'S GOT POWERS!
AND BESIDES-- ONE OF 'EM IS HERS!
YOU'LL HELP-- WON'T YOU, ANGEL?
THIS IS NOT A GOOD IDEA.
I WAS JUST...
I MEAN...
I CAN'T BE THERE ALL THE TIME.
EXACTLY.
BUT WE CAN.
NOW, PLEASE, MRS. DRAGON... LEAVE THE CHILDREN HERE, IN THIS FACILITY--WHERE THEY CAN BE SAFE.

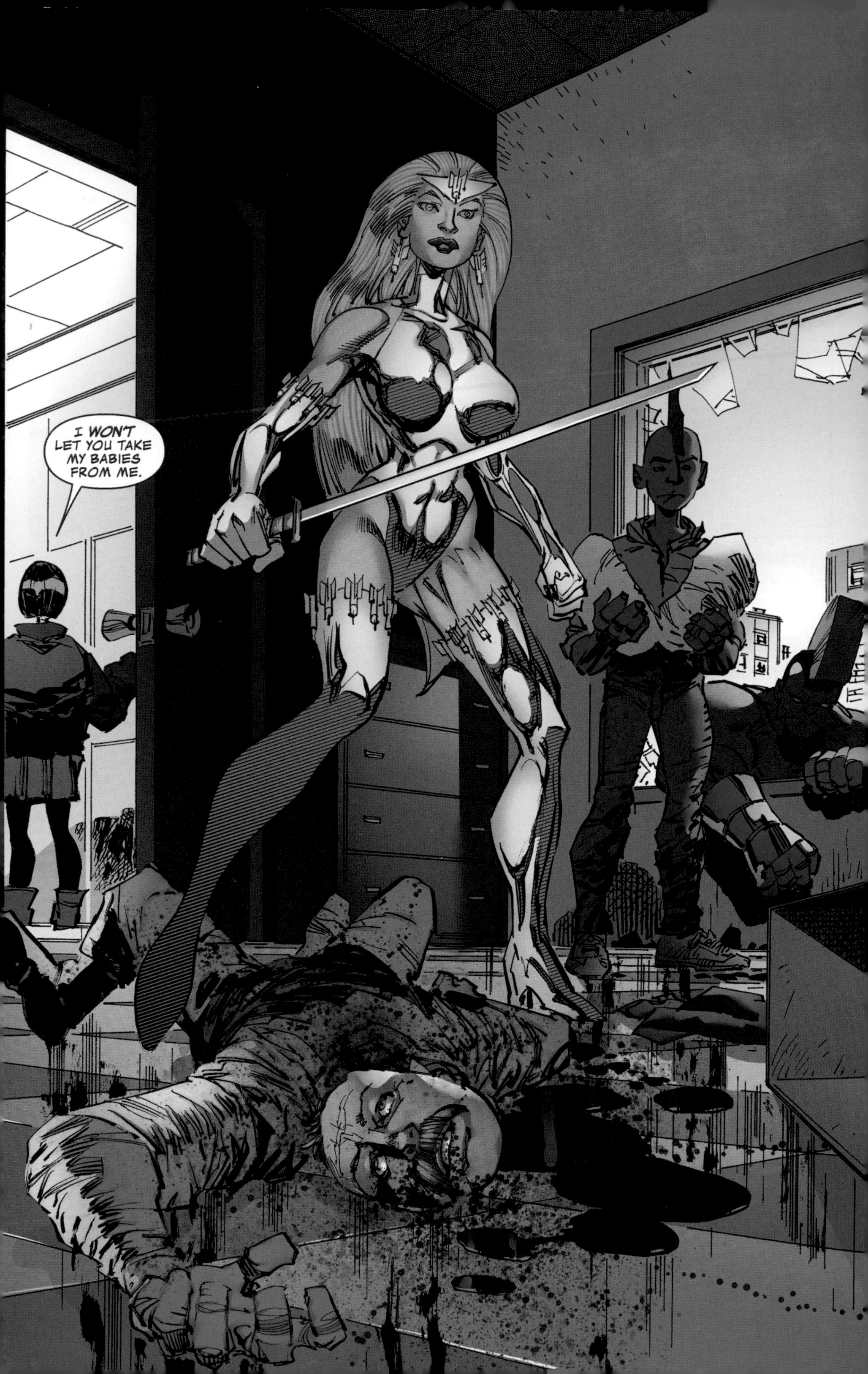
I WON'T LET YOU TAKE MY BABIES FROM ME.

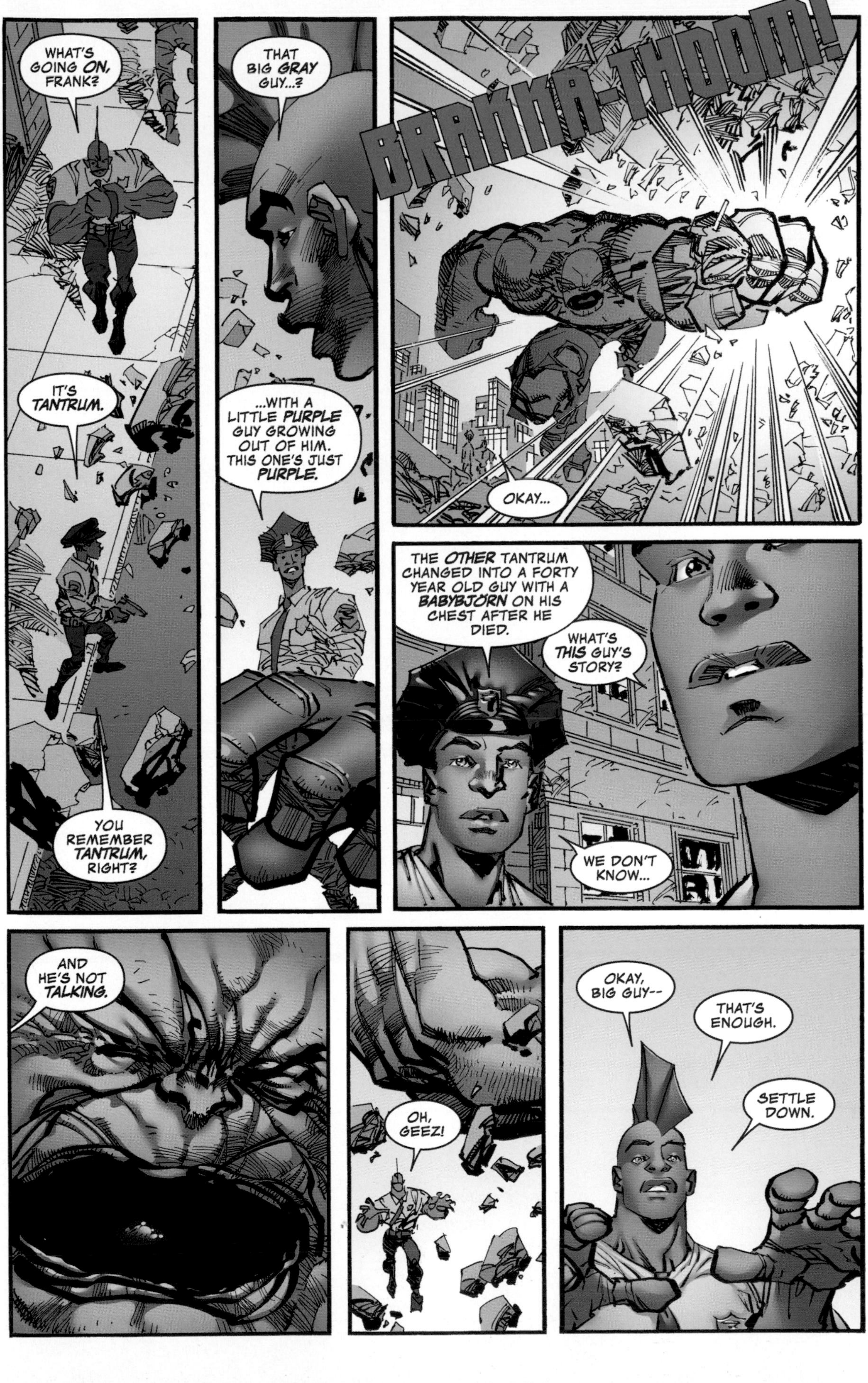
WHAT'S GOING ON, FRANK?
IT'S TANTRUM.
YOU REMEMBER TANTRUM, RIGHT?
THAT BIG GRAY GUY...?
...WITH A LITTLE PURPLE GUY GROWING OUT OF HIM. THIS ONE'S JUST PURPLE.
BRAKKA-THOOM!
OKAY...
THE OTHER TANTRUM CHANGED INTO A FORTY YEAR OLD GUY WITH A BABYBJÖRN ON HIS CHEST AFTER HE DIED.
WHAT'S THIS GUY'S STORY?
WE DON'T KNOW...
AND HE'S NOT TALKING.
OH, GEEZ!
OKAY, BIG GUY--
THAT'S ENOUGH.
SETTLE DOWN.

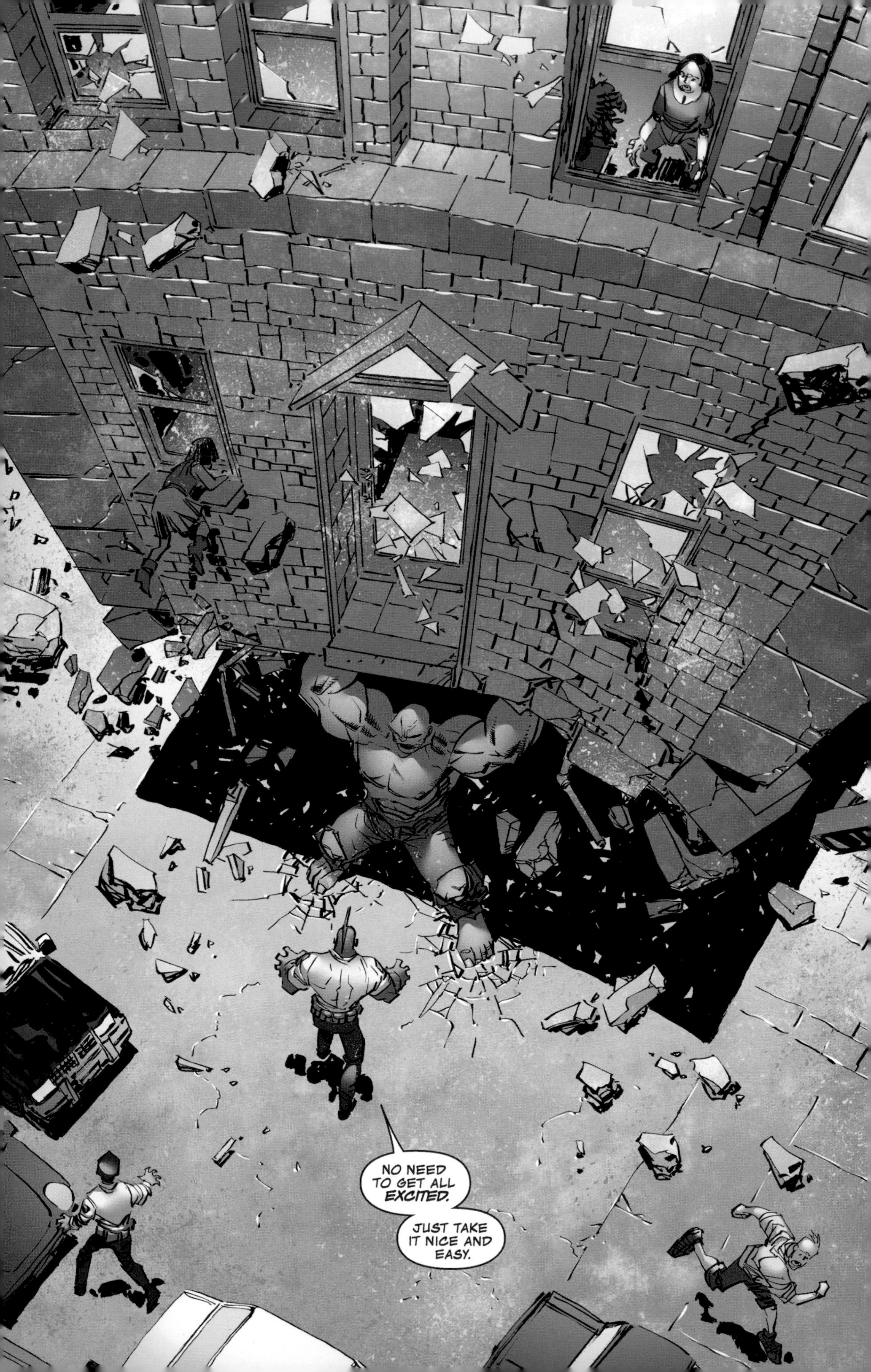
NO NEED TO GET ALL EXCITED.
JUST TAKE IT NICE AND EASY.

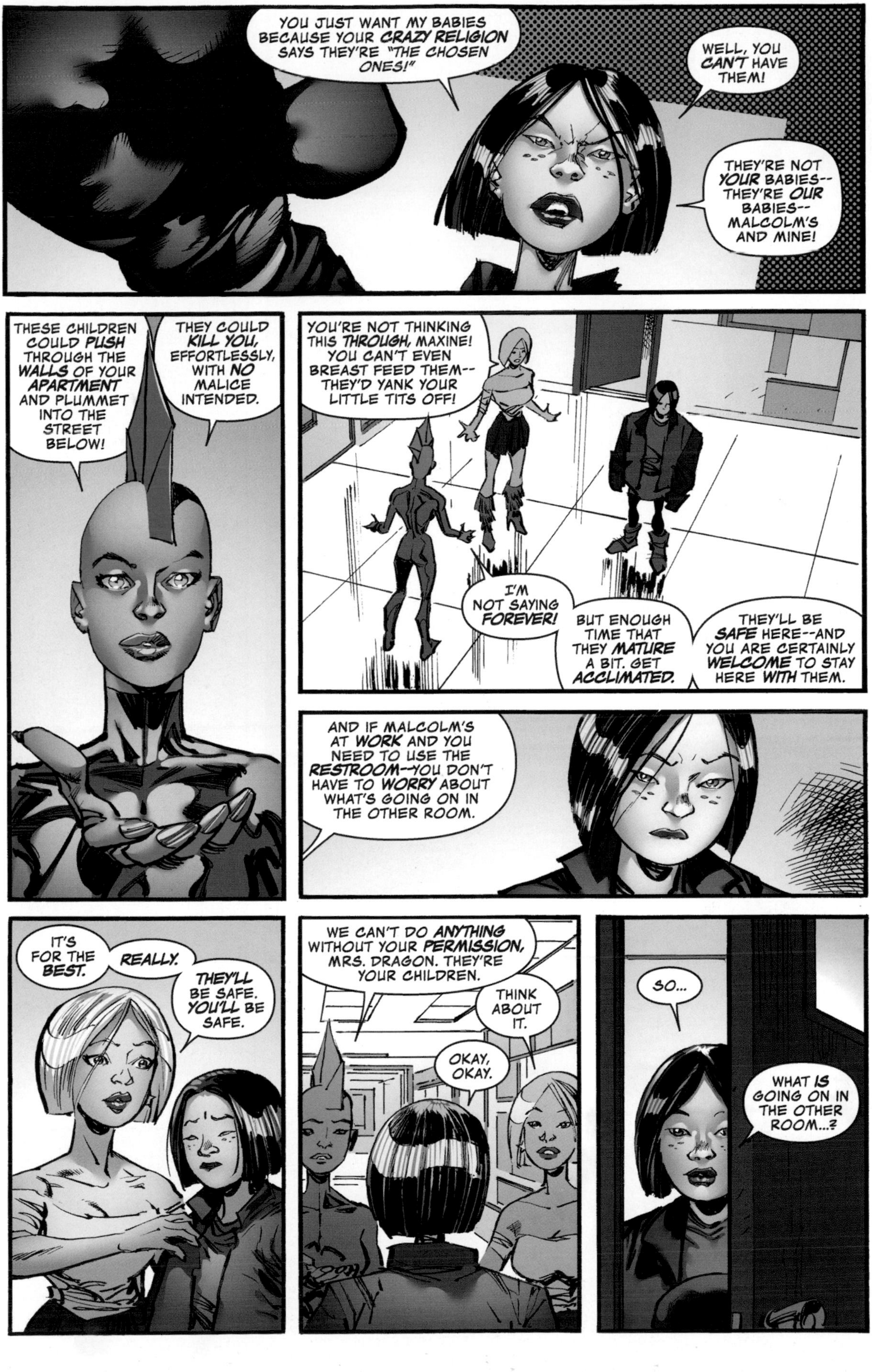
YOU JUST WANT MY BABIES BECAUSE YOUR CRAZY RELIGION SAYS THEY'RE "THE CHOSEN ONES!"
WELL, YOU CAN'T HAVE THEM!
THEY'RE NOT YOUR BABIES-- THEY'RE OUR BABIES-- MALCOLM'S AND MINE!
THESE CHILDREN COULD PUSH THROUGH THE WALLS OF YOUR APARTMENT AND PLUMMET INTO THE STREET BELOW!
THEY COULD KILL YOU, EFFORTLESSLY, WITH NO MALICE INTENDED.
YOU'RE NOT THINKING THIS THROUGH, MAXINE! YOU CAN'T EVEN BREAST FEED THEM-- THEY'D YANK YOUR LITTLE TITS OFF!
I'M NOT SAYING FOREVER!
BUT ENOUGH TIME THAT THEY MATURE A BIT. GET ACCLIMATED.
THEY'LL BE SAFE HERE--AND YOU ARE CERTAINLY WELCOME TO STAY HERE WITH THEM.
AND IF MALCOLM'S AT WORK AND YOU NEED TO USE THE RESTROOM--YOU DON'T HAVE TO WORRY ABOUT WHAT'S GOING ON IN THE OTHER ROOM.
IT'S FOR THE BEST.
REALLY.
THEY'LL BE SAFE. YOU'LL BE SAFE.
WE CAN'T DO ANYTHING WITHOUT YOUR PERMISSION, MRS. DRAGON. THEY'RE YOUR CHILDREN.
THINK ABOUT IT.
OKAY, OKAY.
SO...
WHAT IS GOING ON IN THE OTHER ROOM...?

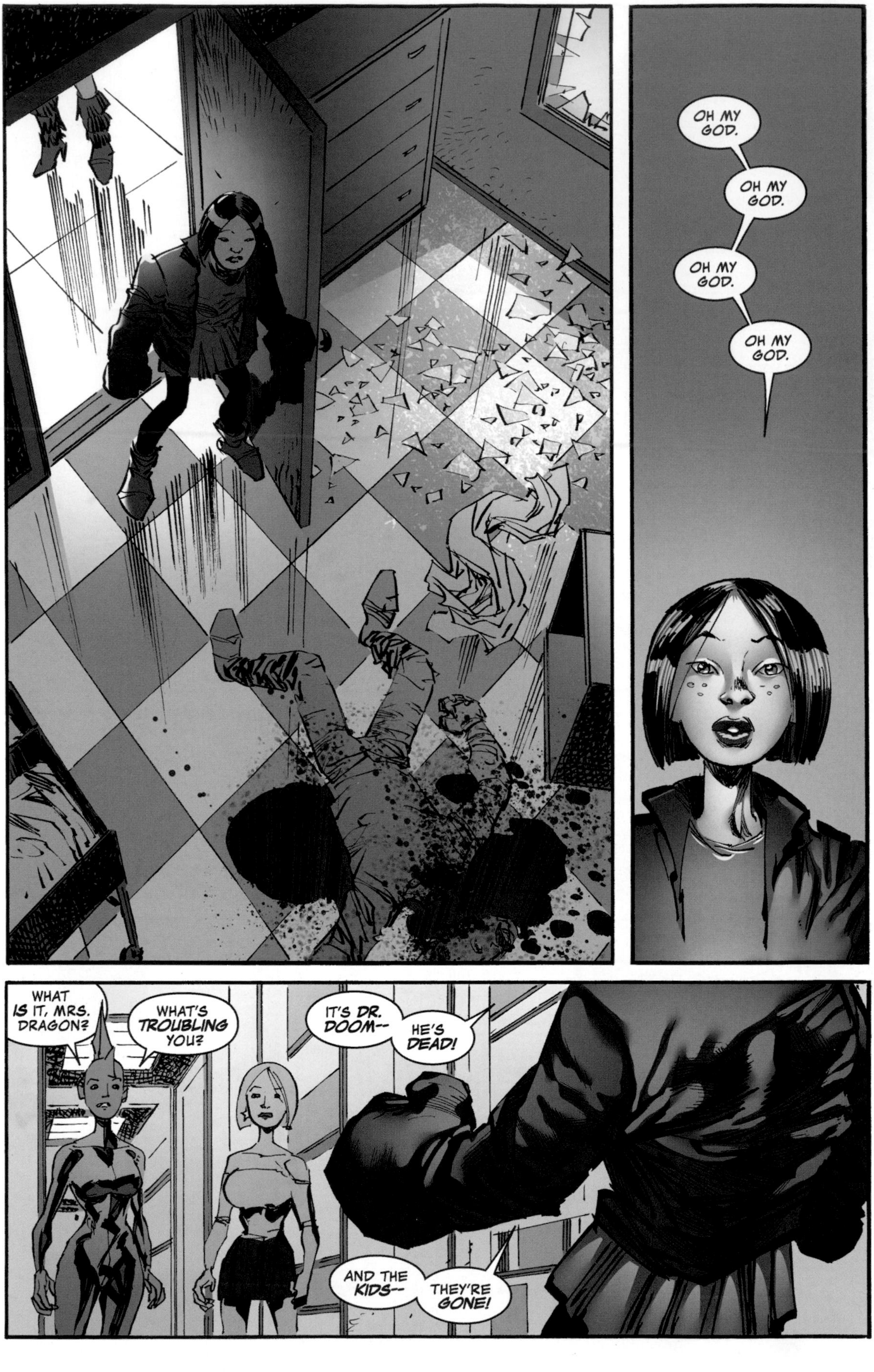
OH MY GOD.
OH MY GOD.
OH MY GOD.
OH MY GOD.
WHAT IS IT, MRS. DRAGON?
WHAT'S TROUBLING YOU?
IT'S DR. DOOM--
HE'S DEAD!
AND THE KIDS--
THEY'RE GONE!

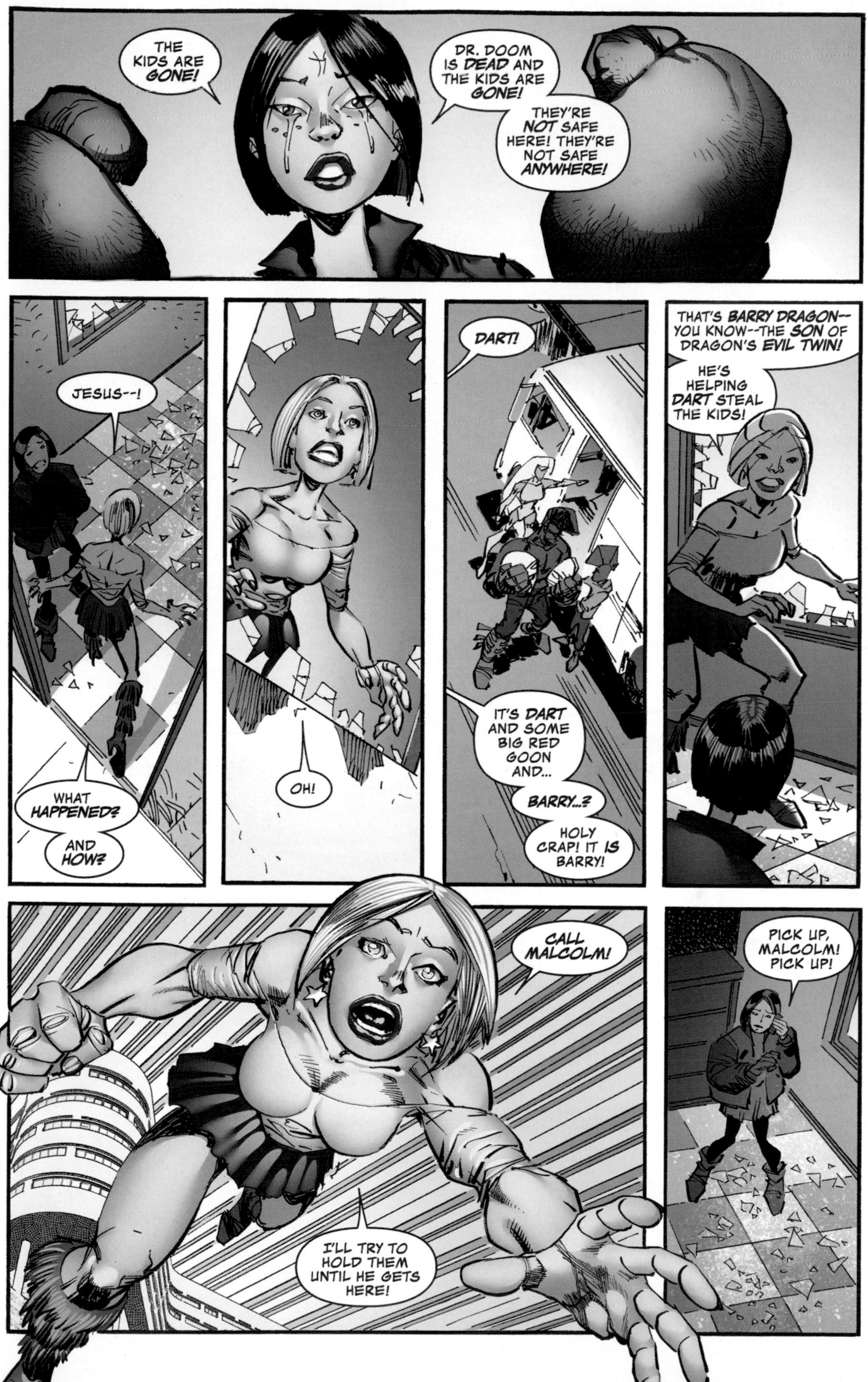
THE KIDS ARE *GONE!*
DR. DOOM IS *DEAD* AND THE KIDS ARE *GONE!*
THEY'RE *NOT* SAFE HERE! THEY'RE NOT SAFE *ANYWHERE!*
JESUS--!
WHAT *HAPPENED?*
AND *HOW?*
OH!
DART!
IT'S *DART* AND SOME BIG RED GOON AND...
BARRY...?
HOLY CRAP! IT *IS* BARRY!
THAT'S *BARRY DRAGON*--YOU KNOW--THE *SON* OF DRAGON'S *EVIL TWIN!*
HE'S HELPING *DART* STEAL THE KIDS!
CALL MALCOLM!
I'LL TRY TO HOLD THEM UNTIL HE GETS HERE!
PICK UP, MALCOLM! PICK UP!

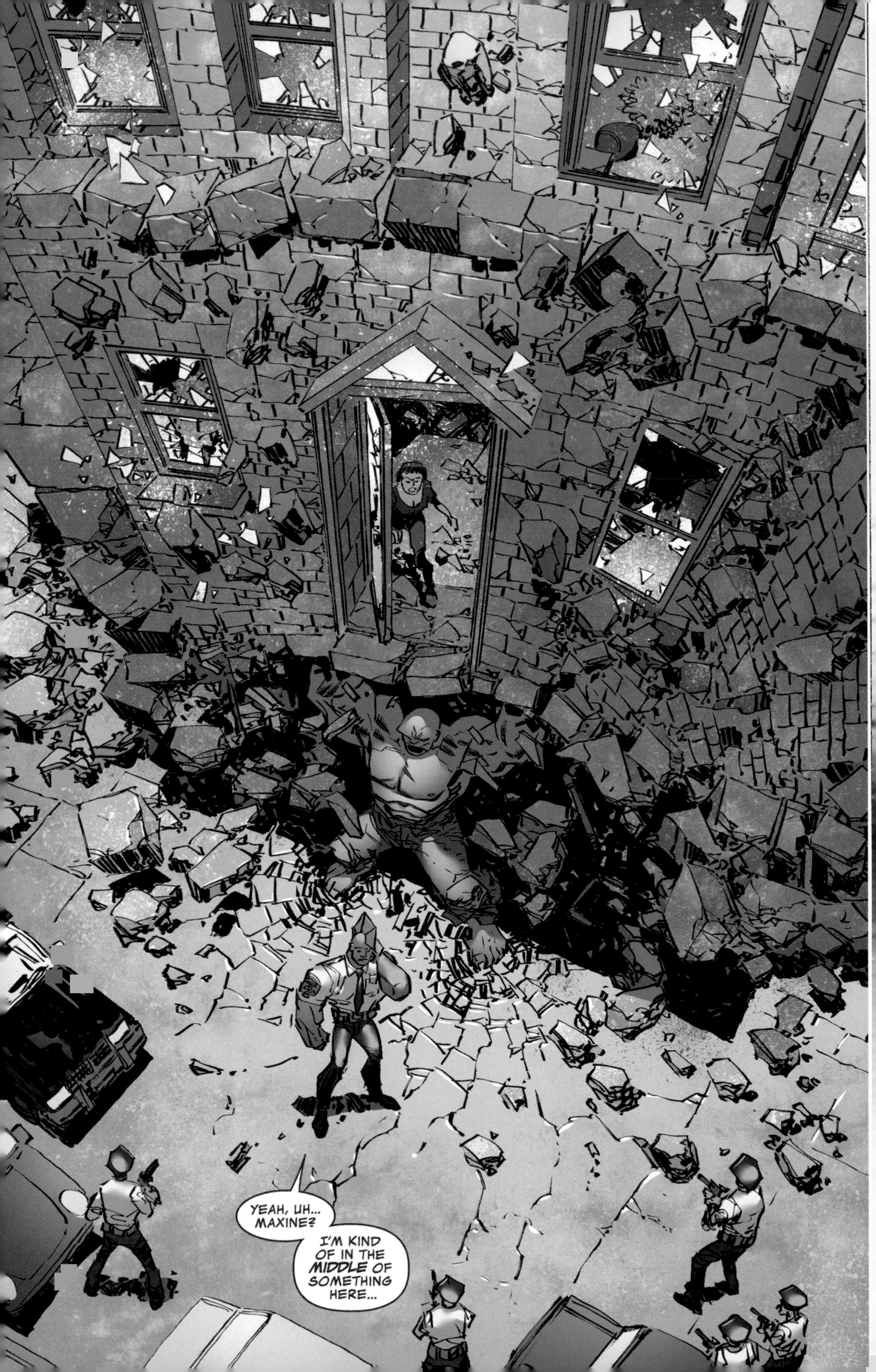
YEAH, UH... MAXINE?
I'M KIND OF IN THE *MIDDLE* OF SOMETHING HERE...

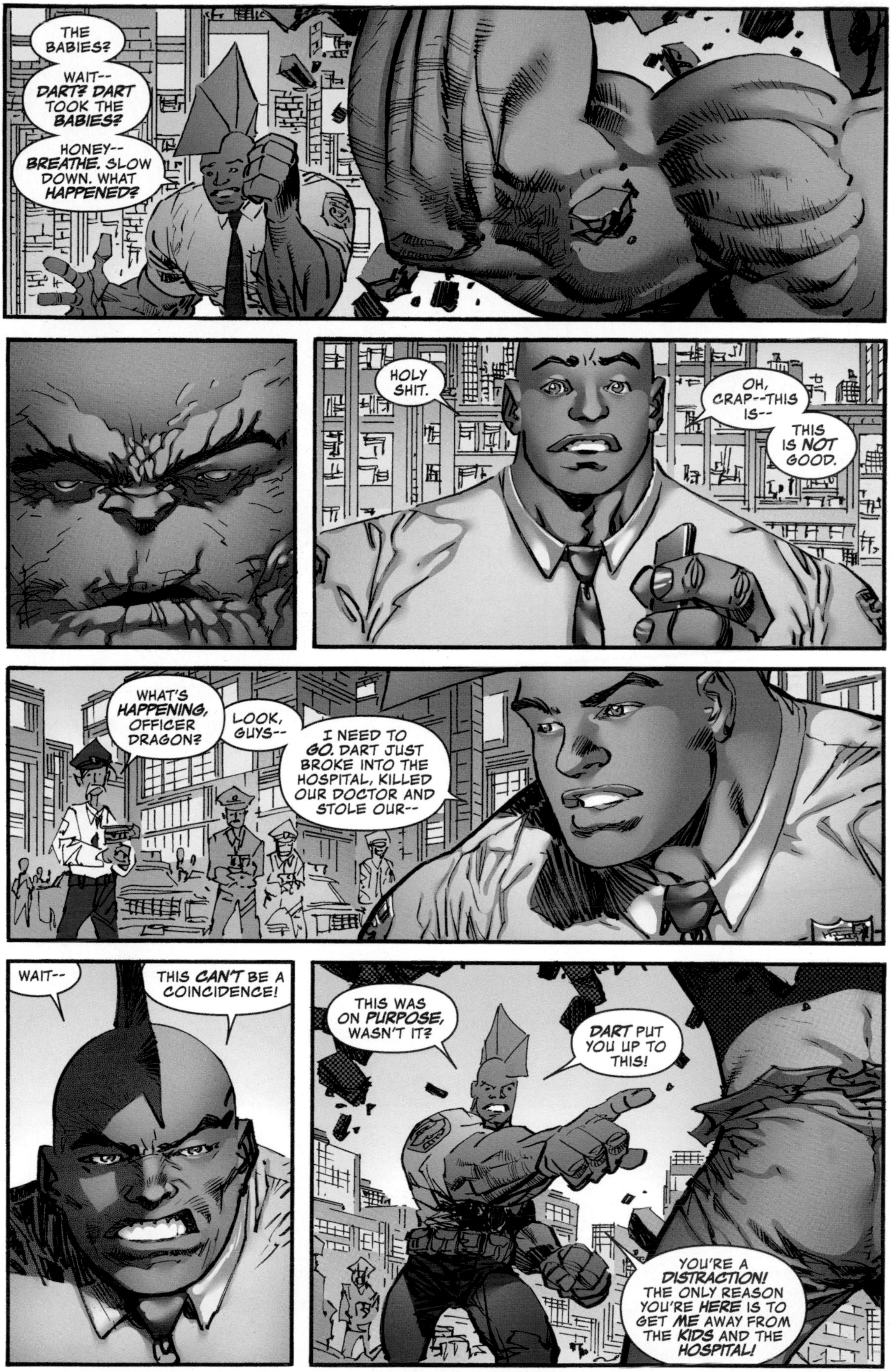
THE BABIES?
WAIT-- DART? DART TOOK THE BABIES?
HONEY-- BREATHE. SLOW DOWN. WHAT HAPPENED?
HOLY SHIT.
OH, CRAP--THIS IS--
THIS IS NOT GOOD.
WHAT'S HAPPENING, OFFICER DRAGON?
LOOK, GUYS--
I NEED TO GO. DART JUST BROKE INTO THE HOSPITAL, KILLED OUR DOCTOR AND STOLE OUR--
WAIT--
THIS CAN'T BE A COINCIDENCE!
THIS WAS ON PURPOSE, WASN'T IT?
DART PUT YOU UP TO THIS!
YOU'RE A DISTRACTION! THE ONLY REASON YOU'RE HERE IS TO GET ME AWAY FROM THE KIDS AND THE HOSPITAL!

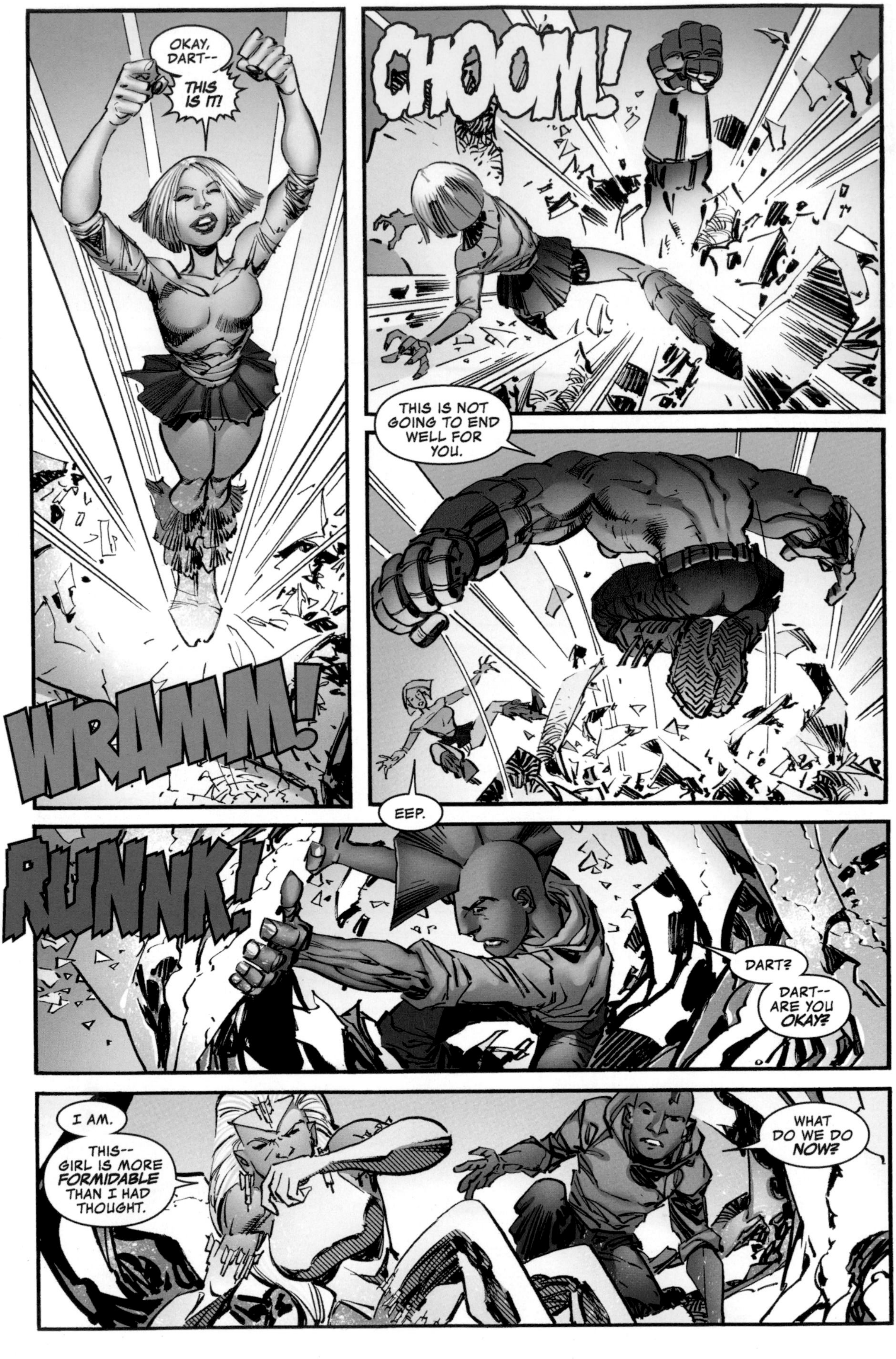
OKAY, DART--
THIS IS IT!
WRAMM!
CHOOM!
THIS IS NOT GOING TO END WELL FOR YOU.
EEP.
RUNNK!
DART?
DART-- ARE YOU OKAY?
I AM.
THIS-- GIRL IS MORE FORMIDABLE THAN I HAD THOUGHT.
WHAT DO WE DO NOW?

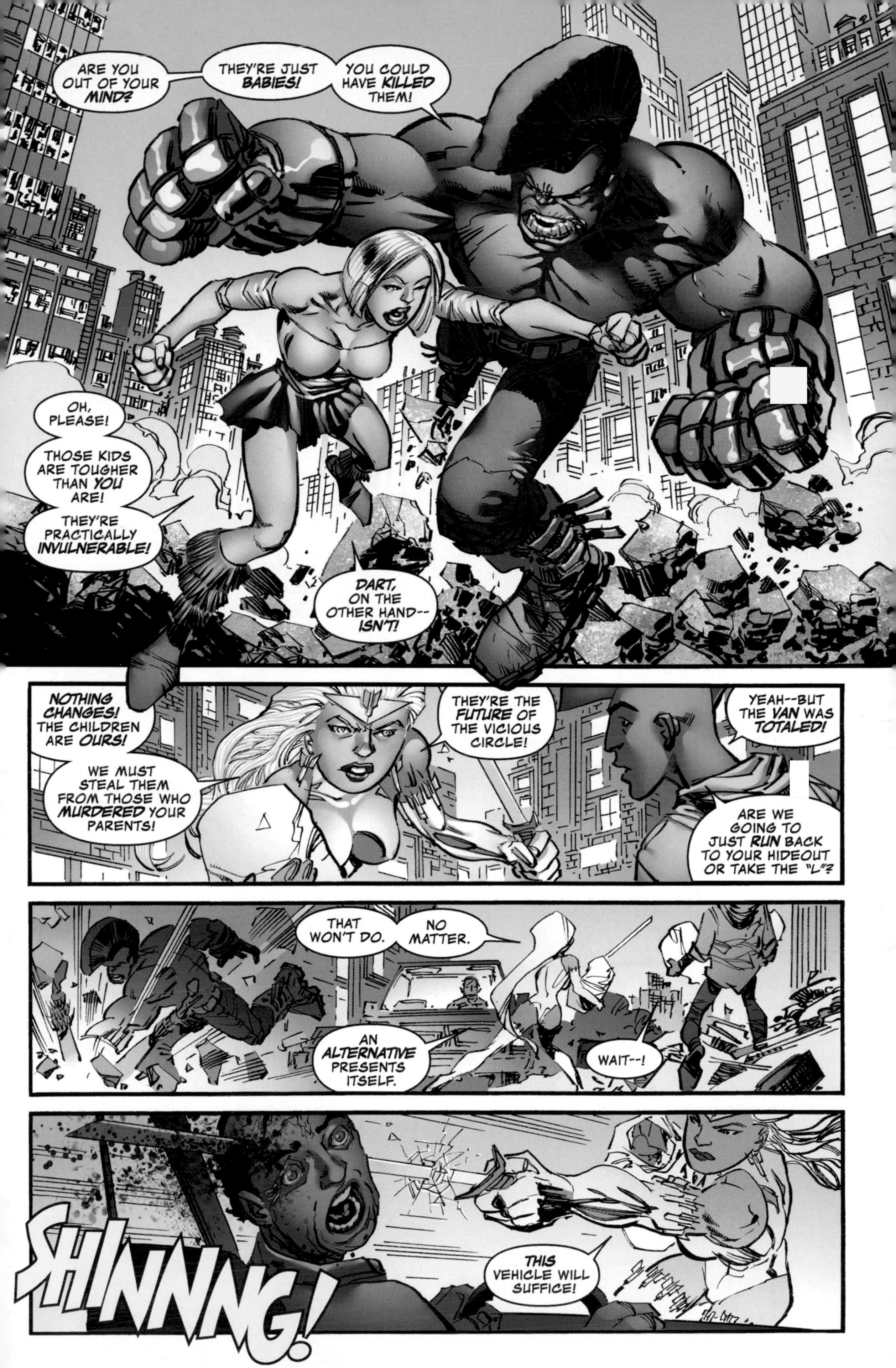

ARE YOU OUT OF YOUR MIND?
THEY'RE JUST BABIES!
YOU COULD HAVE KILLED THEM!
OH, PLEASE!
THOSE KIDS ARE TOUGHER THAN YOU ARE!
THEY'RE PRACTICALLY INVULNERABLE!
DART, ON THE OTHER HAND-- ISN'T!
NOTHING CHANGES! THE CHILDREN ARE OURS!
WE MUST STEAL THEM FROM THOSE WHO MURDERED YOUR PARENTS!
THEY'RE THE FUTURE OF THE VICIOUS CIRCLE!
YEAH--BUT THE VAN WAS TOTALED!
ARE WE GOING TO JUST RUN BACK TO YOUR HIDEOUT OR TAKE THE "L"?
THAT WON'T DO.
NO MATTER.
AN ALTERNATIVE PRESENTS ITSELF.
WAIT--!
SHINNNG!
THIS VEHICLE WILL SUFFICE!

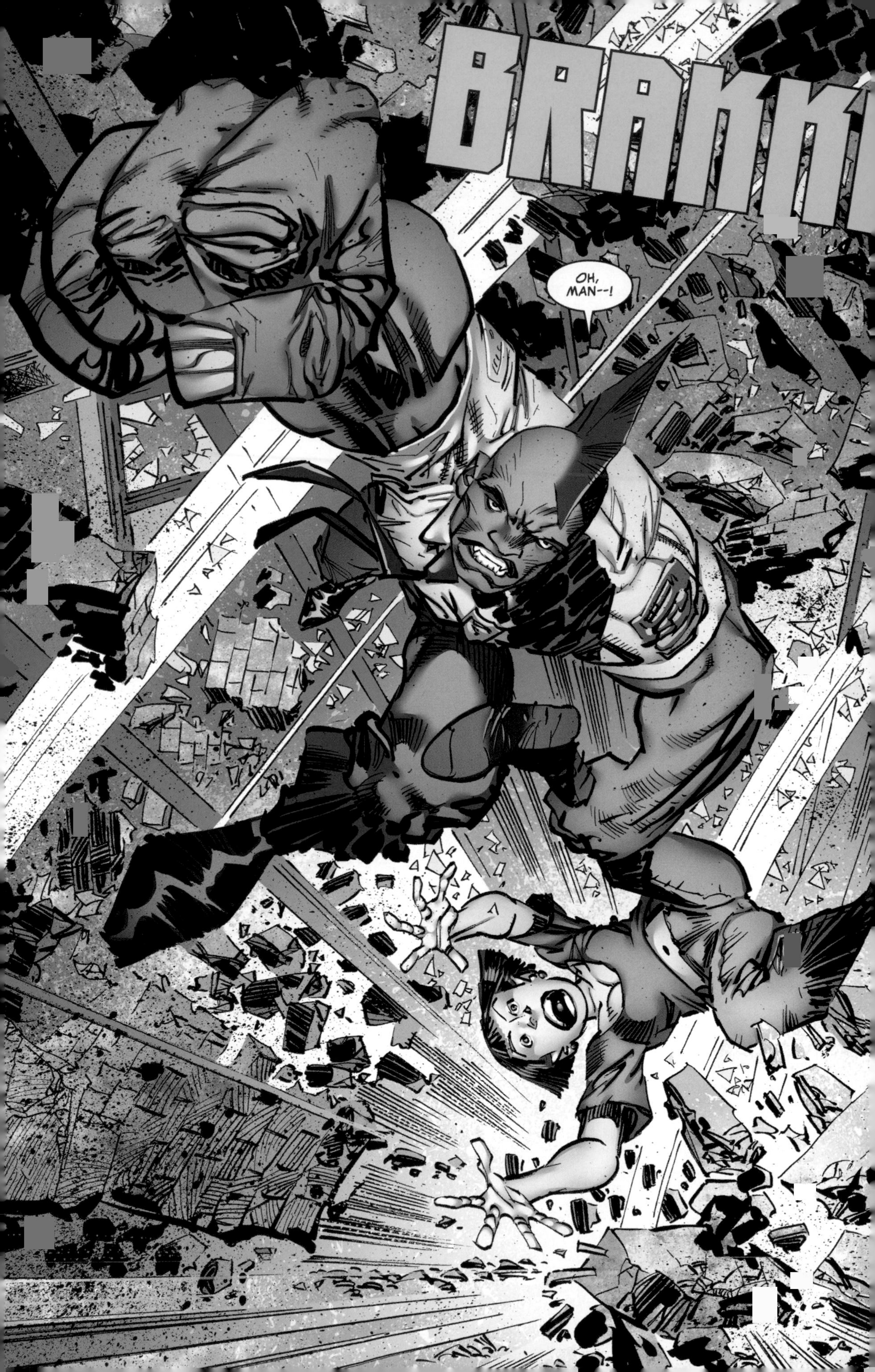
BRAKK
OH, MAN--!

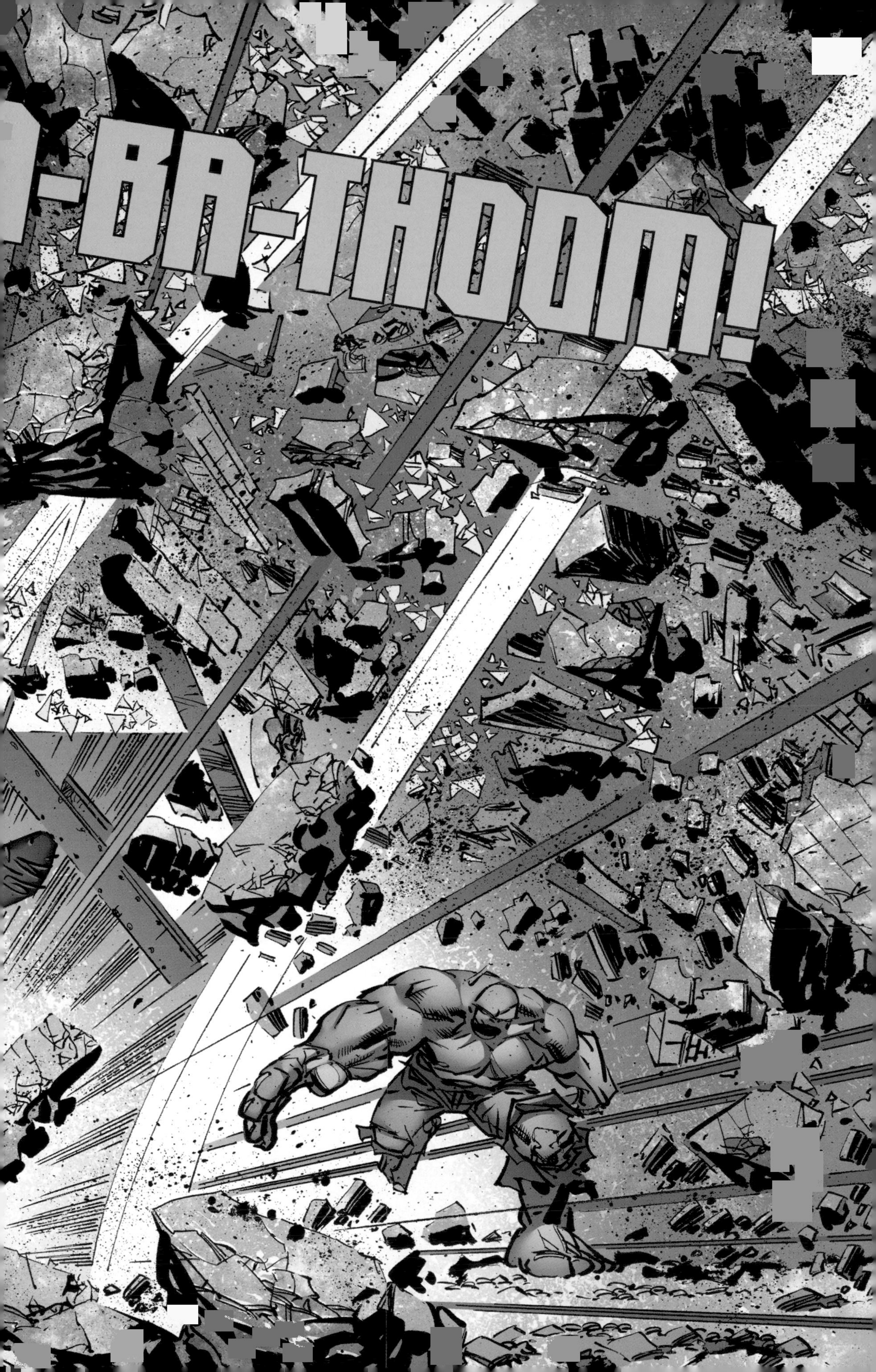
-BA-THOOM!

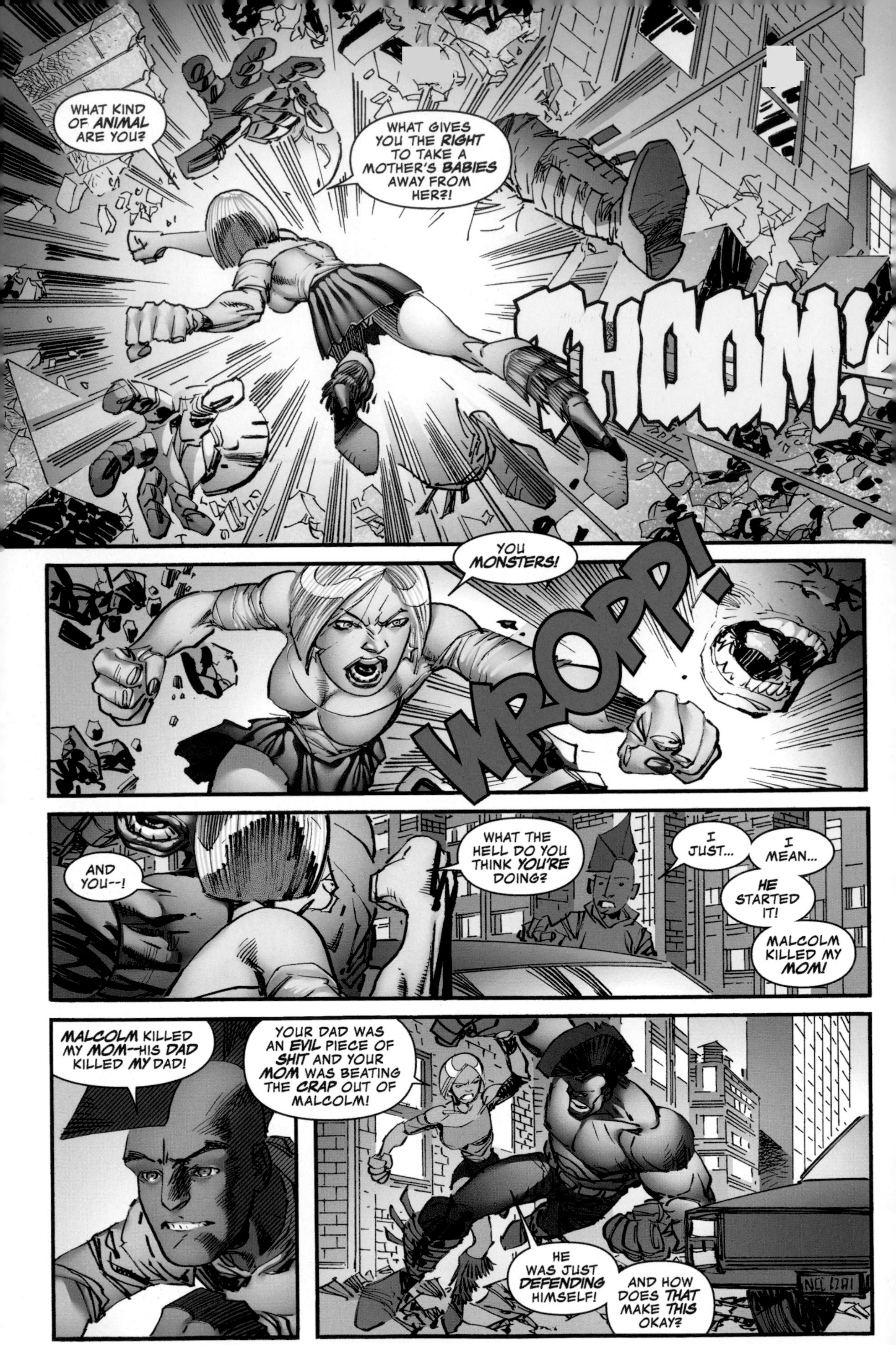
WHAT KIND OF ANIMAL ARE YOU?
WHAT GIVES YOU THE RIGHT TO TAKE A MOTHER'S BABIES AWAY FROM HER?!
THOOM!
YOU MONSTERS!
WROPP!
AND YOU--!
WHAT THE HELL DO YOU THINK YOU'RE DOING?
I JUST...
I MEAN...
HE STARTED IT!
MALCOLM KILLED MY MOM!
MALCOLM KILLED MY MOM--HIS DAD KILLED MY DAD!
YOUR DAD WAS AN EVIL PIECE OF SHIT AND YOUR MOM WAS BEATING THE CRAP OUT OF MALCOLM!
HE WAS JUST DEFENDING HIMSELF!
AND HOW DOES THAT MAKE THIS OKAY?

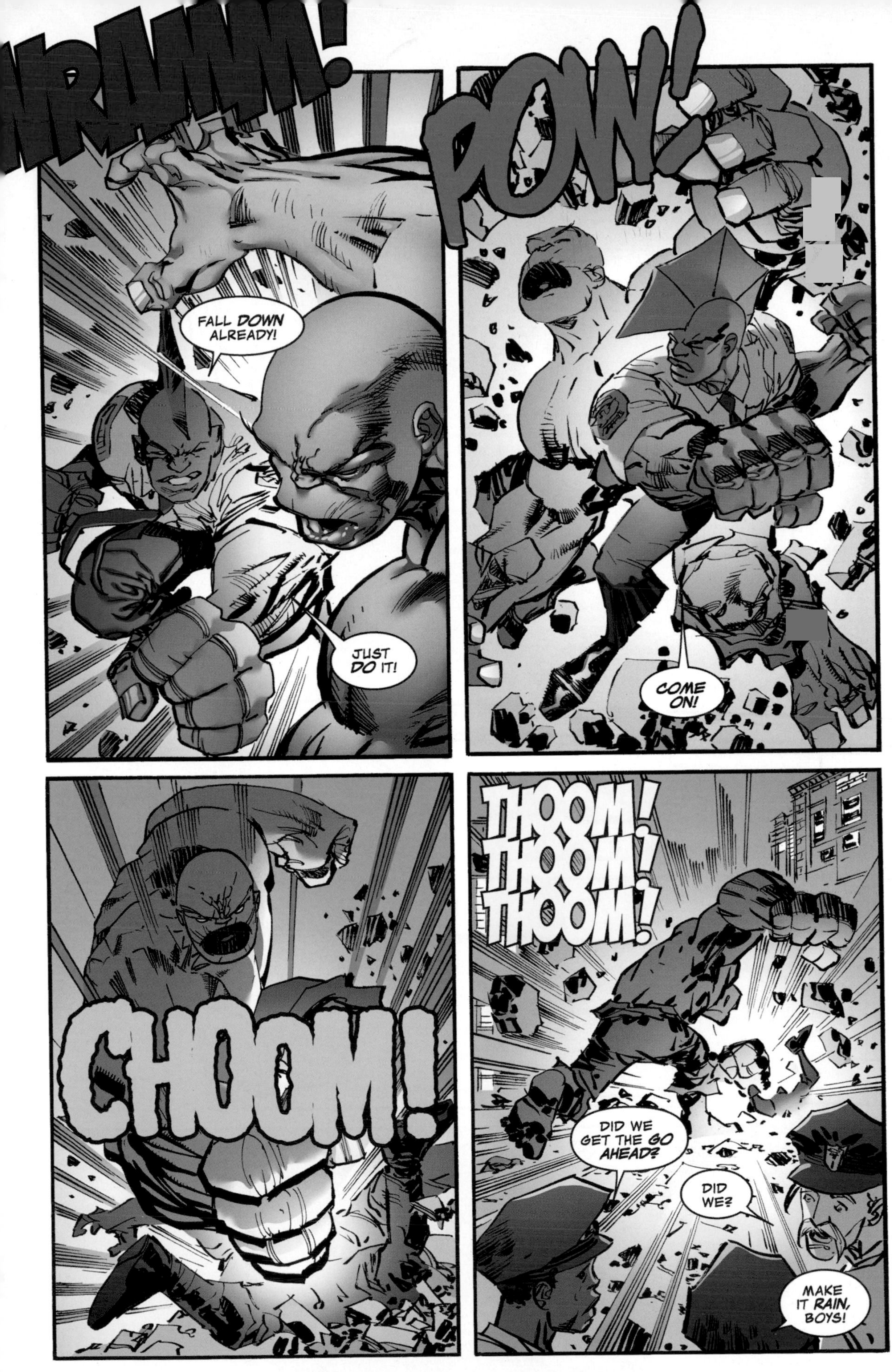
WRAMM!
FALL DOWN ALREADY!
JUST DO IT!
POW!
COME ON!
CHOOM!
THOOM! THOOM! THOOM!
DID WE GET THE GO AHEAD?
DID WE?
MAKE IT RAIN, BOYS!

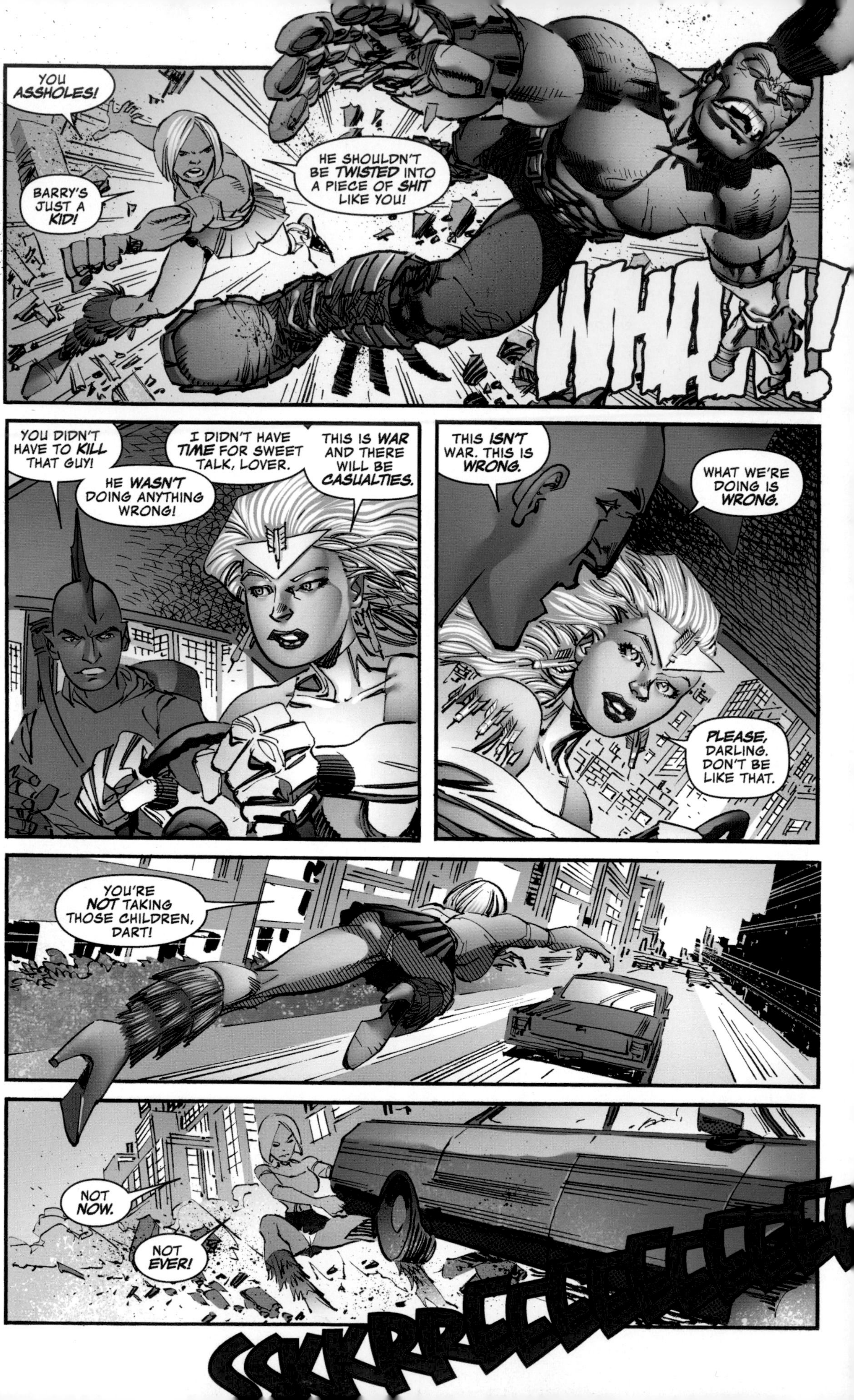
YOU ASSHOLES!
BARRY'S JUST A KID!
HE SHOULDN'T BE TWISTED INTO A PIECE OF SHIT LIKE YOU!
YOU DIDN'T HAVE TO KILL THAT GUY!
HE WASN'T DOING ANYTHING WRONG!
I DIDN'T HAVE TIME FOR SWEET TALK, LOVER.
THIS IS WAR AND THERE WILL BE CASUALTIES.
THIS ISN'T WAR. THIS IS WRONG.
WHAT WE'RE DOING IS WRONG.
PLEASE, DARLING. DON'T BE LIKE THAT.
YOU'RE NOT TAKING THOSE CHILDREN, DART!
NOT NOW.
NOT EVER!

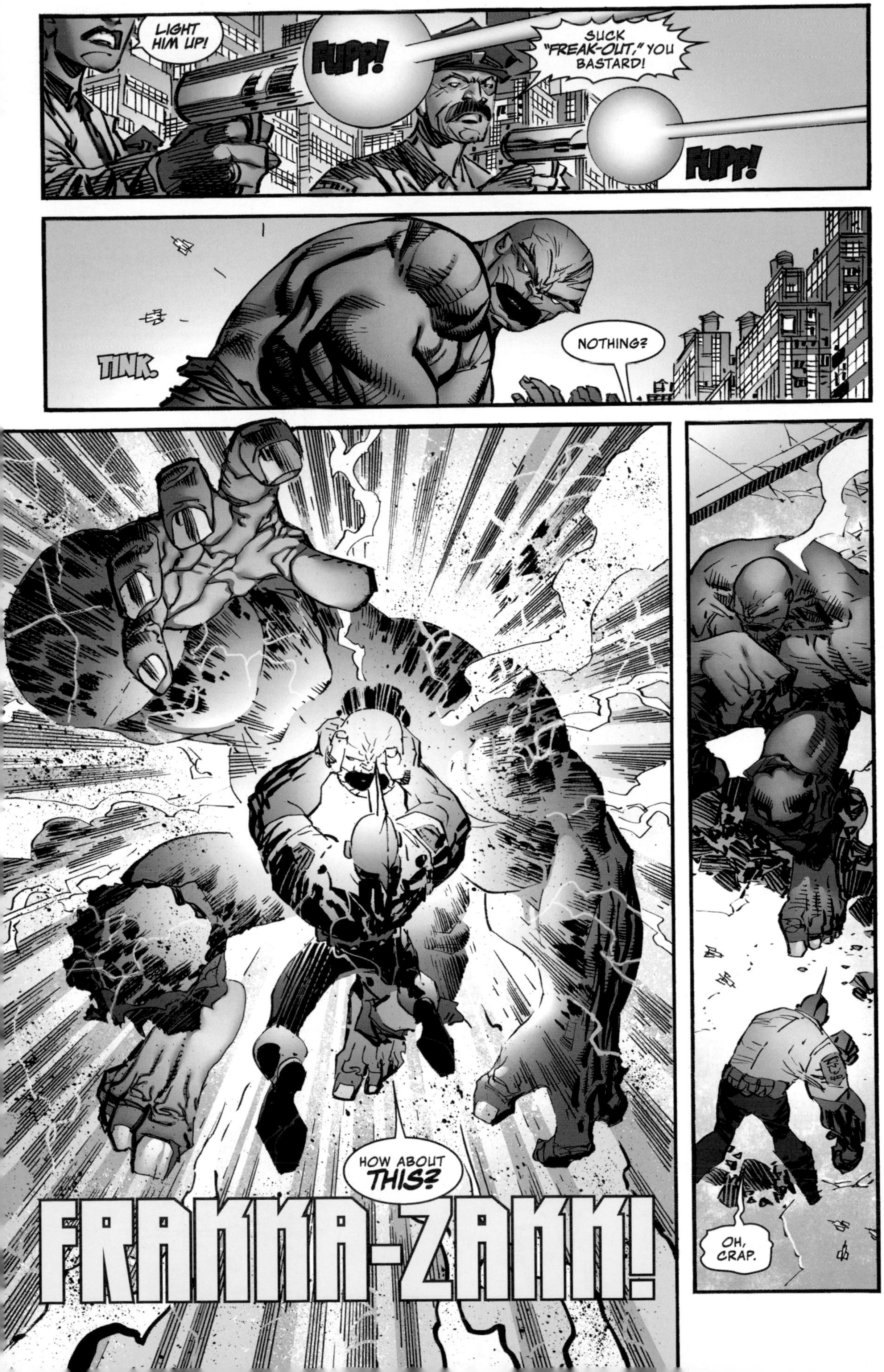
LIGHT HIM UP!
FUPP!
SUCK "FREAK-OUT," YOU BASTARD!
FUPP!
TINK.
NOTHING?
HOW ABOUT THIS?
FRAKKA-ZAKK!
OH, CRAP.

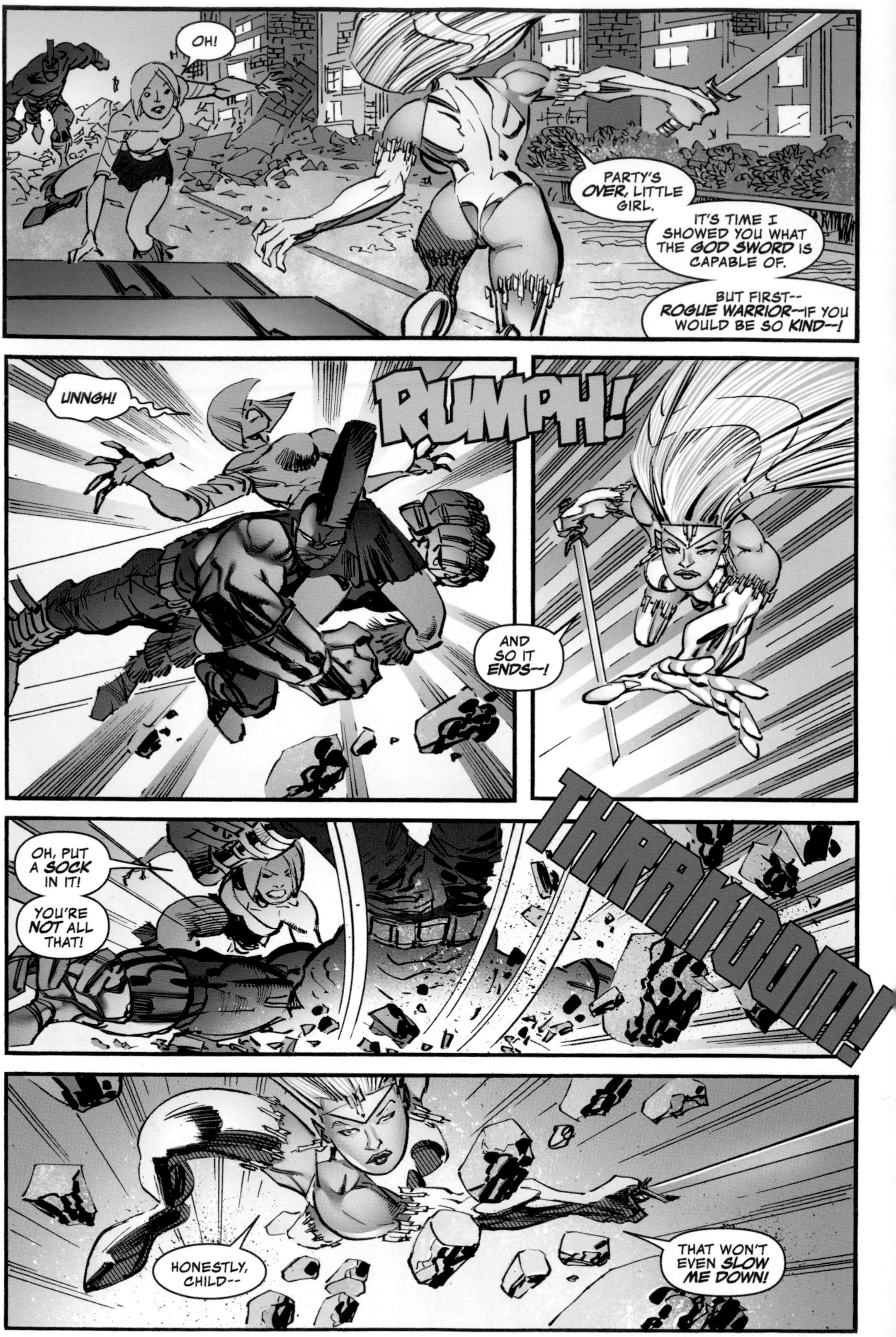
OH!
PARTY'S OVER, LITTLE GIRL.
IT'S TIME I SHOWED YOU WHAT THE GOD SWORD IS CAPABLE OF.
BUT FIRST-- ROGUE WARRIOR--IF YOU WOULD BE SO KIND--!
UNNGH!
RUMPH!
AND SO IT ENDS--!
OH, PUT A SOCK IN IT!
YOU'RE NOT ALL THAT!
THRAKOOM!
HONESTLY, CHILD--
THAT WON'T EVEN SLOW ME DOWN!

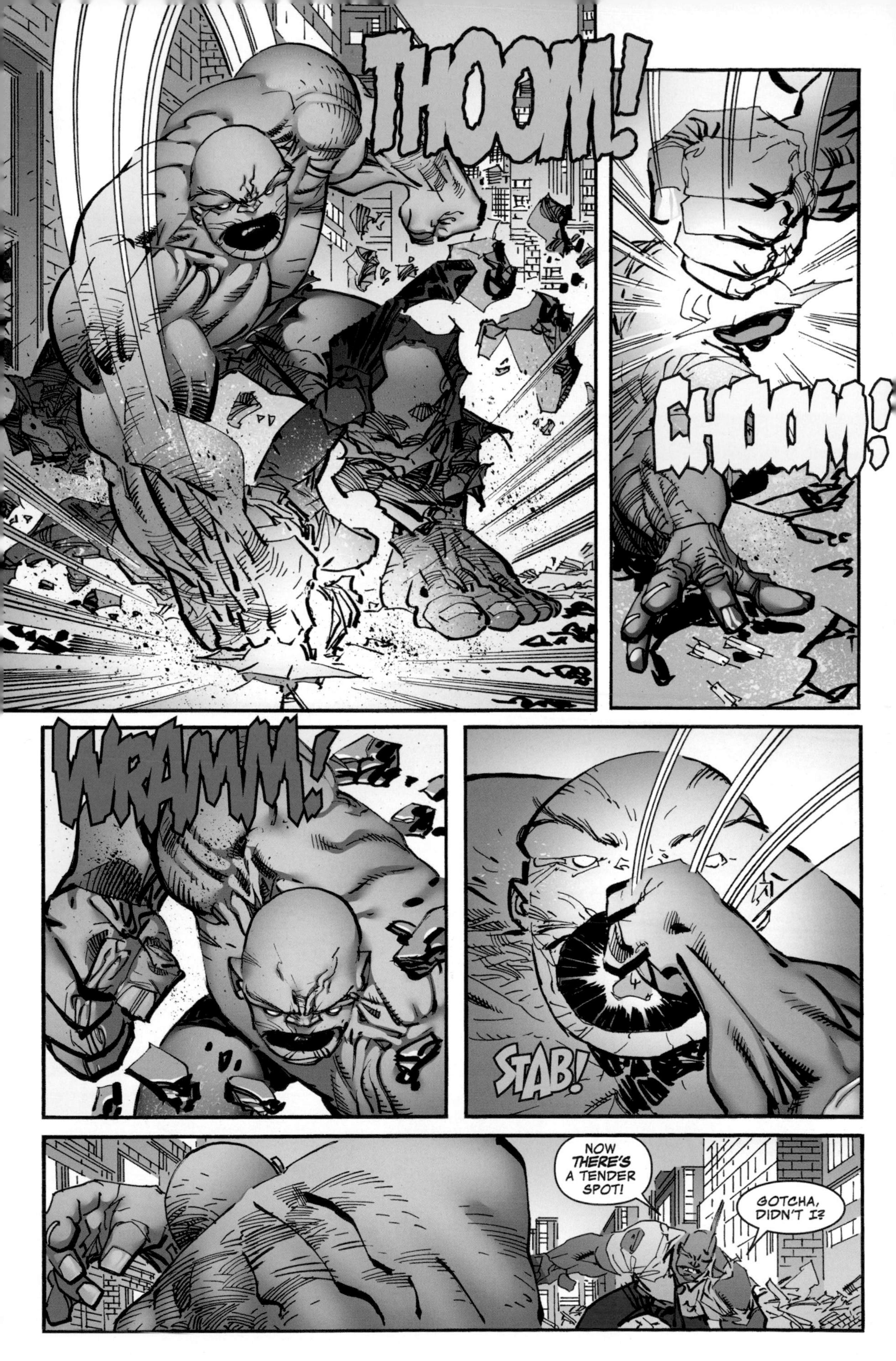
THOOM!
CHOOM!
WRAMM!
STAB!
NOW THERE'S A TENDER SPOT!
GOTCHA, DIDN'T I?

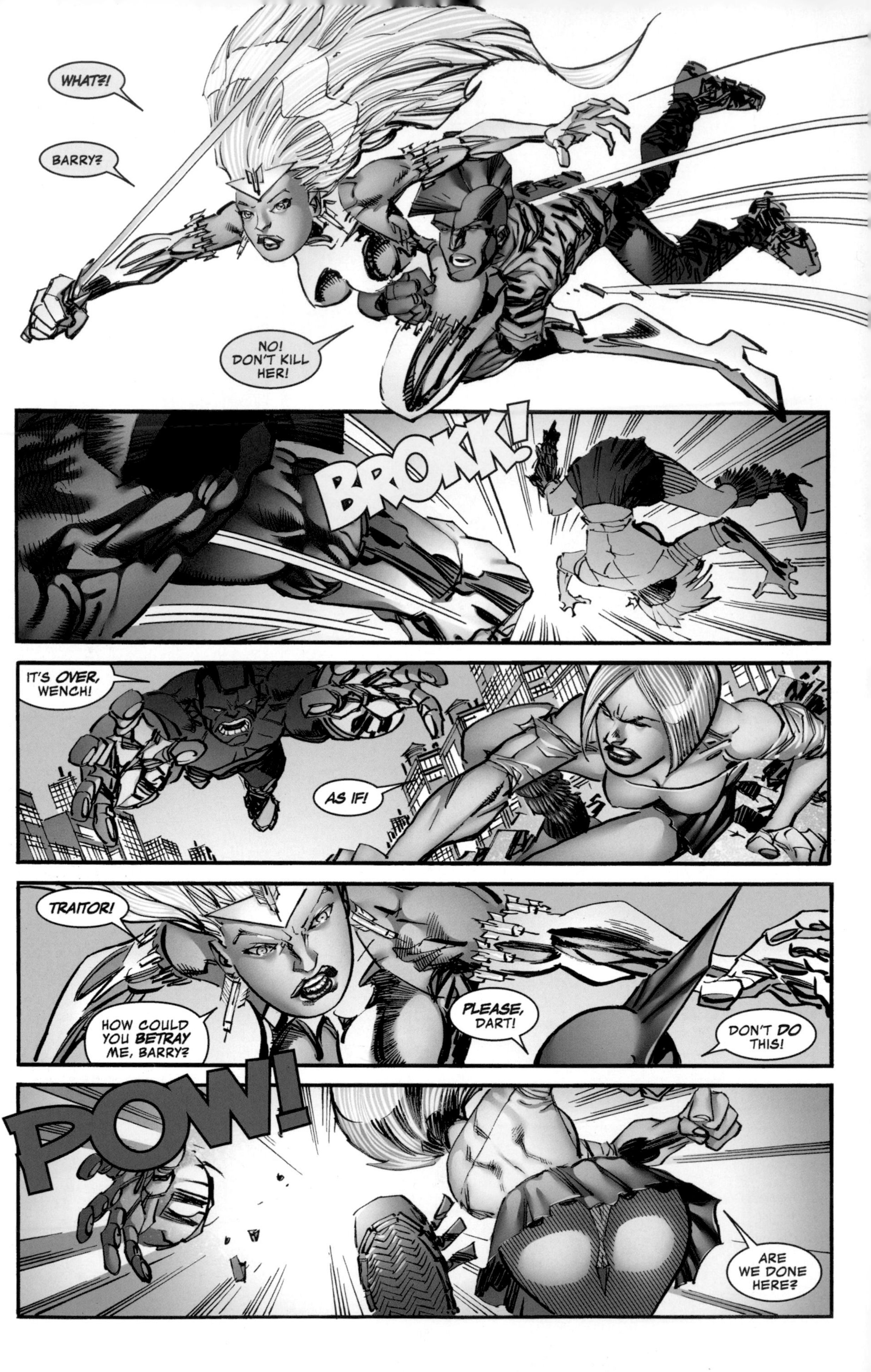
WHAT?!
BARRY?
NO! DON'T KILL HER!
BROKK!
IT'S OVER, WENCH!
AS IF!
TRAITOR!
HOW COULD YOU BETRAY ME, BARRY?
PLEASE, DART!
DON'T DO THIS!
POW!
ARE WE DONE HERE?

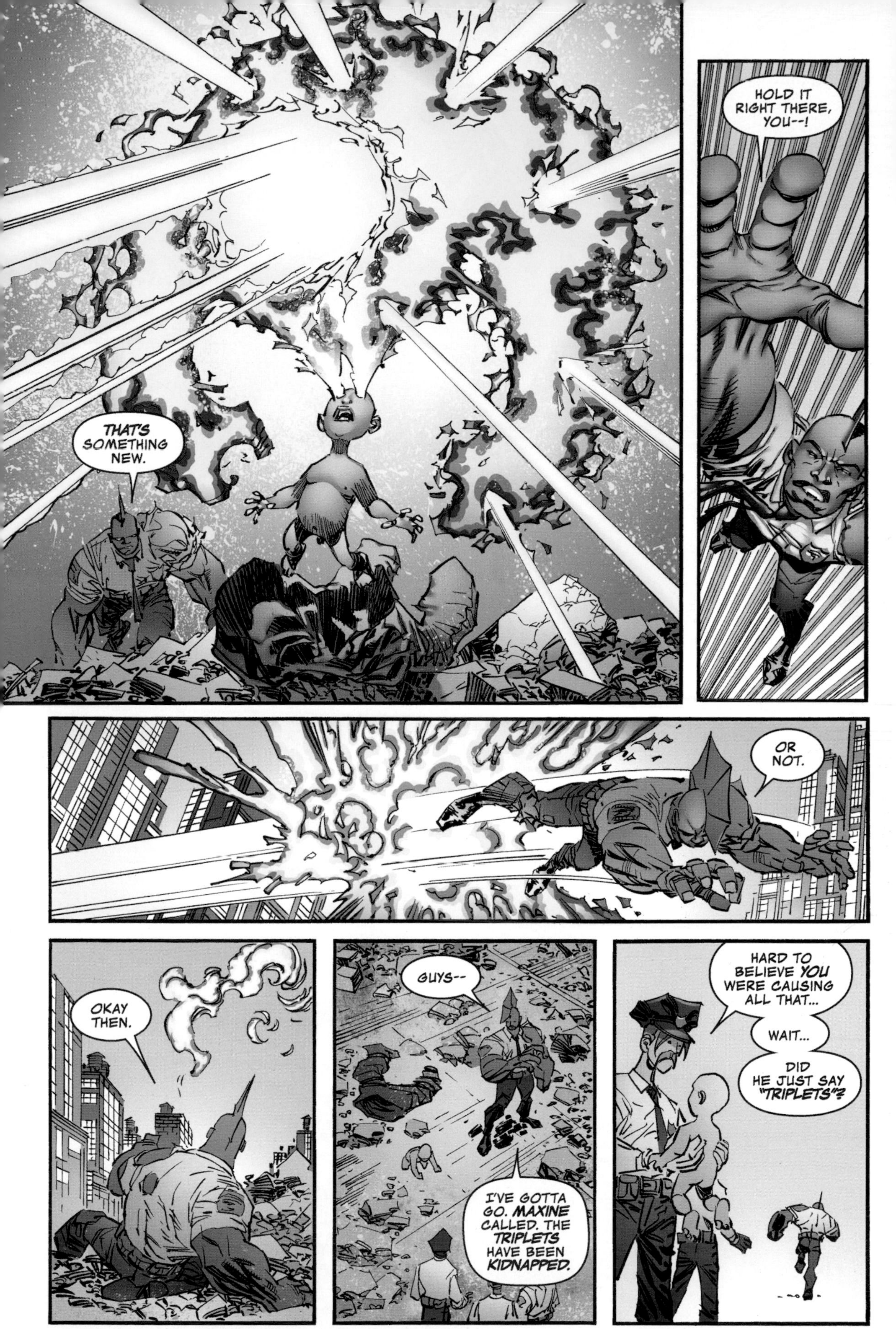
THAT'S SOMETHING NEW.
HOLD IT RIGHT THERE, YOU--!
OR NOT.
OKAY THEN.
GUYS--
I'VE GOTTA GO. MAXINE CALLED. THE TRIPLETS HAVE BEEN KIDNAPPED.
HARD TO BELIEVE YOU WERE CAUSING ALL THAT...
WAIT...
DID HE JUST SAY "TRIPLETS"?

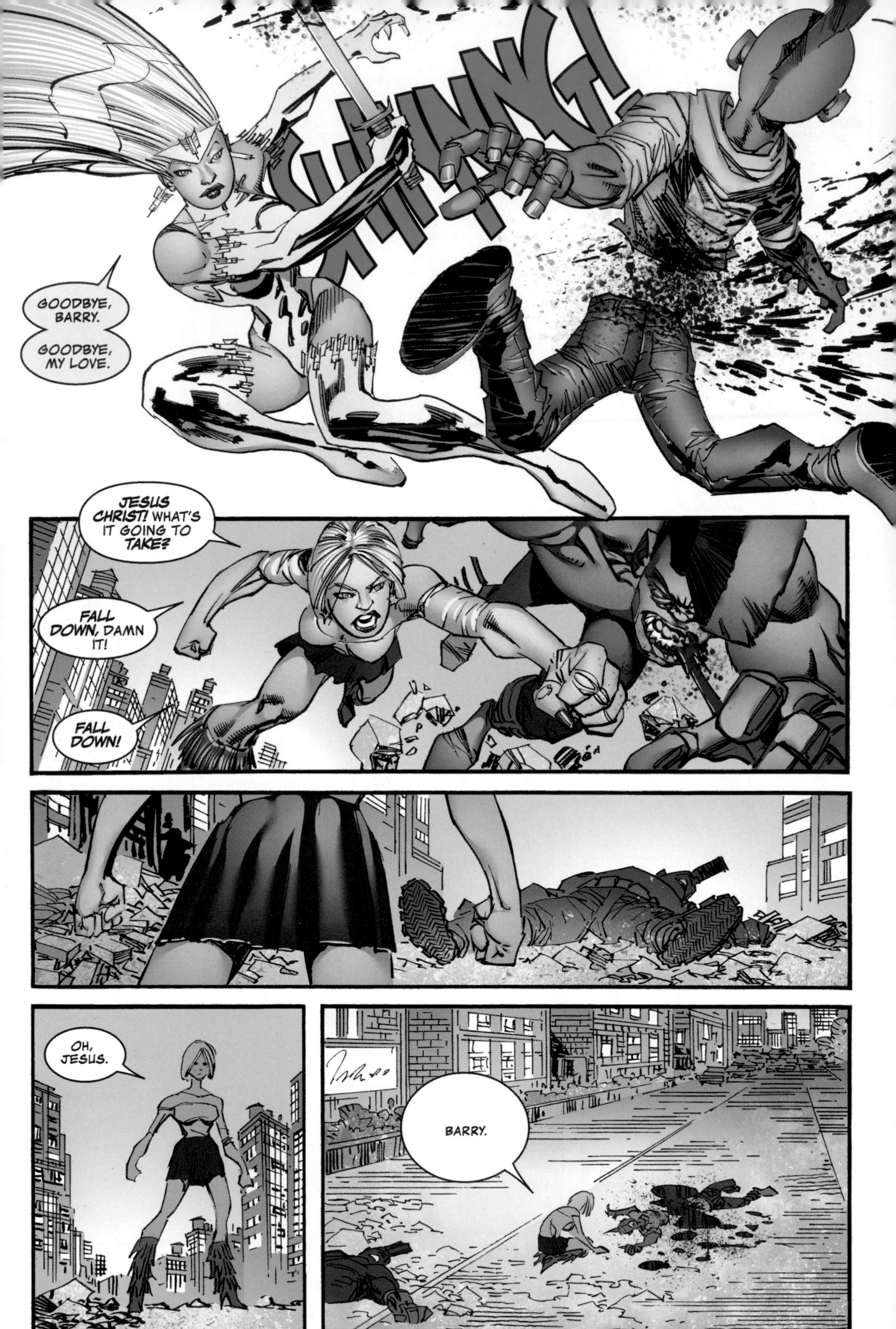
SHHHNNG!
GOODBYE, BARRY.
GOODBYE, MY LOVE.
JESUS CHRIST! WHAT'S IT GOING TO TAKE?
FALL DOWN, DAMN IT!
FALL DOWN!
OH, JESUS.
BARRY.

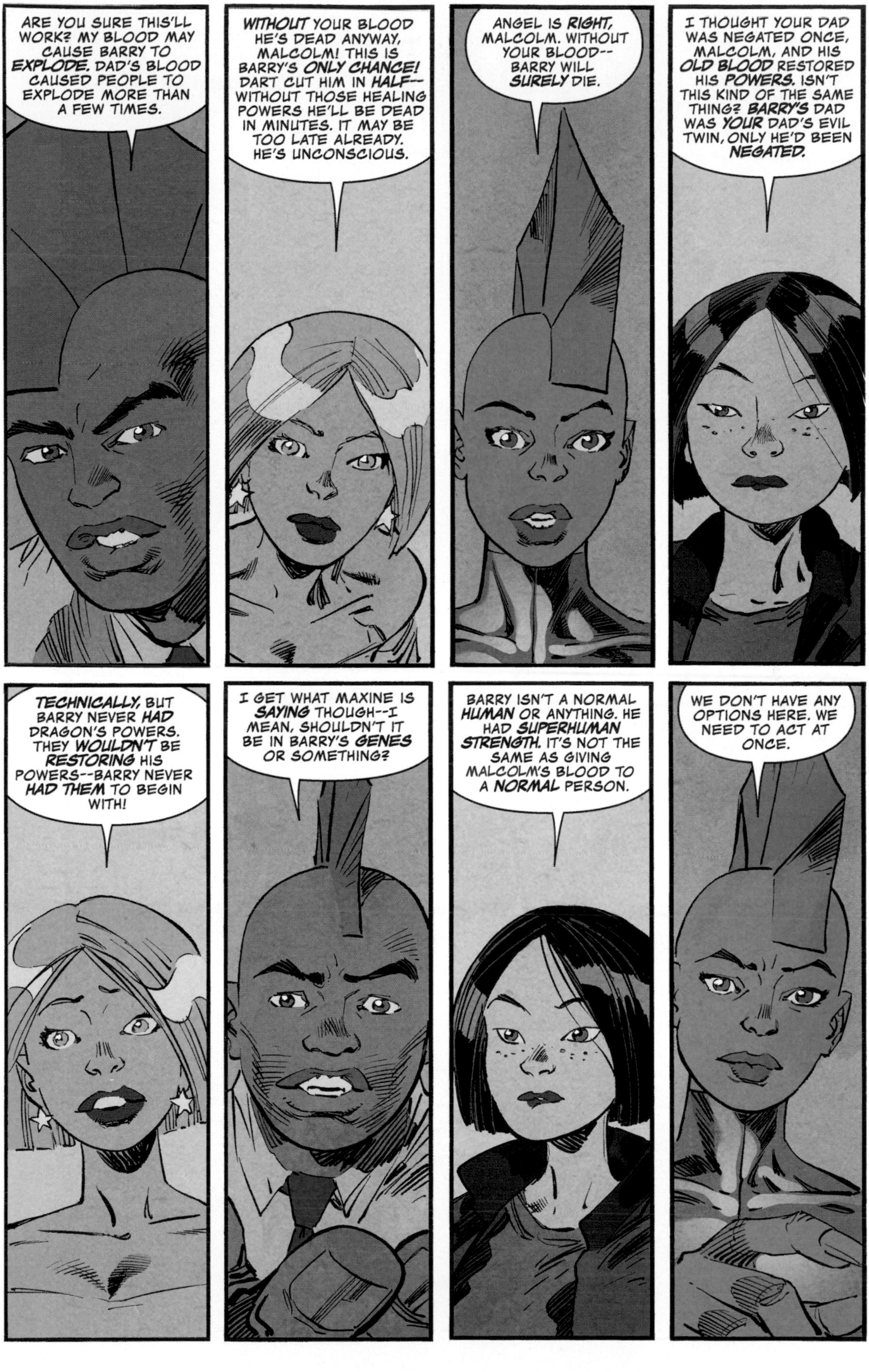
ARE YOU SURE THIS'LL WORK? MY BLOOD MAY CAUSE BARRY TO EXPLODE. DAD'S BLOOD CAUSED PEOPLE TO EXPLODE MORE THAN A FEW TIMES.
WITHOUT YOUR BLOOD HE'S DEAD ANYWAY, MALCOLM! THIS IS BARRY'S ONLY CHANCE! DART CUT HIM IN HALF--WITHOUT THOSE HEALING POWERS HE'LL BE DEAD IN MINUTES. IT MAY BE TOO LATE ALREADY. HE'S UNCONSCIOUS.
ANGEL IS RIGHT, MALCOLM. WITHOUT YOUR BLOOD--BARRY WILL SURELY DIE.
I THOUGHT YOUR DAD WAS NEGATED ONCE, MALCOLM, AND HIS OLD BLOOD RESTORED HIS POWERS. ISN'T THIS KIND OF THE SAME THING? BARRY'S DAD WAS YOUR DAD'S EVIL TWIN, ONLY HE'D BEEN NEGATED.
TECHNICALLY, BUT BARRY NEVER HAD DRAGON'S POWERS. THEY WOULDN'T BE RESTORING HIS POWERS--BARRY NEVER HAD THEM TO BEGIN WITH!
I GET WHAT MAXINE IS SAYING THOUGH--I MEAN, SHOULDN'T IT BE IN BARRY'S GENES OR SOMETHING?
BARRY ISN'T A NORMAL HUMAN OR ANYTHING. HE HAD SUPERHUMAN STRENGTH. IT'S NOT THE SAME AS GIVING MALCOLM'S BLOOD TO A NORMAL PERSON.
WE DON'T HAVE ANY OPTIONS HERE. WE NEED TO ACT AT ONCE.

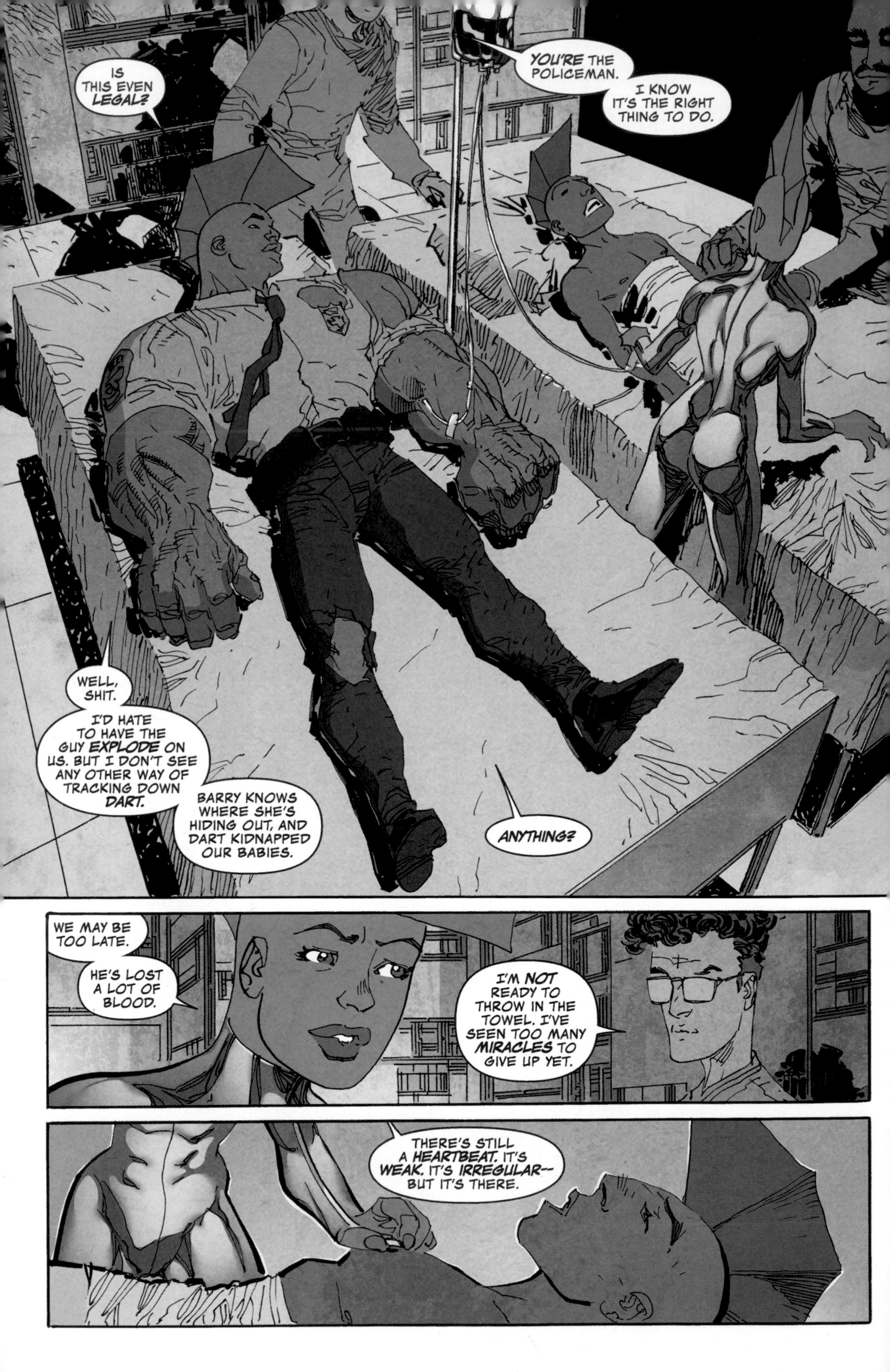
IS THIS EVEN LEGAL?
YOU'RE THE POLICEMAN.
I KNOW IT'S THE RIGHT THING TO DO.
WELL, SHIT.
I'D HATE TO HAVE THE GUY EXPLODE ON US. BUT I DON'T SEE ANY OTHER WAY OF TRACKING DOWN DART.
BARRY KNOWS WHERE SHE'S HIDING OUT, AND DART KIDNAPPED OUR BABIES.
ANYTHING?
WE MAY BE TOO LATE.
HE'S LOST A LOT OF BLOOD.
I'M NOT READY TO THROW IN THE TOWEL. I'VE SEEN TOO MANY MIRACLES TO GIVE UP YET.
THERE'S STILL A HEARTBEAT. IT'S WEAK. IT'S IRREGULAR-- BUT IT'S THERE.

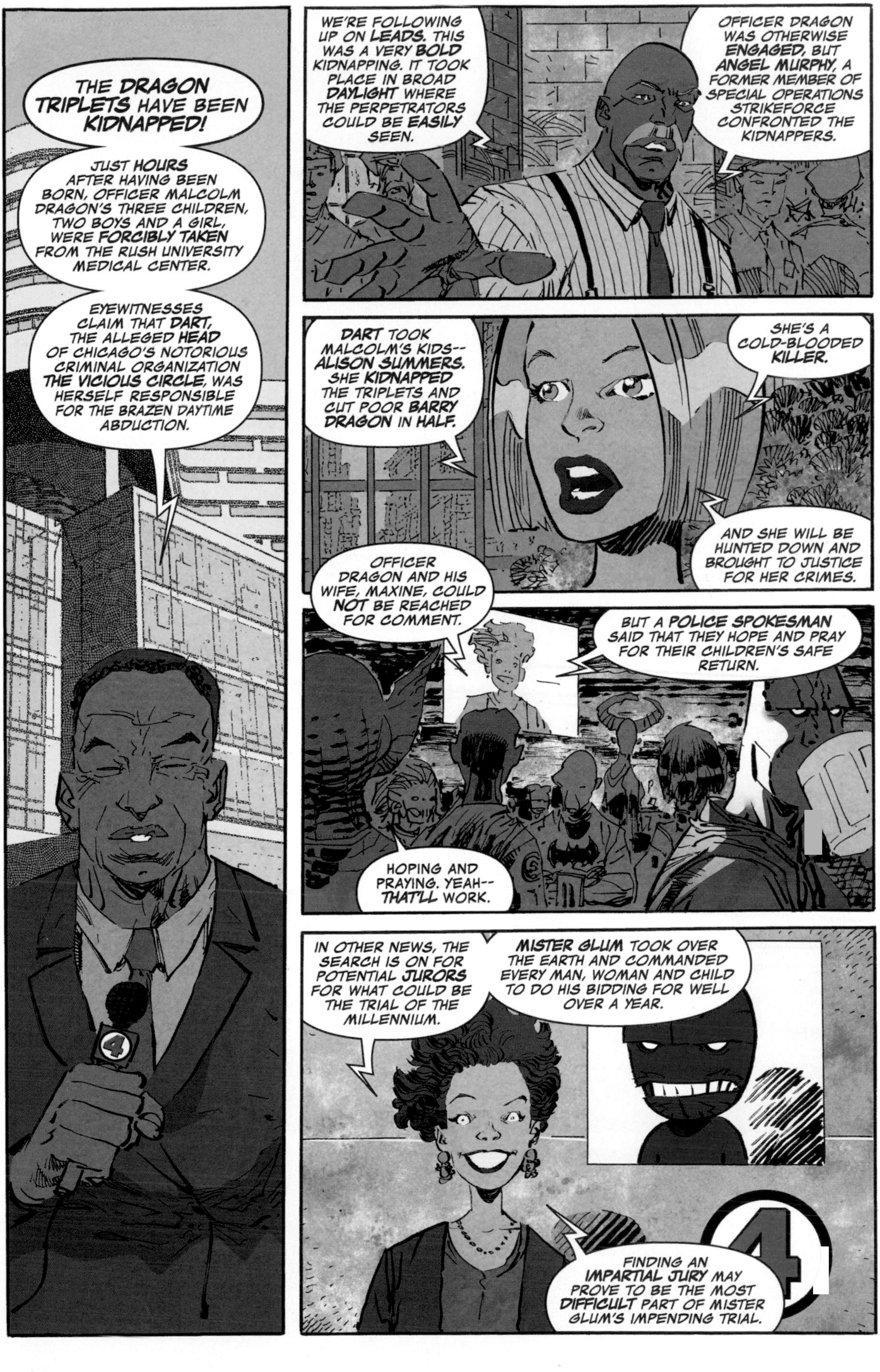
THE DRAGON TRIPLETS HAVE BEEN KIDNAPPED!
JUST HOURS AFTER HAVING BEEN BORN, OFFICER MALCOLM DRAGON'S THREE CHILDREN, TWO BOYS AND A GIRL, WERE FORCIBLY TAKEN FROM THE RUSH UNIVERSITY MEDICAL CENTER.
EYEWITNESSES CLAIM THAT DART, THE ALLEGED HEAD OF CHICAGO'S NOTORIOUS CRIMINAL ORGANIZATION THE VICIOUS CIRCLE, WAS HERSELF RESPONSIBLE FOR THE BRAZEN DAYTIME ABDUCTION.
WE'RE FOLLOWING UP ON LEADS. THIS WAS A VERY BOLD KIDNAPPING. IT TOOK PLACE IN BROAD DAYLIGHT WHERE THE PERPETRATORS COULD BE EASILY SEEN.
OFFICER DRAGON WAS OTHERWISE ENGAGED, BUT ANGEL MURPHY, A FORMER MEMBER OF SPECIAL OPERATIONS STRIKEFORCE CONFRONTED THE KIDNAPPERS.
DART TOOK MALCOLM'S KIDS-- ALISON SUMMERS. SHE KIDNAPPED THE TRIPLETS AND CUT POOR BARRY DRAGON IN HALF.
SHE'S A COLD-BLOODED KILLER.
AND SHE WILL BE HUNTED DOWN AND BROUGHT TO JUSTICE FOR HER CRIMES.
OFFICER DRAGON AND HIS WIFE, MAXINE, COULD NOT BE REACHED FOR COMMENT.
BUT A POLICE SPOKESMAN SAID THAT THEY HOPE AND PRAY FOR THEIR CHILDREN'S SAFE RETURN.
HOPING AND PRAYING. YEAH-- THAT'LL WORK.
IN OTHER NEWS, THE SEARCH IS ON FOR POTENTIAL JURORS FOR WHAT COULD BE THE TRIAL OF THE MILLENNIUM.
MISTER GLUM TOOK OVER THE EARTH AND COMMANDED EVERY MAN, WOMAN AND CHILD TO DO HIS BIDDING FOR WELL OVER A YEAR.
FINDING AN IMPARTIAL JURY MAY PROVE TO BE THE MOST DIFFICULT PART OF MISTER GLUM'S IMPENDING TRIAL.

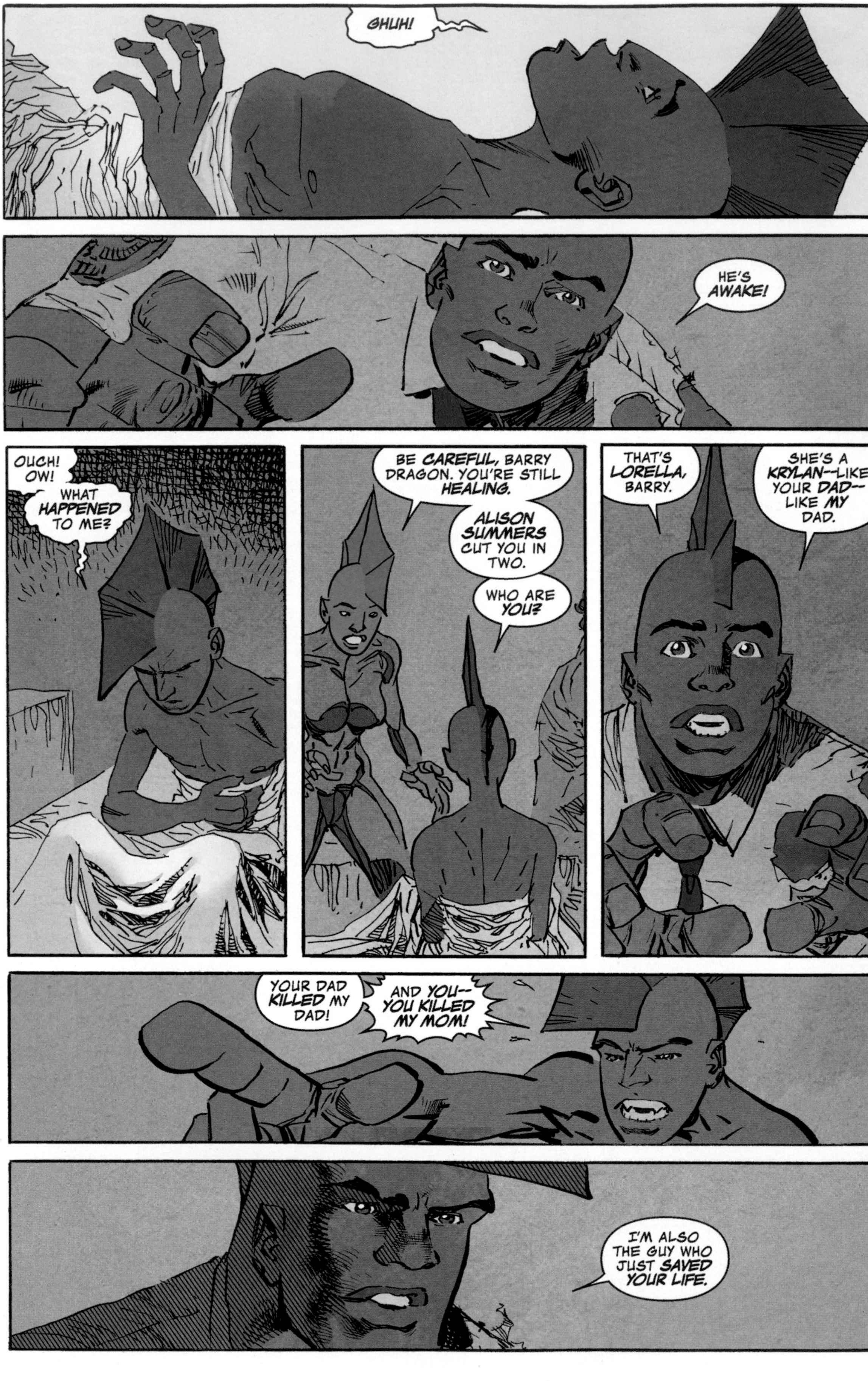
GHUH!
HE'S AWAKE!
OUCH! OW!
WHAT HAPPENED TO ME?
BE CAREFUL, BARRY DRAGON. YOU'RE STILL HEALING.
ALISON SUMMERS CUT YOU IN TWO.
WHO ARE YOU?
THAT'S LORELLA, BARRY.
SHE'S A KRYLAN--LIKE YOUR DAD--LIKE MY DAD.
YOUR DAD KILLED MY DAD!
AND YOU--YOU KILLED MY MOM!
I'M ALSO THE GUY WHO JUST SAVED YOUR LIFE.

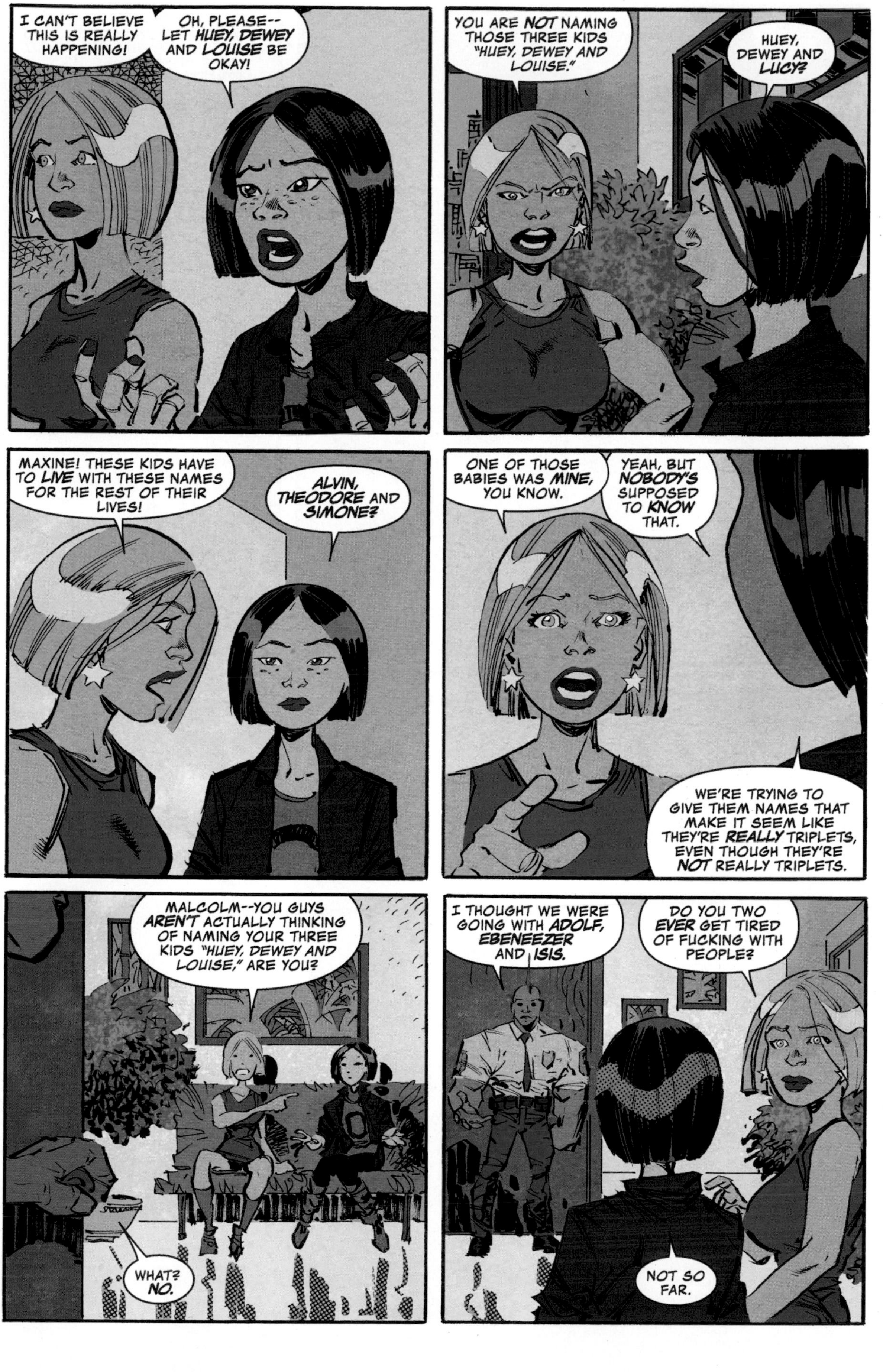
I CAN'T BELIEVE THIS IS REALLY HAPPENING!
OH, PLEASE-- LET HUEY, DEWEY AND LOUISE BE OKAY!
YOU ARE NOT NAMING THOSE THREE KIDS "HUEY, DEWEY AND LOUISE."
HUEY, DEWEY AND LUCY?
MAXINE! THESE KIDS HAVE TO LIVE WITH THESE NAMES FOR THE REST OF THEIR LIVES!
ALVIN, THEODORE AND SIMONE?
ONE OF THOSE BABIES WAS MINE, YOU KNOW.
YEAH, BUT NOBODY'S SUPPOSED TO KNOW THAT.
WE'RE TRYING TO GIVE THEM NAMES THAT MAKE IT SEEM LIKE THEY'RE REALLY TRIPLETS, EVEN THOUGH THEY'RE NOT REALLY TRIPLETS.
MALCOLM--YOU GUYS AREN'T ACTUALLY THINKING OF NAMING YOUR THREE KIDS "HUEY, DEWEY AND LOUISE," ARE YOU?
WHAT? NO.
I THOUGHT WE WERE GOING WITH ADOLF, EBENEEZER AND ISIS.
DO YOU TWO EVER GET TIRED OF FUCKING WITH PEOPLE?
NOT SO FAR.

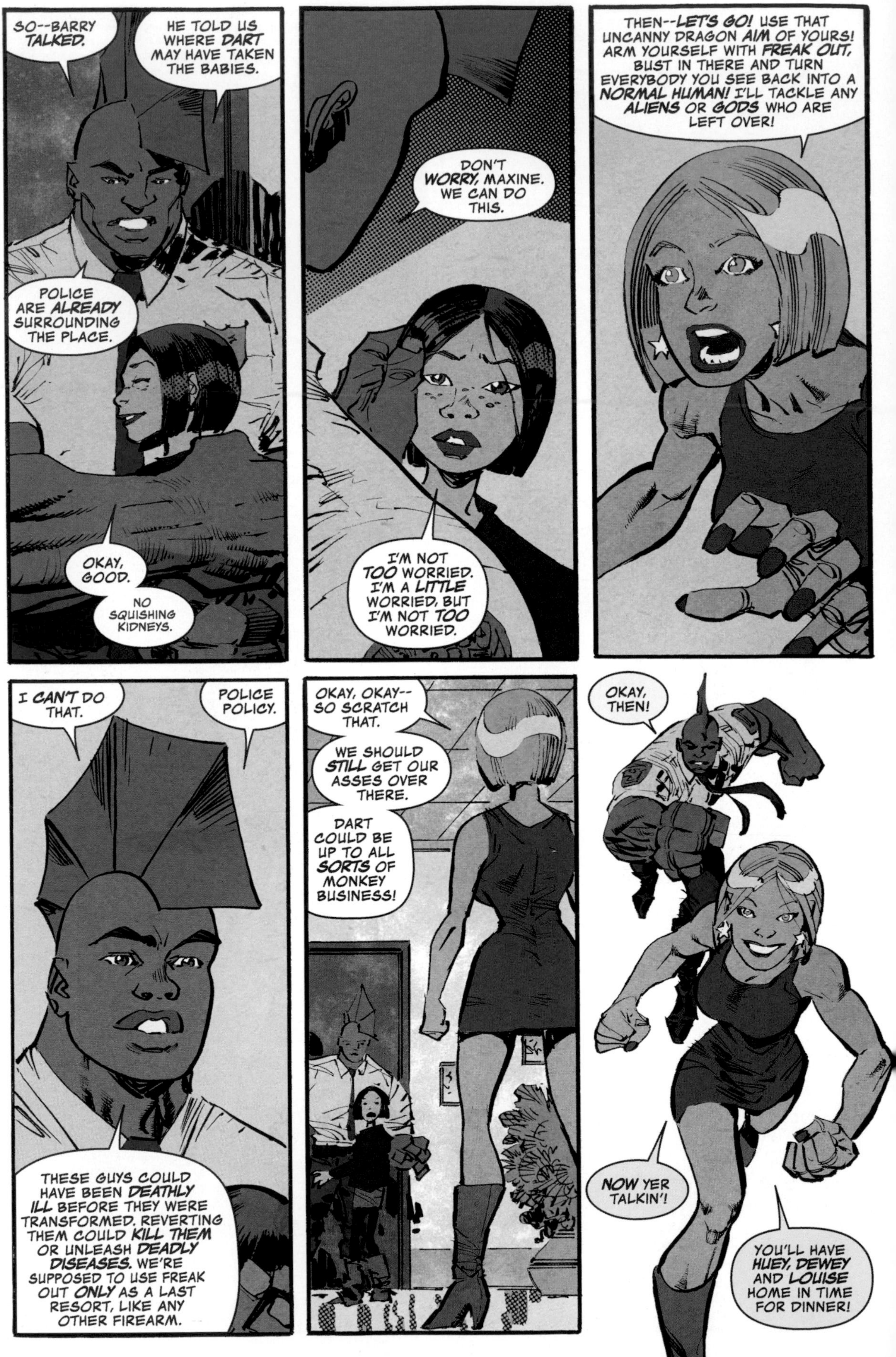
SO--BARRY TALKED.
HE TOLD US WHERE DART MAY HAVE TAKEN THE BABIES.
POLICE ARE ALREADY SURROUNDING THE PLACE.
OKAY, GOOD.
NO SQUISHING KIDNEYS.
DON'T WORRY, MAXINE. WE CAN DO THIS.
I'M NOT TOO WORRIED. I'M A LITTLE WORRIED, BUT I'M NOT TOO WORRIED.
THEN--LET'S GO! USE THAT UNCANNY DRAGON AIM OF YOURS! ARM YOURSELF WITH FREAK OUT, BUST IN THERE AND TURN EVERYBODY YOU SEE BACK INTO A NORMAL HUMAN! I'LL TACKLE ANY ALIENS OR GODS WHO ARE LEFT OVER!
I CAN'T DO THAT.
POLICE POLICY.
THESE GUYS COULD HAVE BEEN DEATHLY ILL BEFORE THEY WERE TRANSFORMED. REVERTING THEM COULD KILL THEM OR UNLEASH DEADLY DISEASES. WE'RE SUPPOSED TO USE FREAK OUT ONLY AS A LAST RESORT, LIKE ANY OTHER FIREARM.
OKAY, OKAY-- SO SCRATCH THAT.
WE SHOULD STILL GET OUR ASSES OVER THERE.
DART COULD BE UP TO ALL SORTS OF MONKEY BUSINESS!
OKAY, THEN!
NOW YER TALKIN'!
YOU'LL HAVE HUEY, DEWEY AND LOUISE HOME IN TIME FOR DINNER!

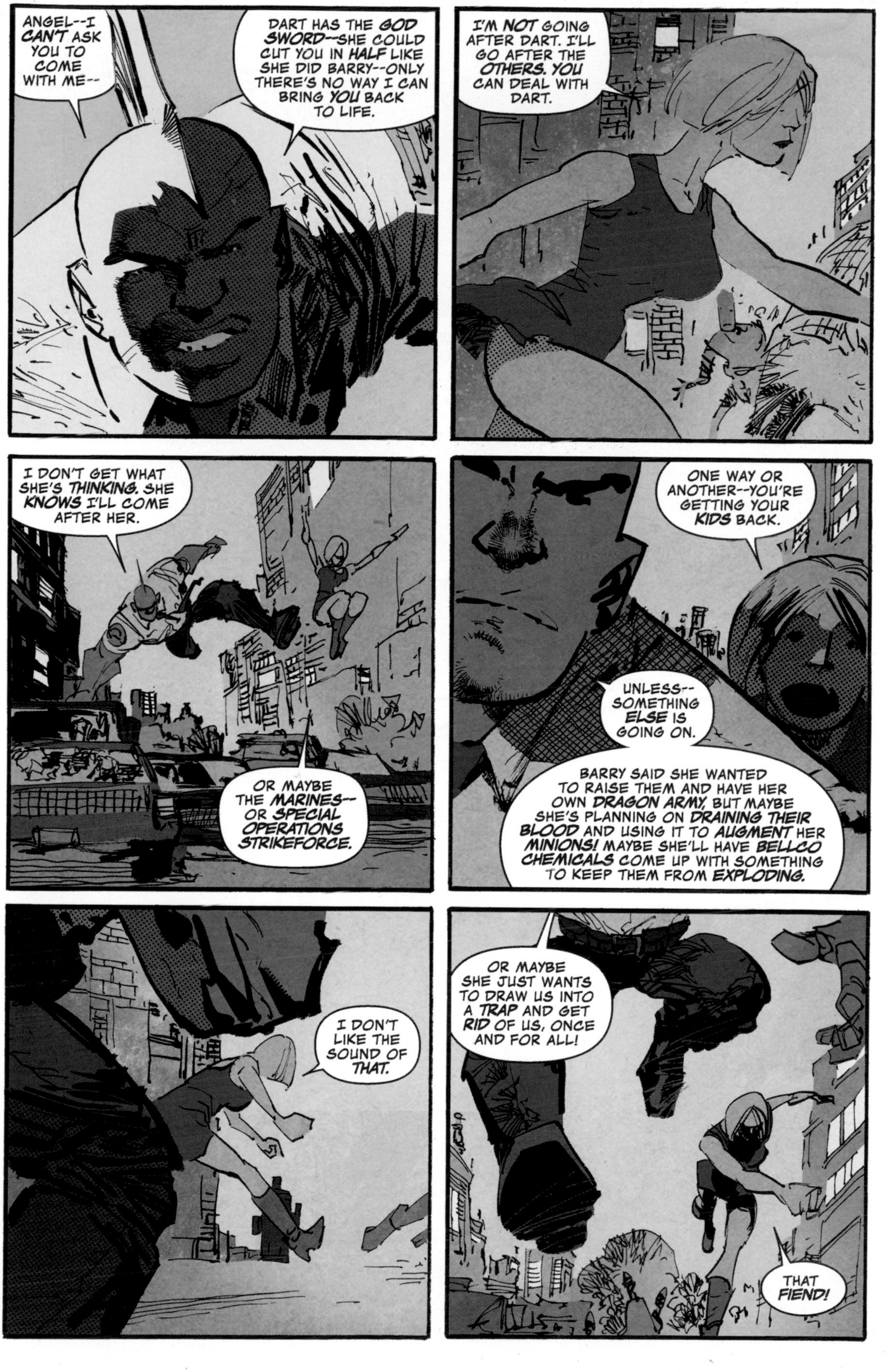
ANGEL--I CAN'T ASK YOU TO COME WITH ME--
DART HAS THE GOD SWORD--SHE COULD CUT YOU IN HALF LIKE SHE DID BARRY--ONLY THERE'S NO WAY I CAN BRING YOU BACK TO LIFE.
I'M NOT GOING AFTER DART. I'LL GO AFTER THE OTHERS. YOU CAN DEAL WITH DART.
I DON'T GET WHAT SHE'S THINKING. SHE KNOWS I'LL COME AFTER HER.
OR MAYBE THE MARINES--OR SPECIAL OPERATIONS STRIKEFORCE.
ONE WAY OR ANOTHER--YOU'RE GETTING YOUR KIDS BACK.
UNLESS--SOMETHING ELSE IS GOING ON.
BARRY SAID SHE WANTED TO RAISE THEM AND HAVE HER OWN DRAGON ARMY, BUT MAYBE SHE'S PLANNING ON DRAINING THEIR BLOOD AND USING IT TO AUGMENT HER MINIONS! MAYBE SHE'LL HAVE BELLCO CHEMICALS COME UP WITH SOMETHING TO KEEP THEM FROM EXPLODING.
I DON'T LIKE THE SOUND OF THAT.
OR MAYBE SHE JUST WANTS TO DRAW US INTO A TRAP AND GET RID OF US, ONCE AND FOR ALL!
THAT FIEND!

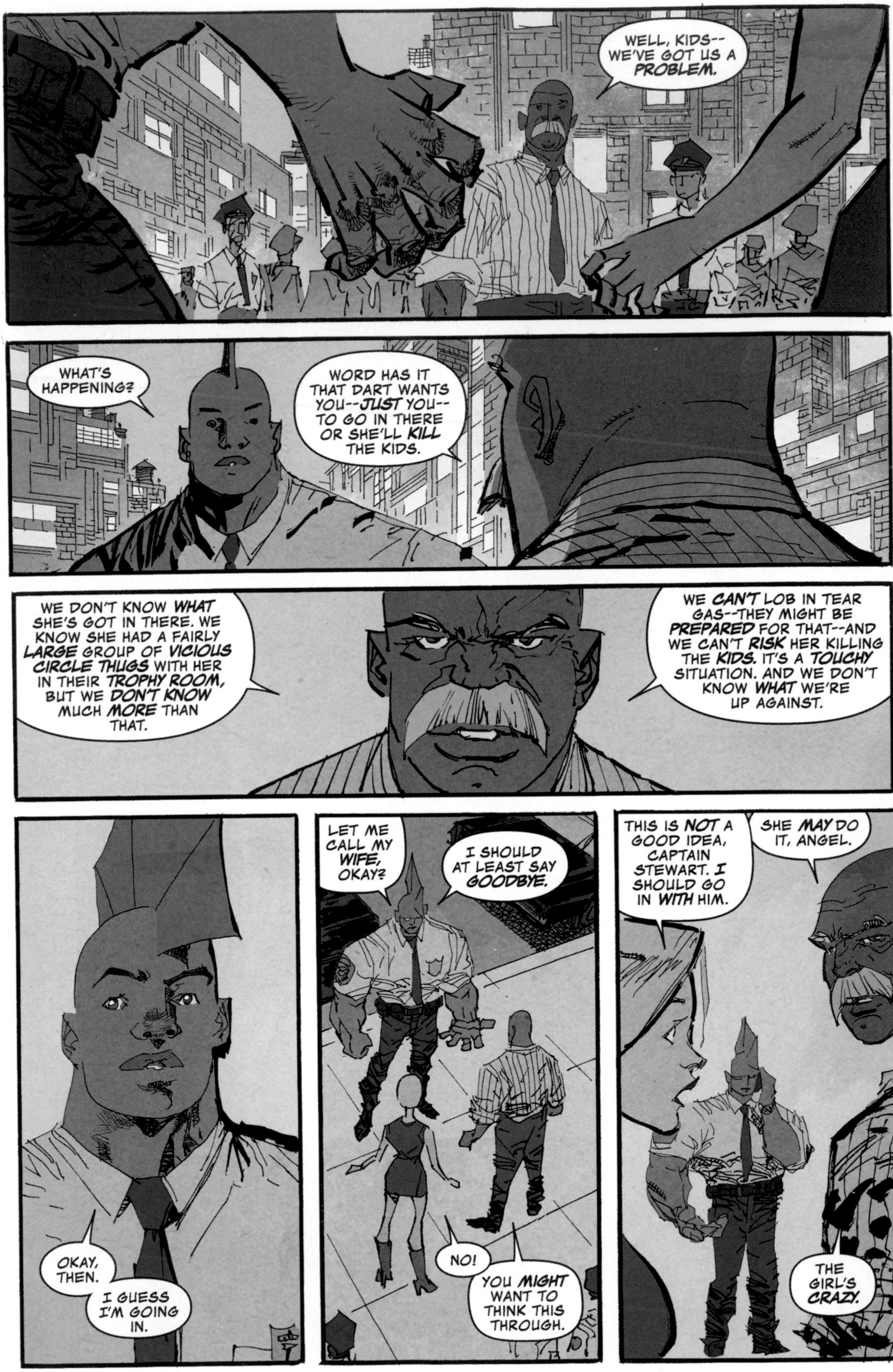
WELL, KIDS-- WE'VE GOT US A PROBLEM.
WHAT'S HAPPENING?
WORD HAS IT THAT DART WANTS YOU--JUST YOU-- TO GO IN THERE OR SHE'LL KILL THE KIDS.
WE DON'T KNOW WHAT SHE'S GOT IN THERE. WE KNOW SHE HAD A FAIRLY LARGE GROUP OF VICIOUS CIRCLE THUGS WITH HER IN THEIR TROPHY ROOM, BUT WE DON'T KNOW MUCH MORE THAN THAT.
WE CAN'T LOB IN TEAR GAS--THEY MIGHT BE PREPARED FOR THAT--AND WE CAN'T RISK HER KILLING THE KIDS. IT'S A TOUCHY SITUATION. AND WE DON'T KNOW WHAT WE'RE UP AGAINST.
OKAY, THEN.
I GUESS I'M GOING IN.
LET ME CALL MY WIFE, OKAY?
I SHOULD AT LEAST SAY GOODBYE.
NO!
YOU MIGHT WANT TO THINK THIS THROUGH.
THIS IS NOT A GOOD IDEA, CAPTAIN STEWART. I SHOULD GO IN WITH HIM.
SHE MAY DO IT, ANGEL.
THE GIRL'S CRAZY.

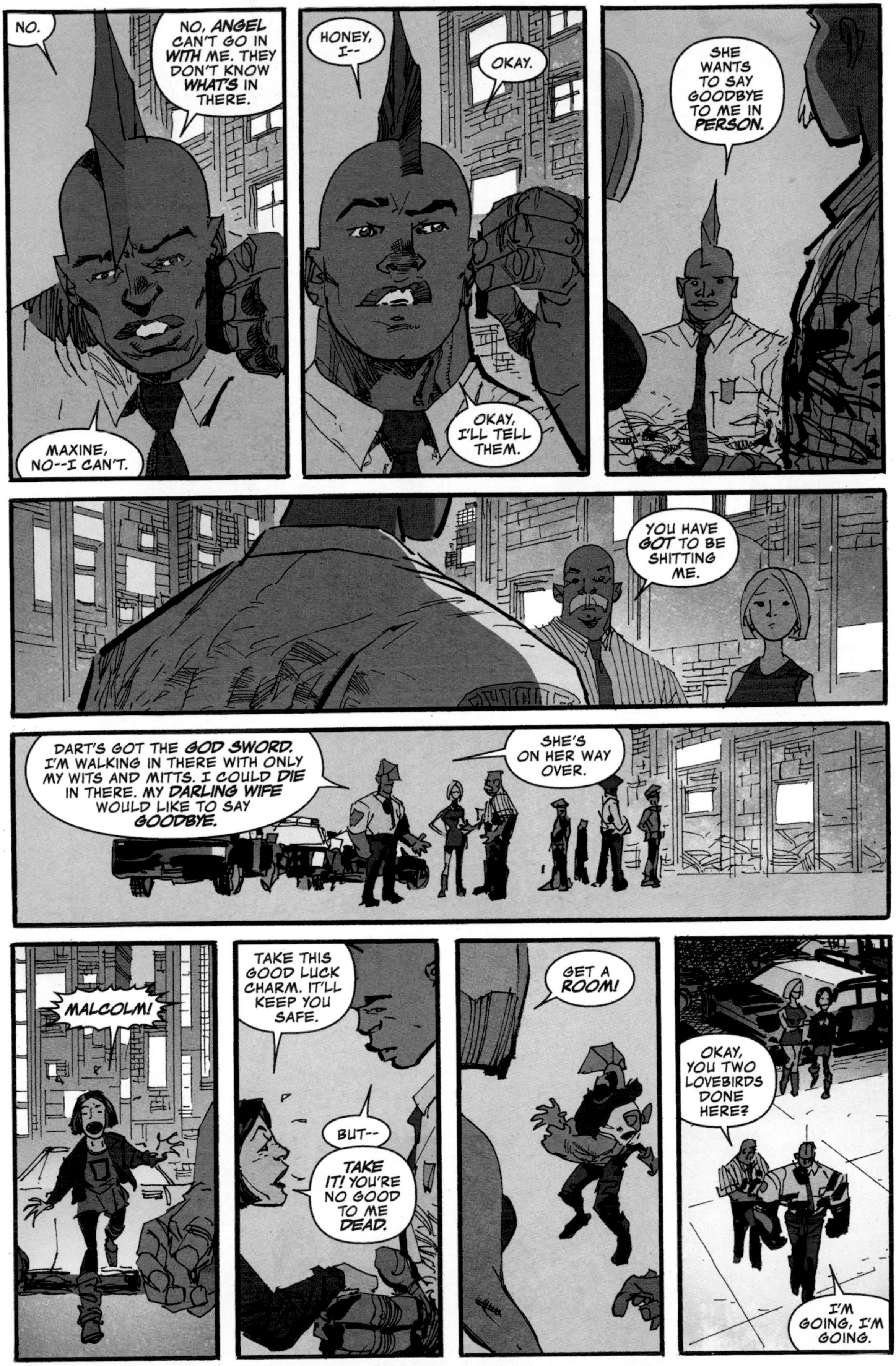
NO.
NO, *ANGEL* CAN'T GO IN *WITH* ME. THEY DON'T KNOW *WHAT'S* IN THERE.
MAXINE, NO--I CAN'T.
HONEY, I--
OKAY.
OKAY, I'LL TELL THEM.
SHE WANTS TO SAY GOODBYE TO ME IN *PERSON*.
YOU HAVE *GOT* TO BE SHITTING ME.
DART'S GOT THE *GOD SWORD*. I'M WALKING IN THERE WITH ONLY MY WITS AND MITTS. I COULD *DIE* IN THERE. MY *DARLING WIFE* WOULD LIKE TO SAY *GOODBYE*.
SHE'S ON HER WAY OVER.
MALCOLM!
TAKE THIS GOOD LUCK CHARM. IT'LL KEEP YOU SAFE.
BUT--
TAKE IT! YOU'RE NO GOOD TO ME *DEAD*.
GET A *ROOM!*
OKAY, YOU TWO LOVEBIRDS DONE HERE?
I'M GOING, I'M GOING.

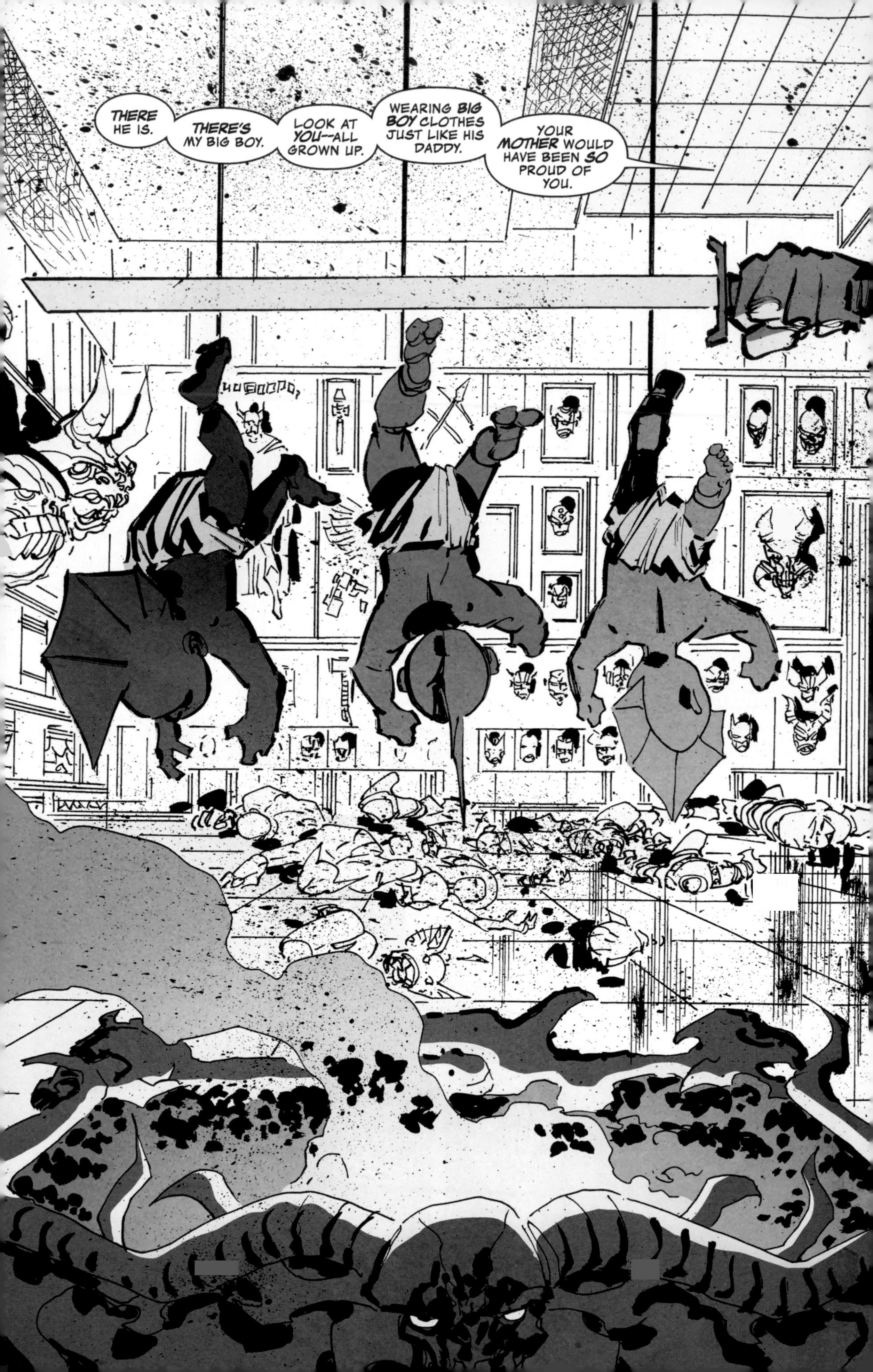
THERE HE IS.
THERE'S MY BIG BOY.
LOOK AT YOU--ALL GROWN UP.
WEARING BIG BOY CLOTHES JUST LIKE HIS DADDY.
YOUR MOTHER WOULD HAVE BEEN SO PROUD OF YOU.

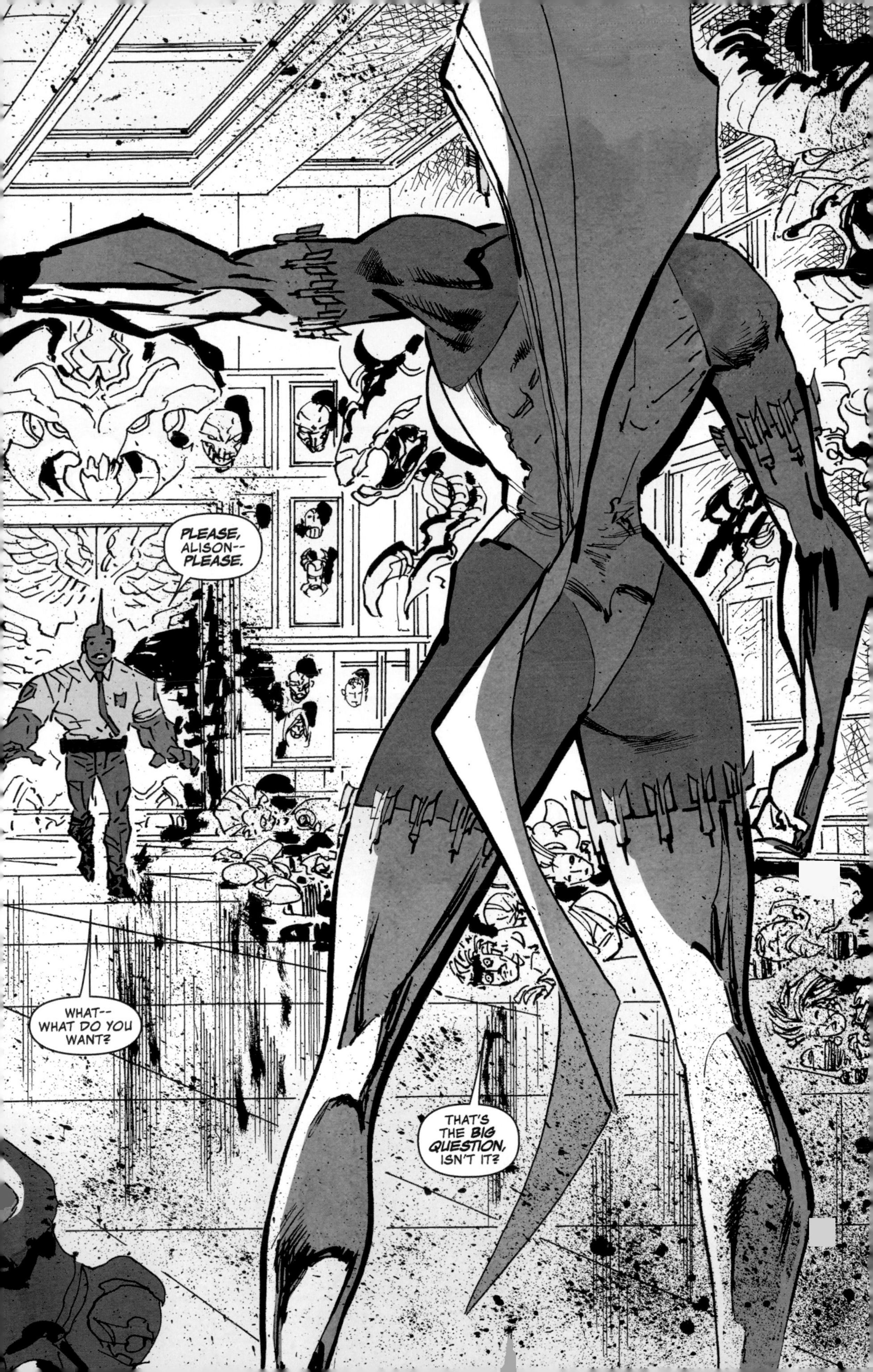
PLEASE, ALISON-- PLEASE.
WHAT-- WHAT DO YOU WANT?
THAT'S THE BIG QUESTION, ISN'T IT?

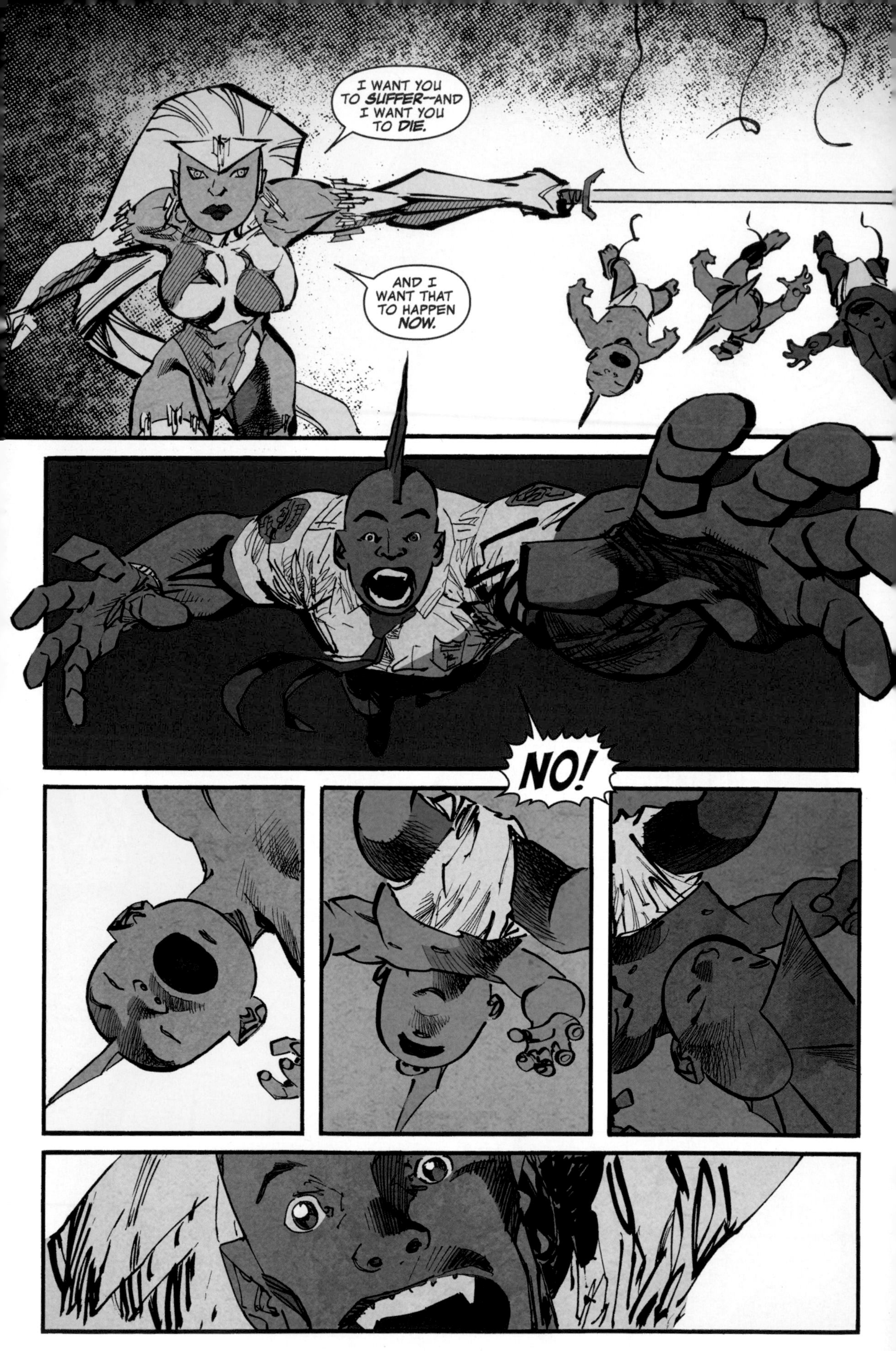
I WANT YOU TO SUFFER--AND I WANT YOU TO DIE.
AND I WANT THAT TO HAPPEN NOW.
NO!

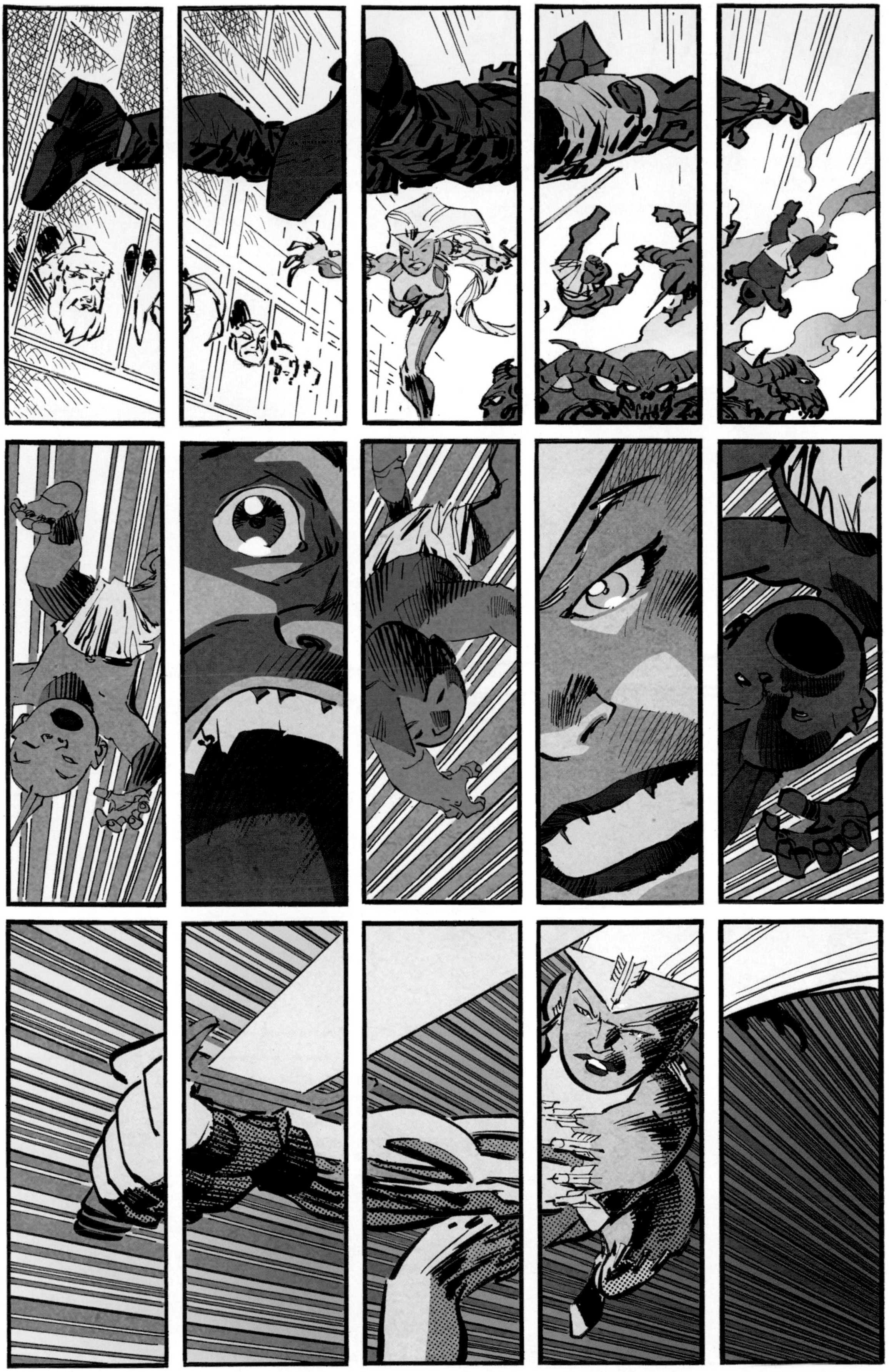

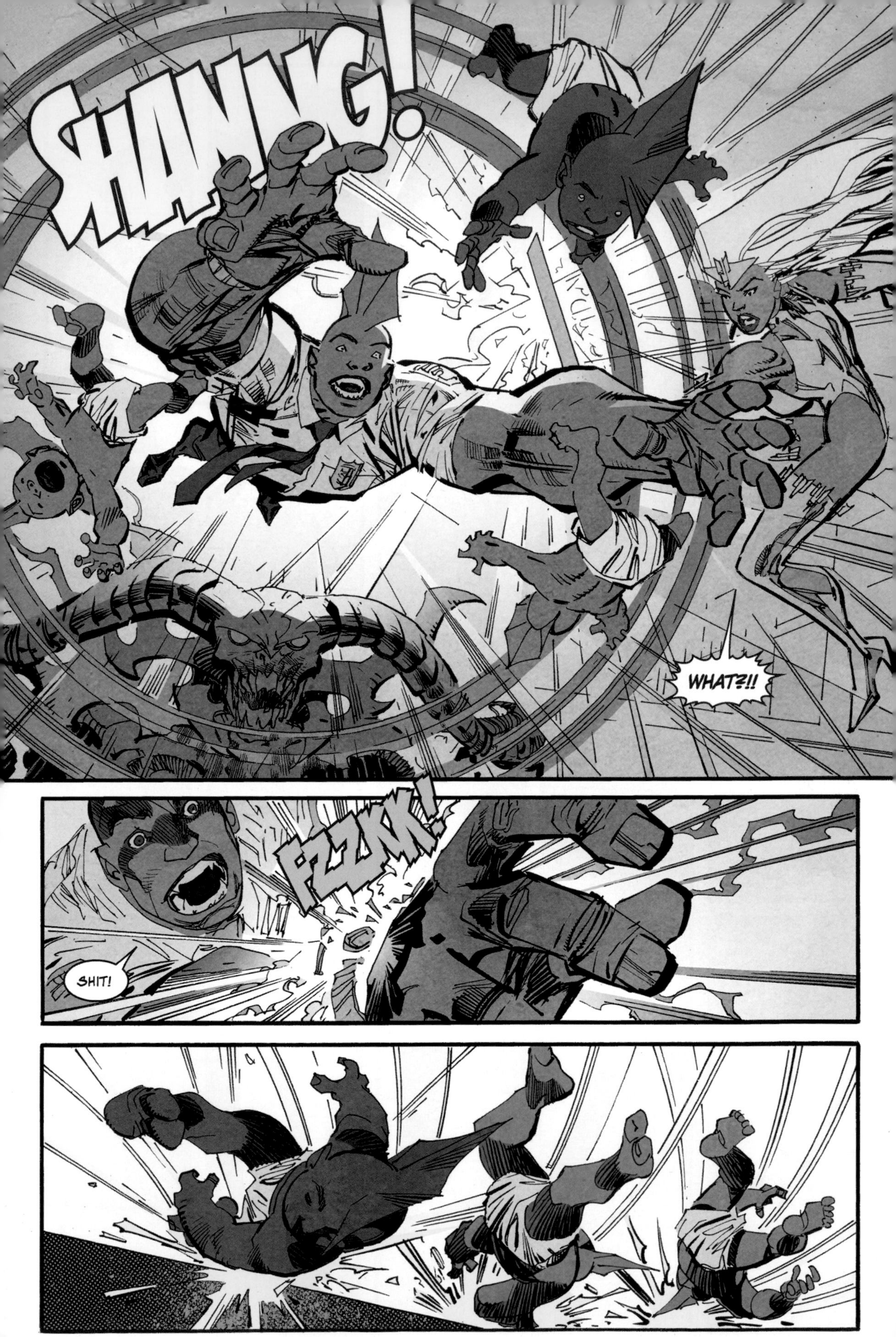
SHANNG!
WHAT?!!
FZZKK!
SHIT!

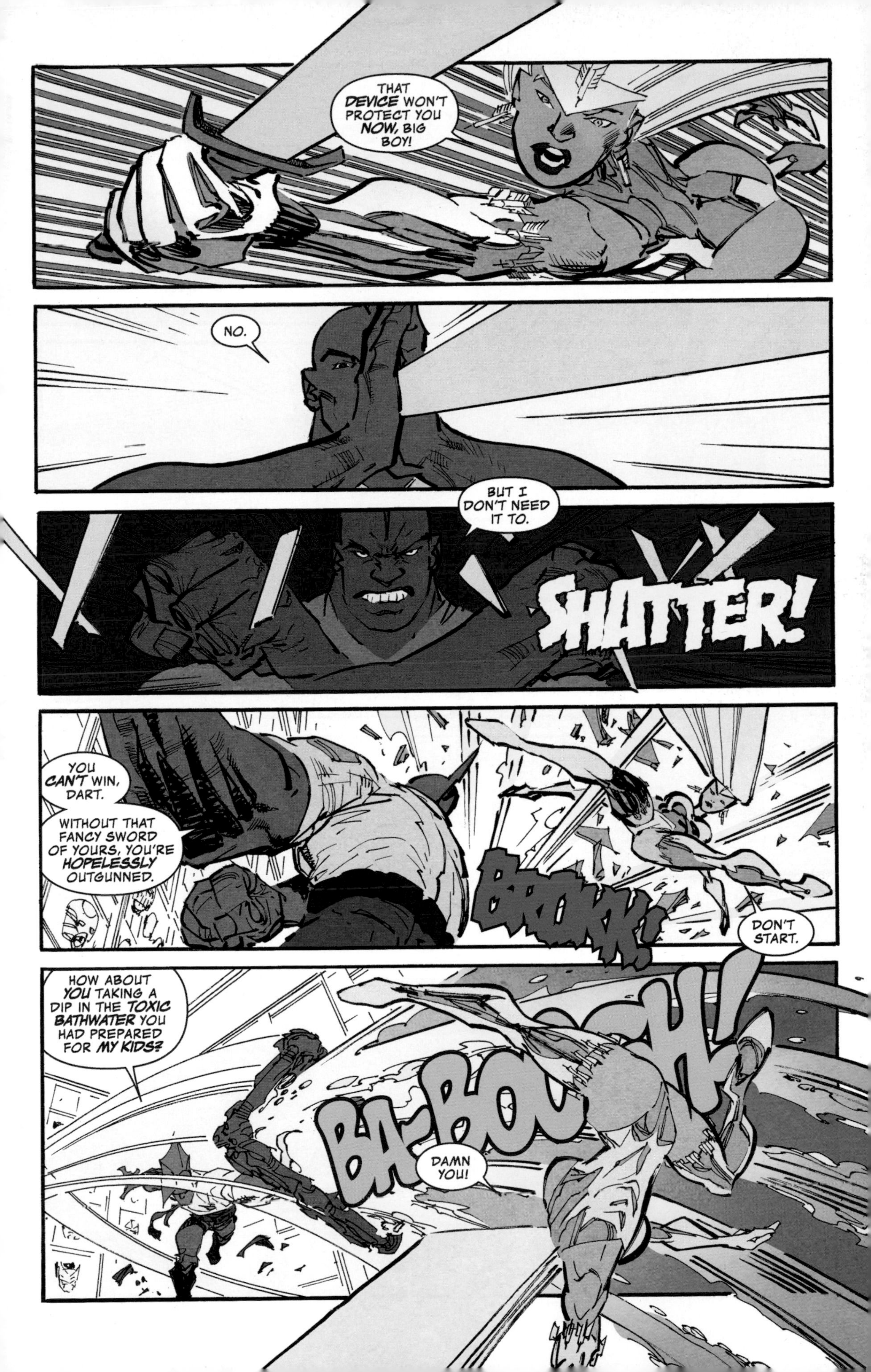
THAT DEVICE WON'T PROTECT YOU NOW, BIG BOY!
NO.
BUT I DON'T NEED IT TO.
SHATTER!
YOU CAN'T WIN, DART.
WITHOUT THAT FANCY SWORD OF YOURS, YOU'RE HOPELESSLY OUTGUNNED.
BROKK!
DON'T START.
HOW ABOUT YOU TAKING A DIP IN THE TOXIC BATHWATER YOU HAD PREPARED FOR MY KIDS?
BA-BOOOOSH!
DAMN YOU!

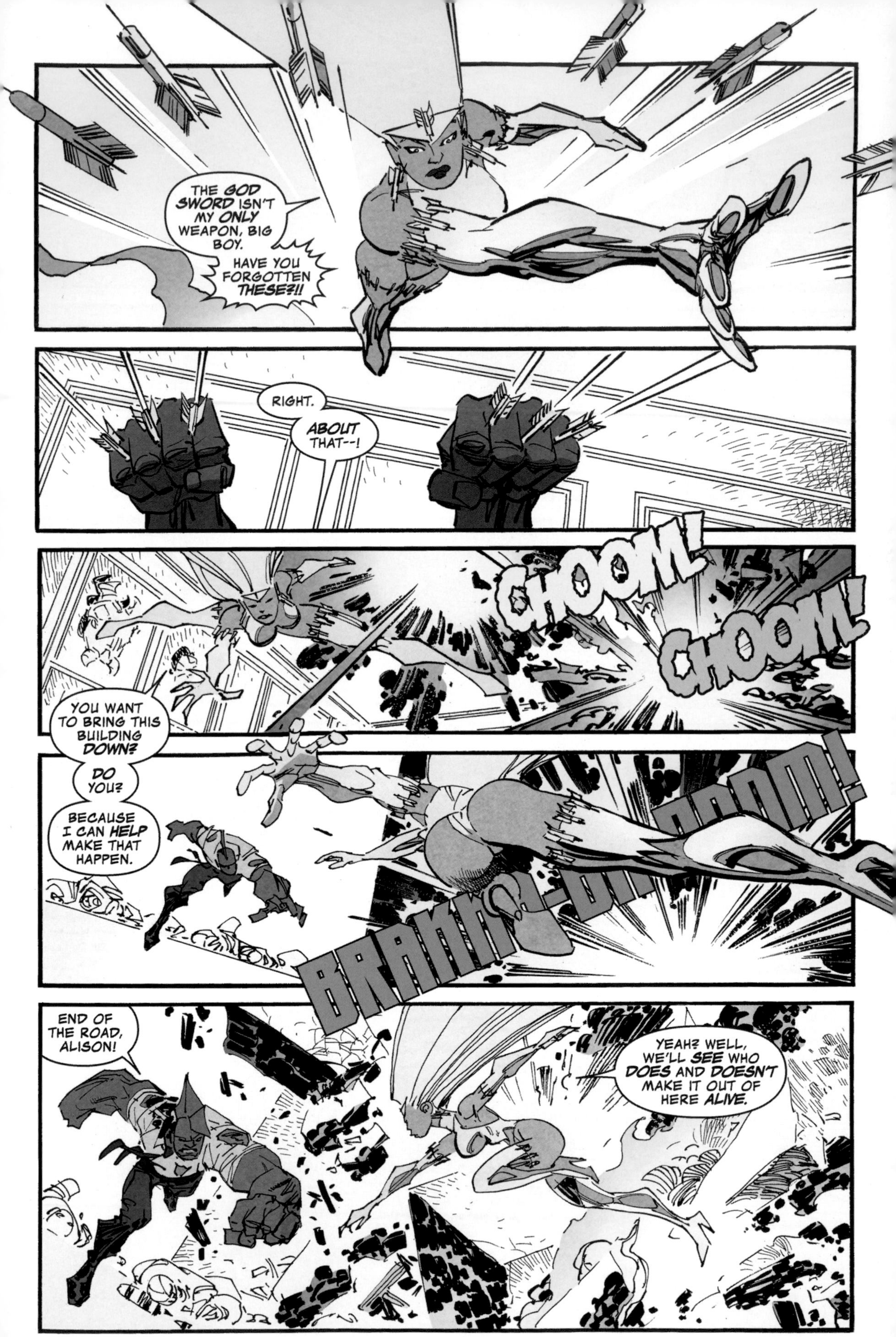
THE GOD SWORD ISN'T MY ONLY WEAPON, BIG BOY.
HAVE YOU FORGOTTEN THESE?!!
RIGHT.
ABOUT THAT--!
CHOOM!
CHOOM!
YOU WANT TO BRING THIS BUILDING DOWN?
DO YOU?
BECAUSE I CAN HELP MAKE THAT HAPPEN.
END OF THE ROAD, ALISON!
YEAH? WELL, WE'LL SEE WHO DOES AND DOESN'T MAKE IT OUT OF HERE ALIVE.

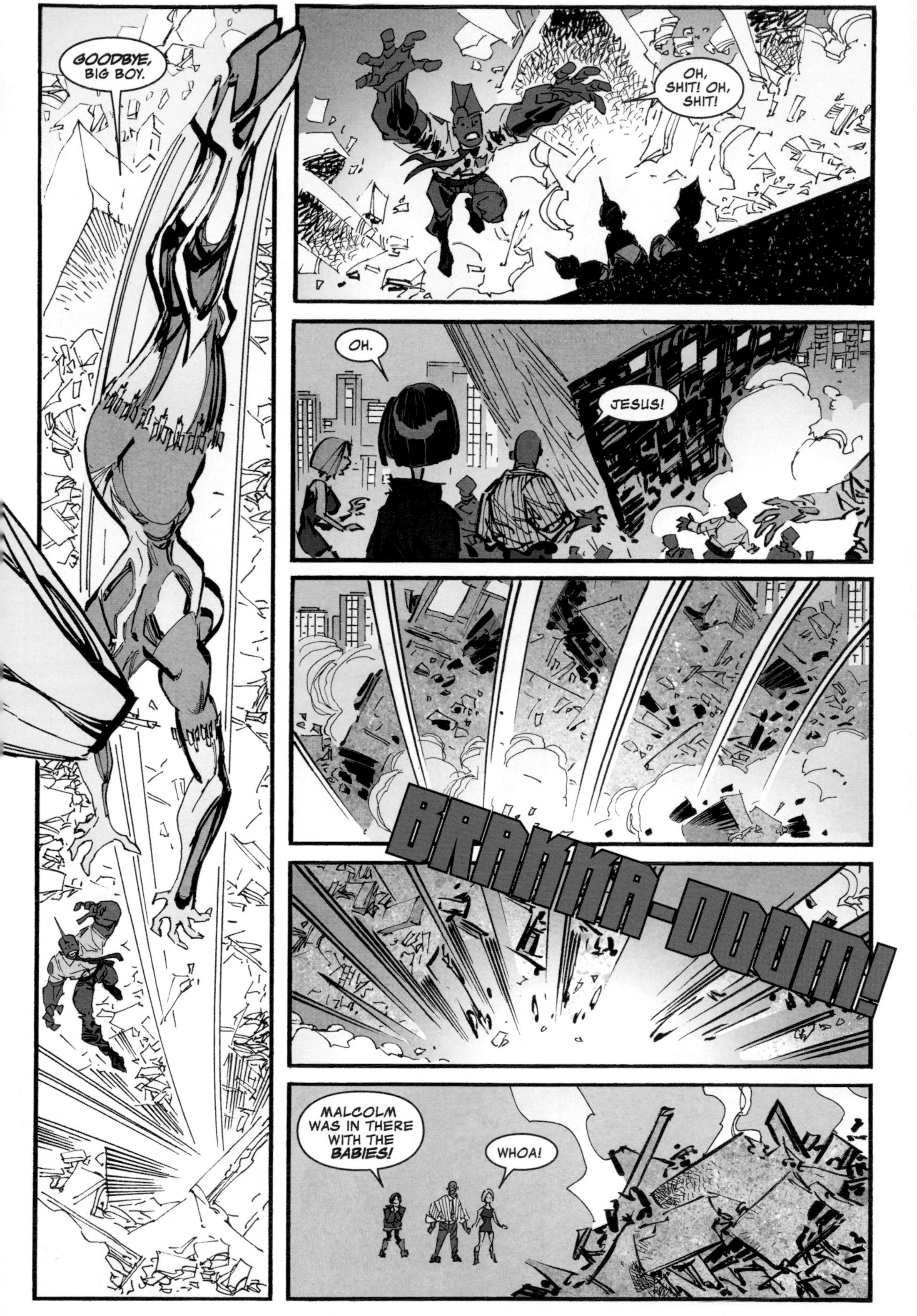
GOODBYE, BIG BOY.
OH, SHIT! OH, SHIT!
OH.
JESUS!
BRAKKA-DOOM!
MALCOLM WAS IN THERE WITH THE *BABIES!*
WHOA!

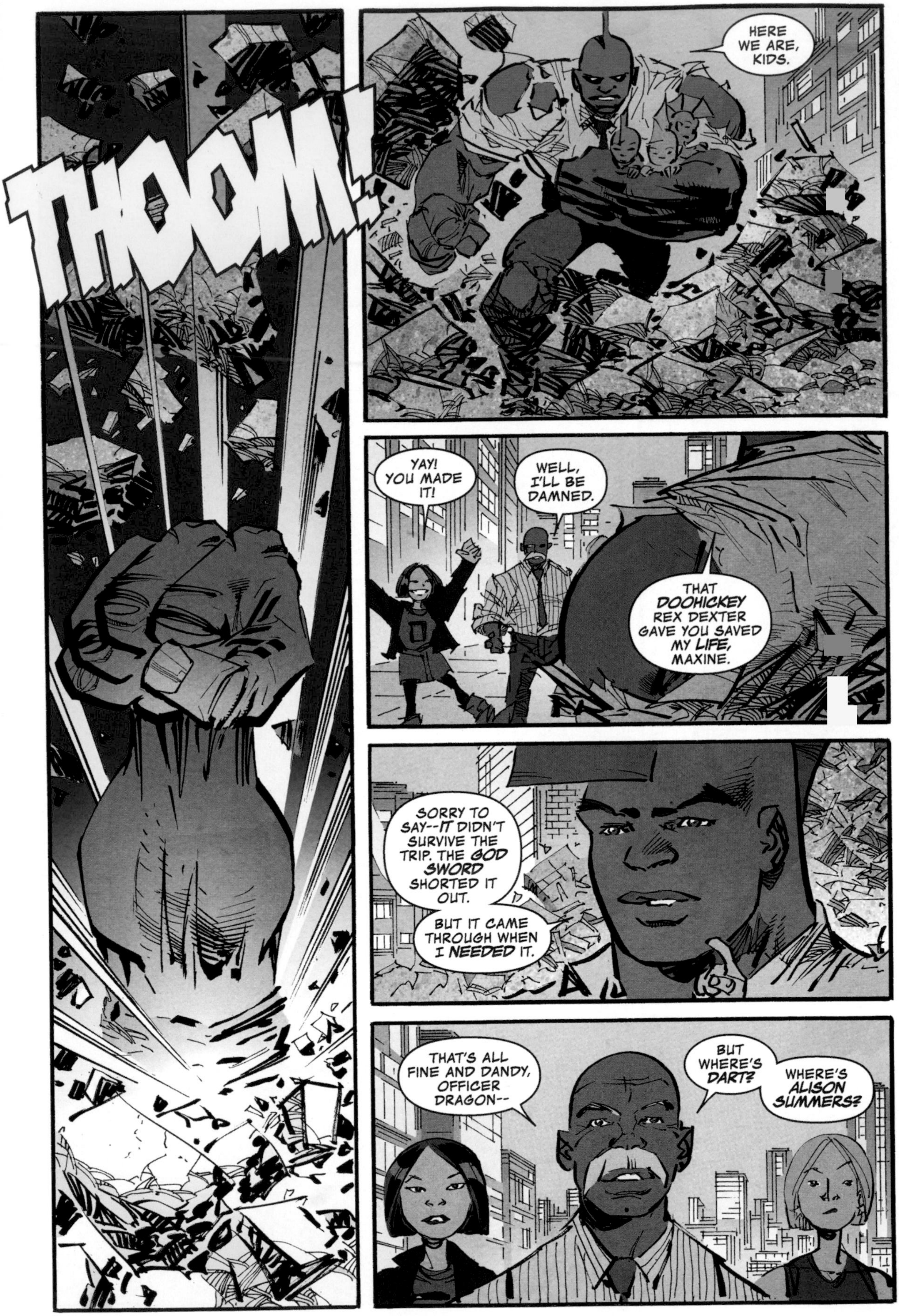
THOOM!!
HERE WE ARE, KIDS.
YAY! YOU MADE IT!
WELL, I'LL BE DAMNED.
THAT DOOHICKEY REX DEXTER GAVE YOU SAVED MY LIFE, MAXINE.
SORRY TO SAY--IT DIDN'T SURVIVE THE TRIP. THE GOD SWORD SHORTED IT OUT.
BUT IT CAME THROUGH WHEN I NEEDED IT.
THAT'S ALL FINE AND DANDY, OFFICER DRAGON--
BUT WHERE'S DART?
WHERE'S ALISON SUMMERS?

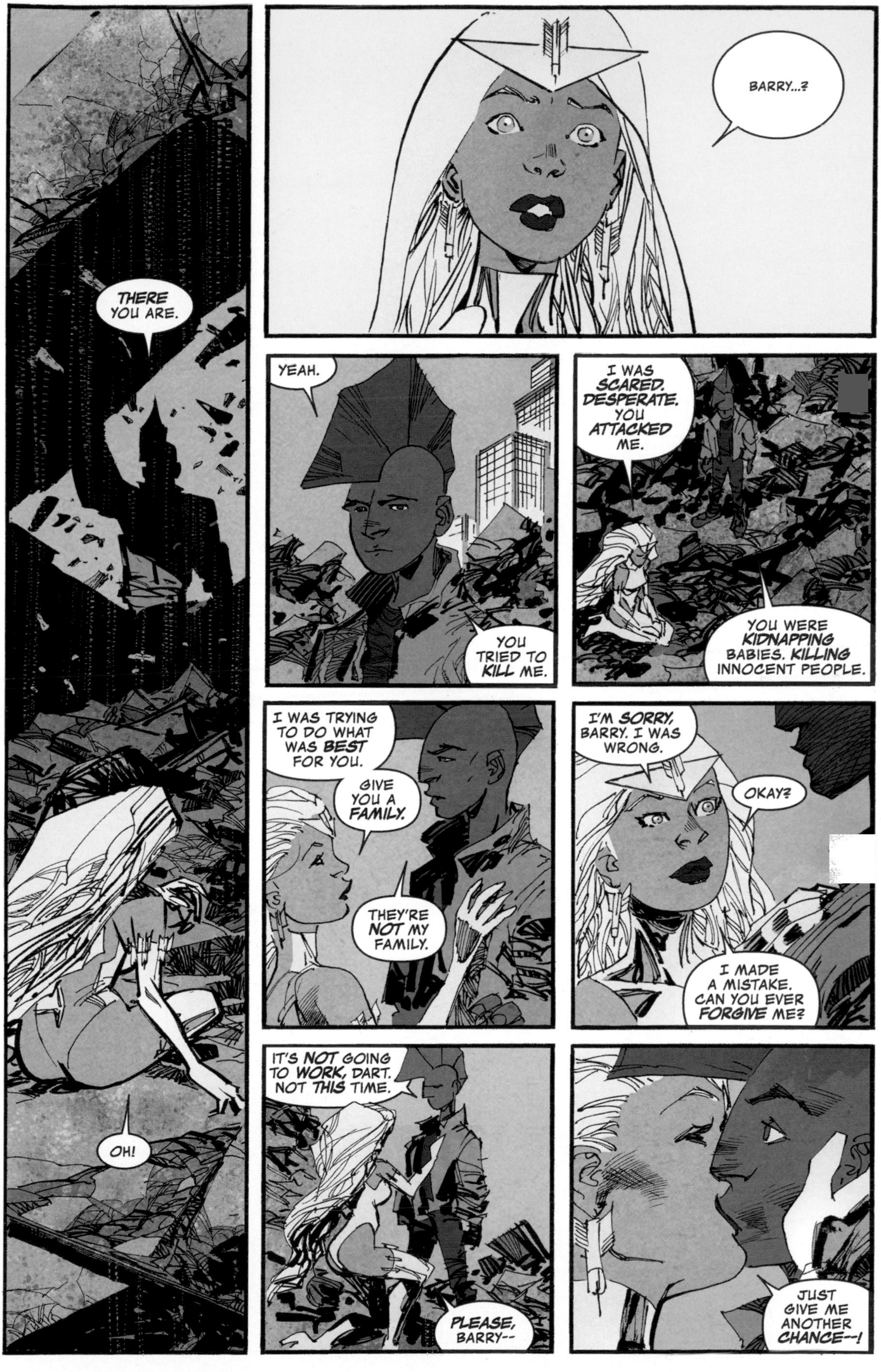
THERE YOU ARE.
OH!
BARRY...?
YEAH.
YOU TRIED TO KILL ME.
I WAS SCARED. DESPERATE. YOU ATTACKED ME.
YOU WERE KIDNAPPING BABIES. KILLING INNOCENT PEOPLE.
I WAS TRYING TO DO WHAT WAS BEST FOR YOU.
GIVE YOU A FAMILY.
THEY'RE NOT MY FAMILY.
I'M SORRY, BARRY. I WAS WRONG.
OKAY?
I MADE A MISTAKE. CAN YOU EVER FORGIVE ME?
IT'S NOT GOING TO WORK, DART. NOT THIS TIME.
PLEASE, BARRY--
JUST GIVE ME ANOTHER CHANCE--!

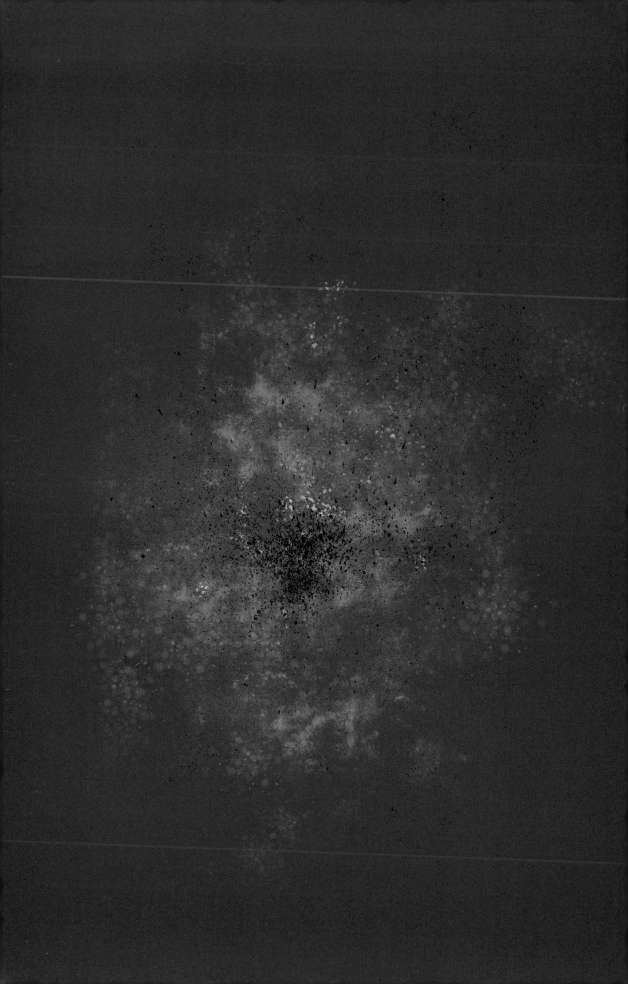

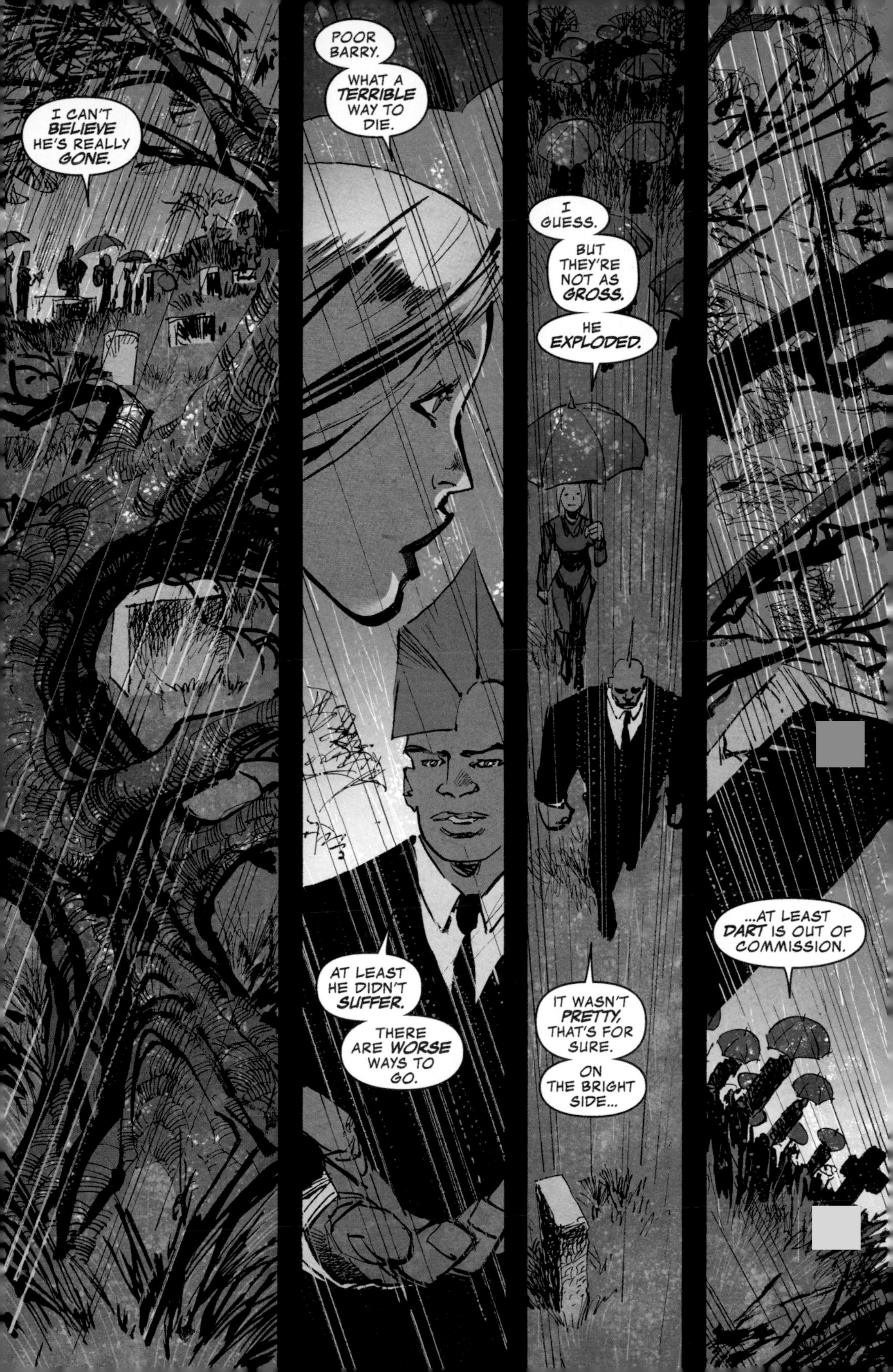
I CAN'T BELIEVE HE'S REALLY GONE.
POOR BARRY.
WHAT A TERRIBLE WAY TO DIE.
AT LEAST HE DIDN'T SUFFER.
THERE ARE WORSE WAYS TO GO.
I GUESS.
BUT THEY'RE NOT AS GROSS.
HE EXPLODED.
IT WASN'T PRETTY, THAT'S FOR SURE.
ON THE BRIGHT SIDE...
...AT LEAST DART IS OUT OF COMMISSION.

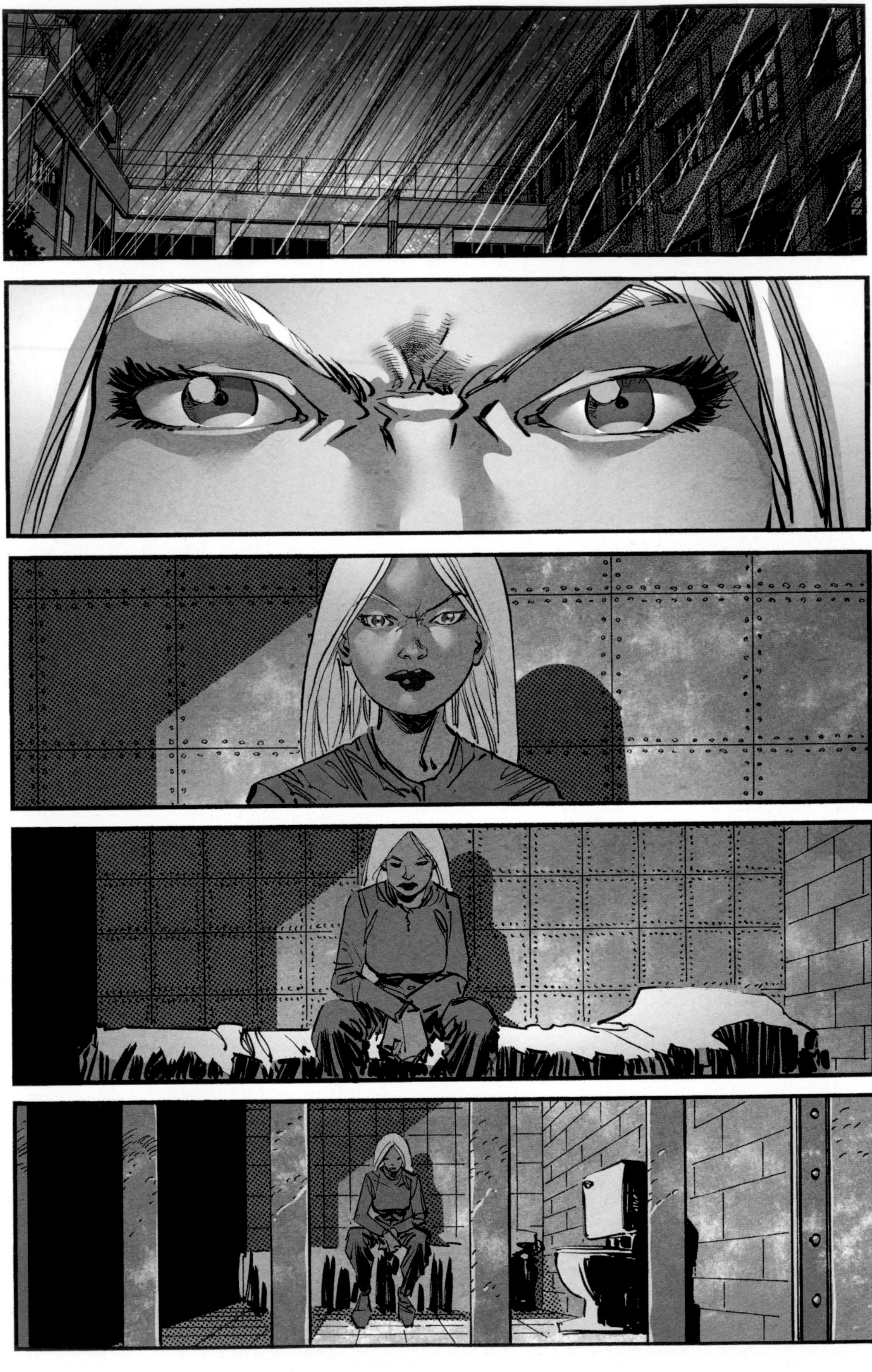

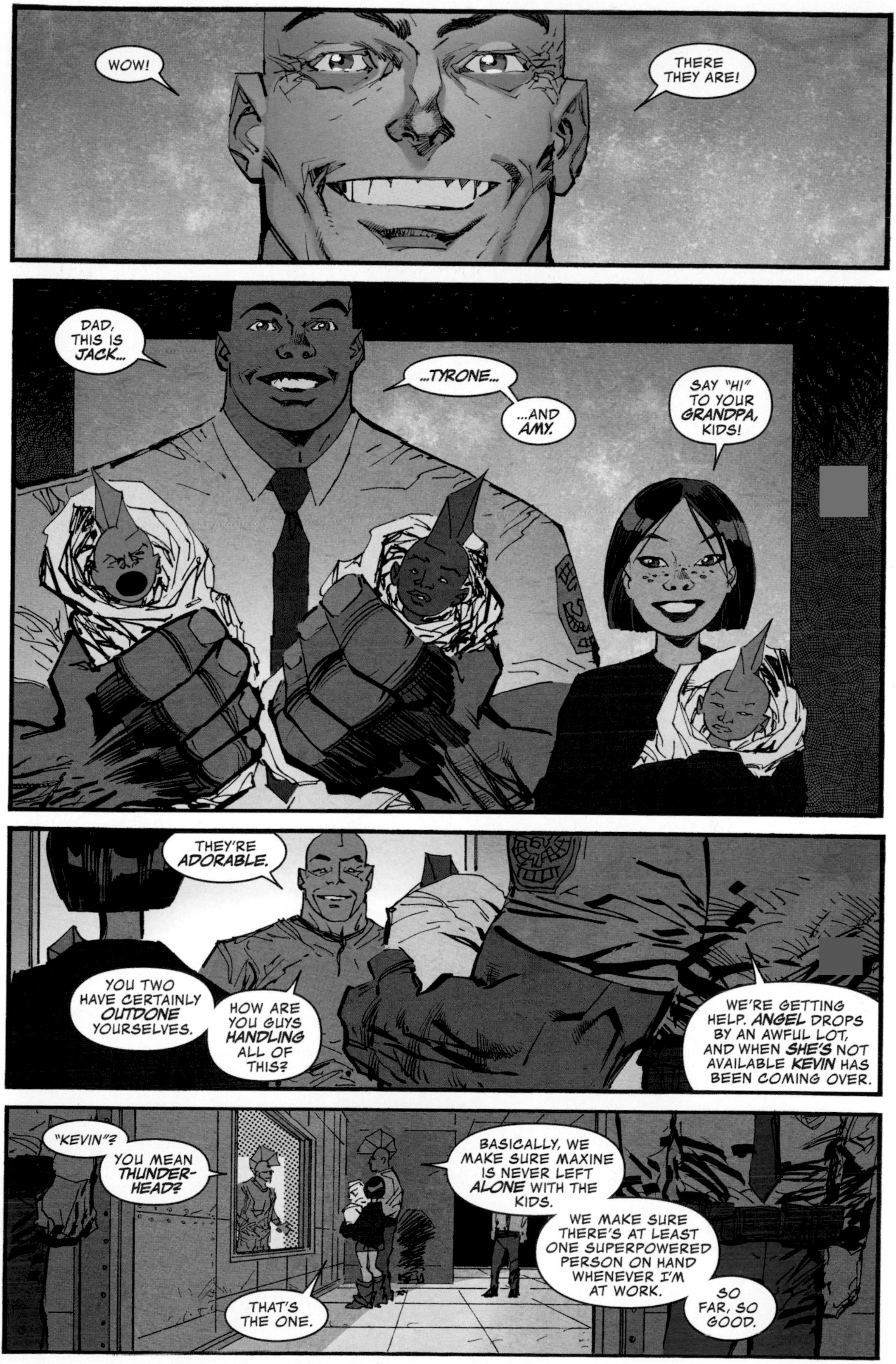
WOW!
THERE THEY ARE!
DAD, THIS IS JACK...
...TYRONE...
...AND AMY.
SAY "HI" TO YOUR GRANDPA, KIDS!
THEY'RE ADORABLE.
YOU TWO HAVE CERTAINLY OUTDONE YOURSELVES.
HOW ARE YOU GUYS HANDLING ALL OF THIS?
WE'RE GETTING HELP. ANGEL DROPS BY AN AWFUL LOT, AND WHEN SHE'S NOT AVAILABLE KEVIN HAS BEEN COMING OVER.
"KEVIN"?
YOU MEAN THUNDER-HEAD?
THAT'S THE ONE.
BASICALLY, WE MAKE SURE MAXINE IS NEVER LEFT ALONE WITH THE KIDS.
WE MAKE SURE THERE'S AT LEAST ONE SUPERPOWERED PERSON ON HAND WHENEVER I'M AT WORK.
SO FAR, SO GOOD.

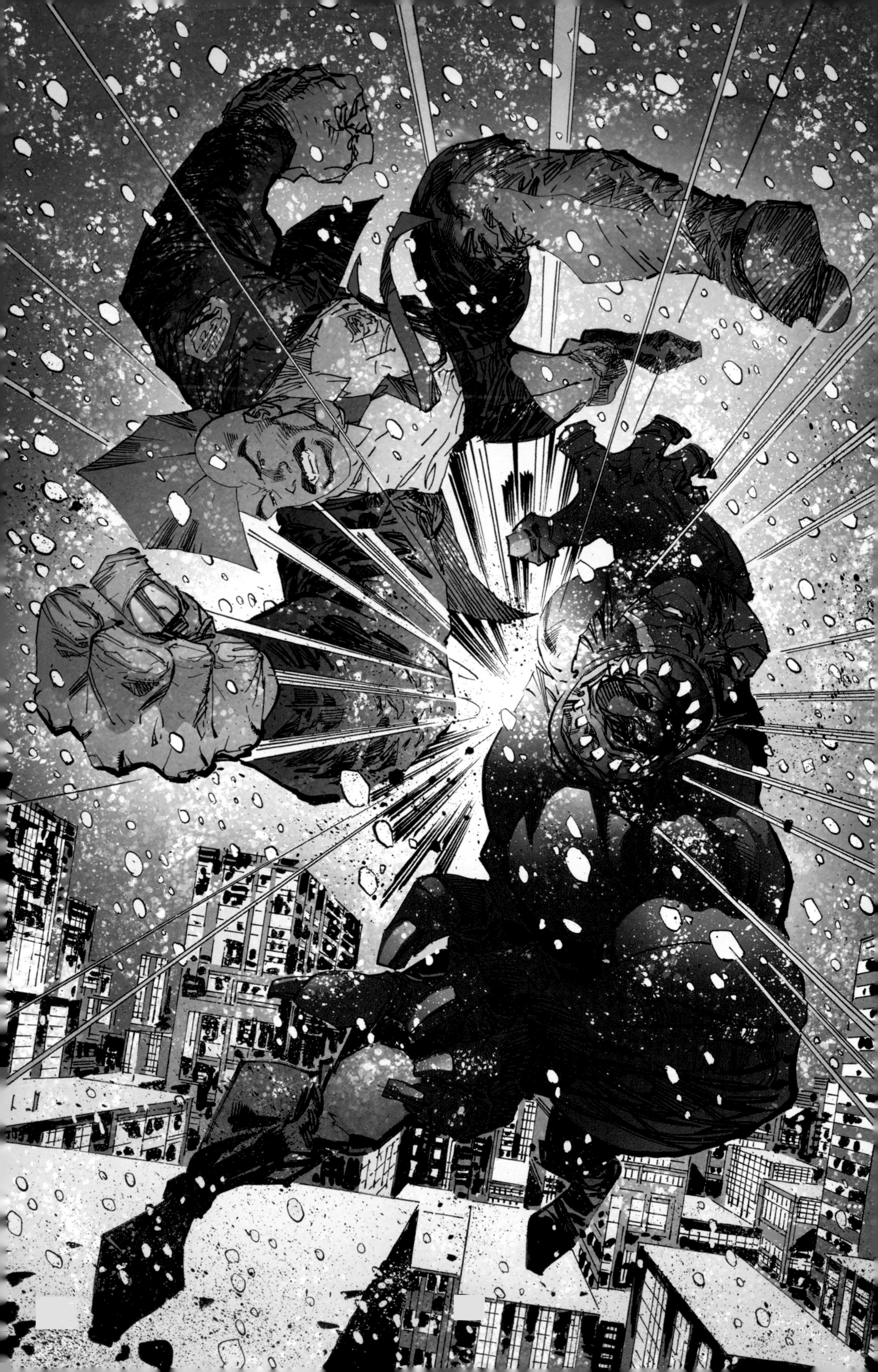

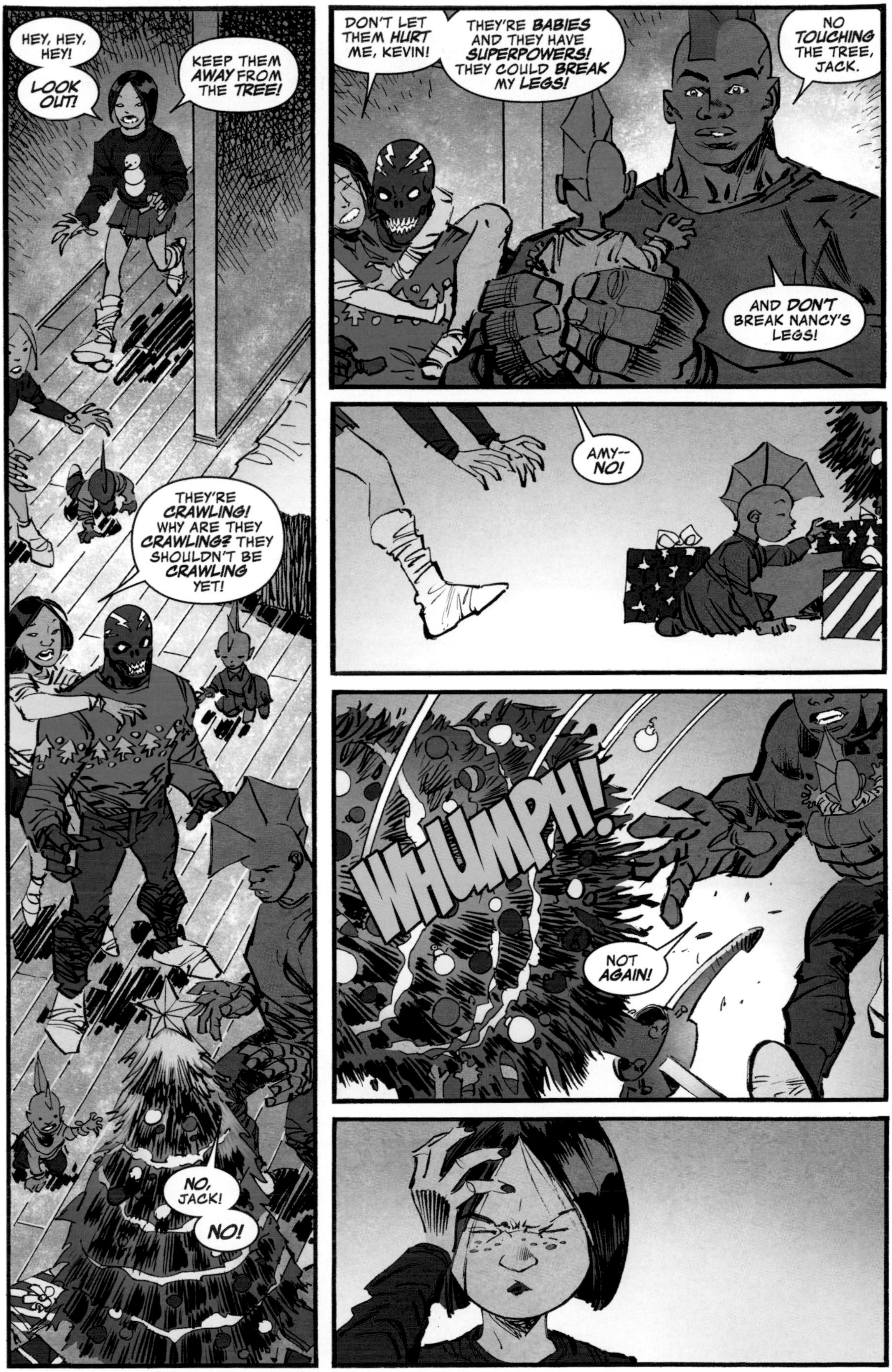
HEY, HEY, HEY!
LOOK OUT!
KEEP THEM AWAY FROM THE TREE!
THEY'RE CRAWLING! WHY ARE THEY CRAWLING? THEY SHOULDN'T BE CRAWLING YET!
NO, JACK!
NO!
DON'T LET THEM HURT ME, KEVIN!
THEY'RE BABIES AND THEY HAVE SUPERPOWERS! THEY COULD BREAK MY LEGS!
NO TOUCHING THE TREE, JACK.
AND DON'T BREAK NANCY'S LEGS!
AMY-- NO!
WHUMPH!
NOT AGAIN!

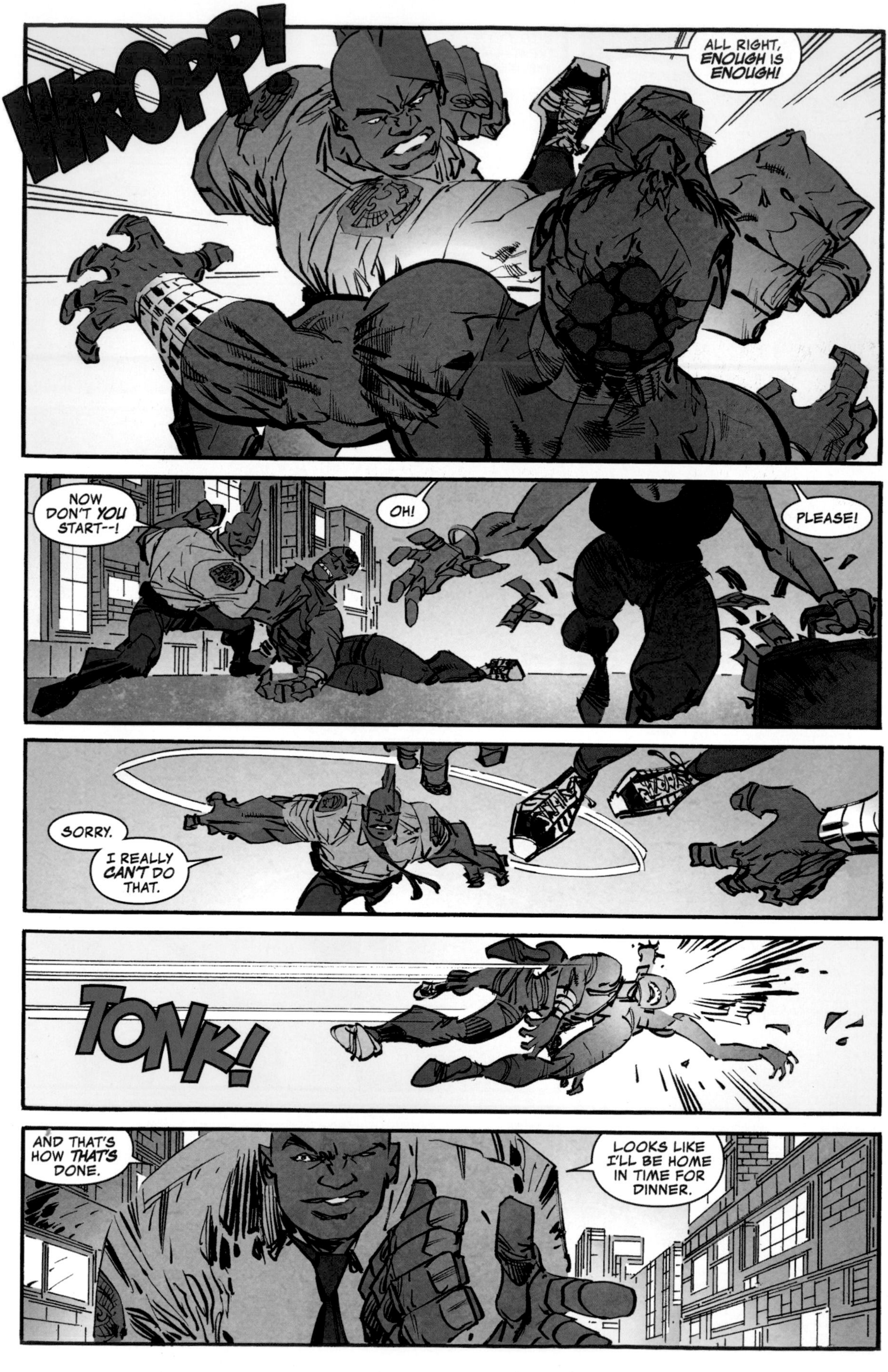
WHROPP!
ALL RIGHT, ENOUGH IS ENOUGH!
NOW DON'T YOU START--!
OH!
PLEASE!
SORRY.
I REALLY CAN'T DO THAT.
TONK!
AND THAT'S HOW THAT'S DONE.
LOOKS LIKE I'LL BE HOME IN TIME FOR DINNER.

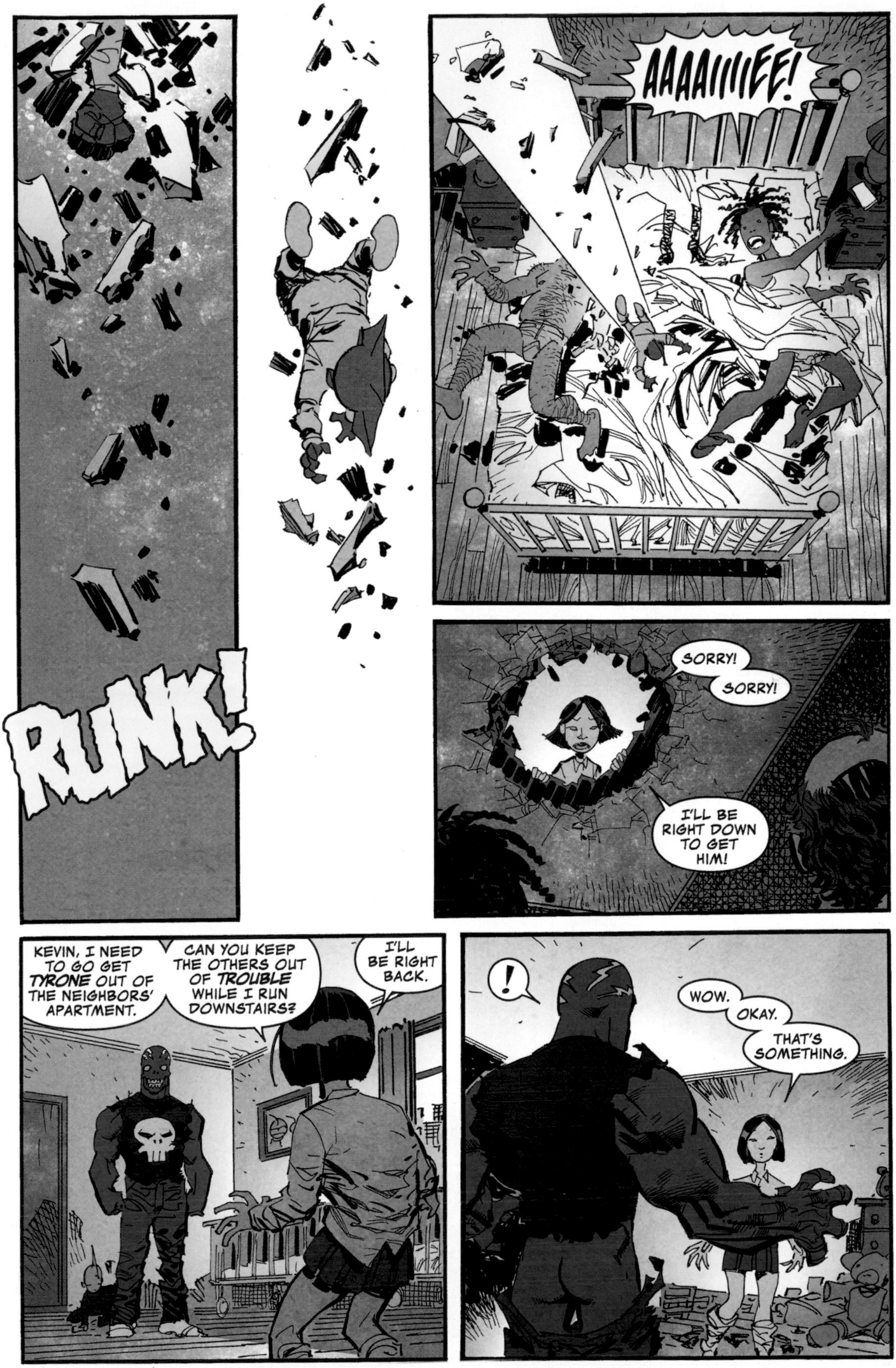
RUNK!
AAAAIIIIIEE!
SORRY!
SORRY!
I'LL BE RIGHT DOWN TO GET HIM!
KEVIN, I NEED TO GO GET TYRONE OUT OF THE NEIGHBORS' APARTMENT.
CAN YOU KEEP THE OTHERS OUT OF TROUBLE WHILE I RUN DOWNSTAIRS?
I'LL BE RIGHT BACK.
!
WOW.
OKAY.
THAT'S SOMETHING.

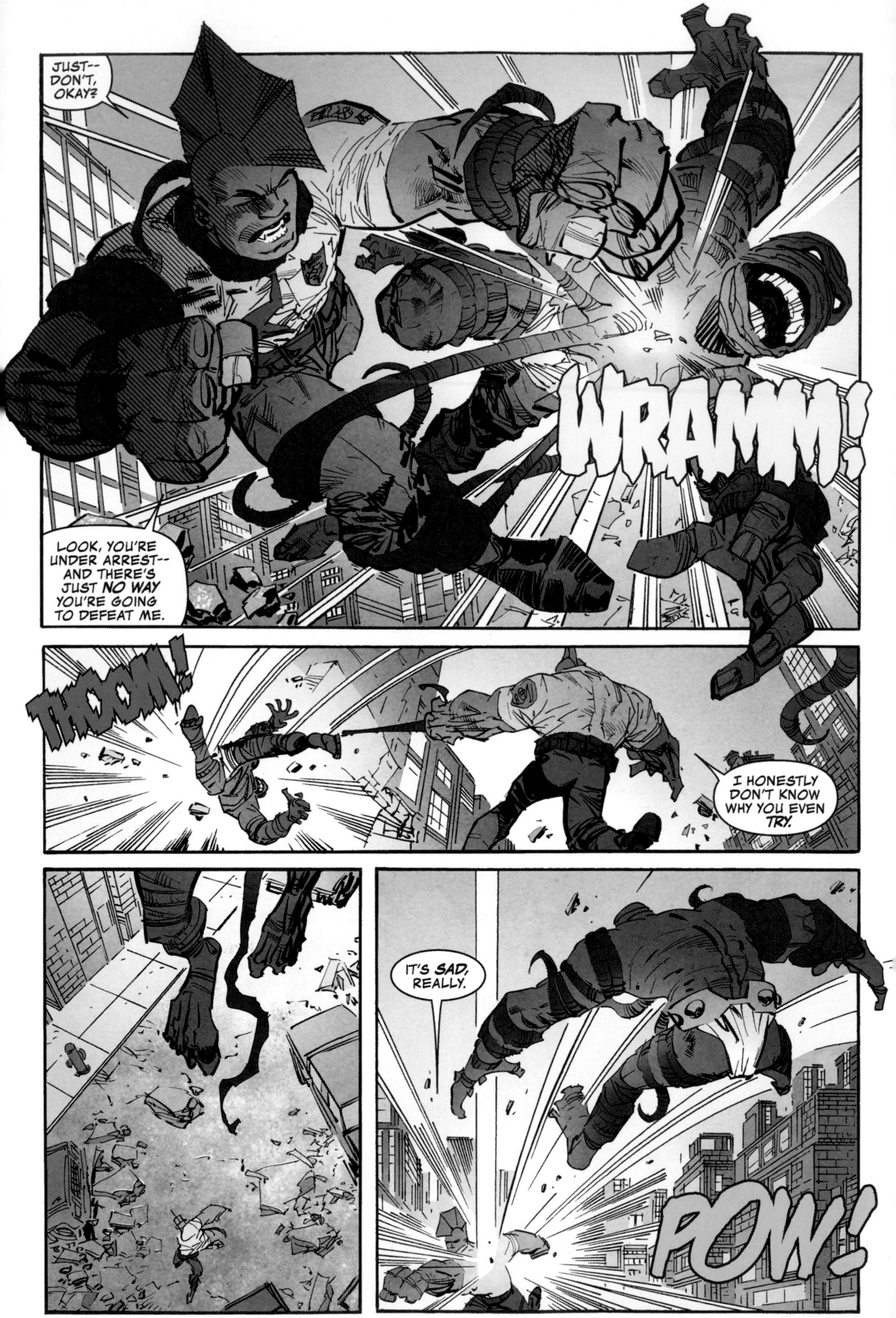
JUST--
DON'T, OKAY?
WRAMM!
LOOK, YOU'RE UNDER ARREST-- AND THERE'S JUST NO WAY YOU'RE GOING TO DEFEAT ME.
THOOM!
I HONESTLY DON'T KNOW WHY YOU EVEN TRY.
IT'S SAD, REALLY.
POW!

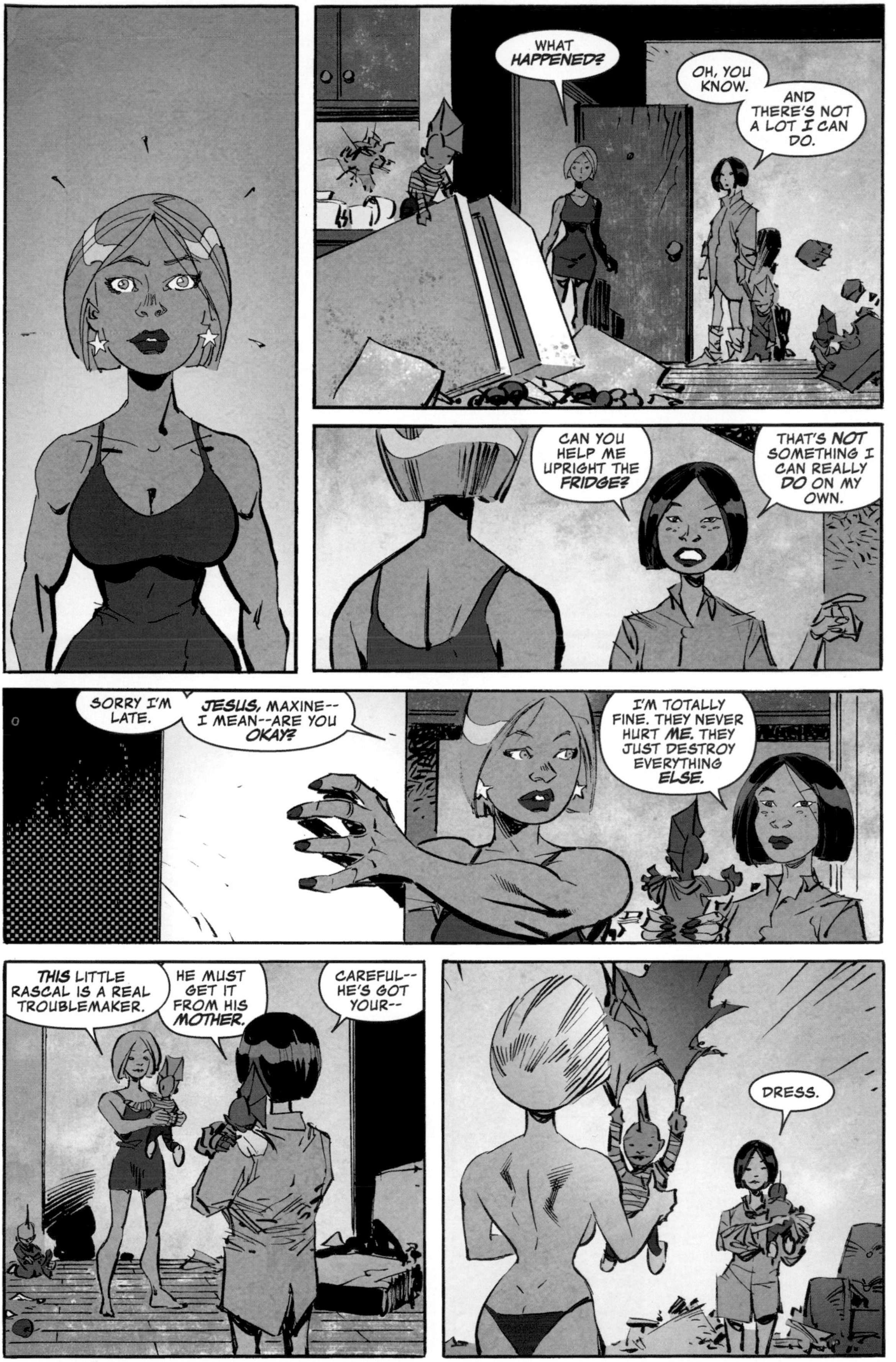
WHAT HAPPENED?
OH, YOU KNOW.
AND THERE'S NOT A LOT I CAN DO.
CAN YOU HELP ME UPRIGHT THE FRIDGE?
THAT'S NOT SOMETHING I CAN REALLY DO ON MY OWN.
SORRY I'M LATE.
JESUS, MAXINE-- I MEAN--ARE YOU OKAY?
I'M TOTALLY FINE. THEY NEVER HURT ME. THEY JUST DESTROY EVERYTHING ELSE.
THIS LITTLE RASCAL IS A REAL TROUBLEMAKER.
HE MUST GET IT FROM HIS MOTHER.
CAREFUL-- HE'S GOT YOUR--
DRESS.

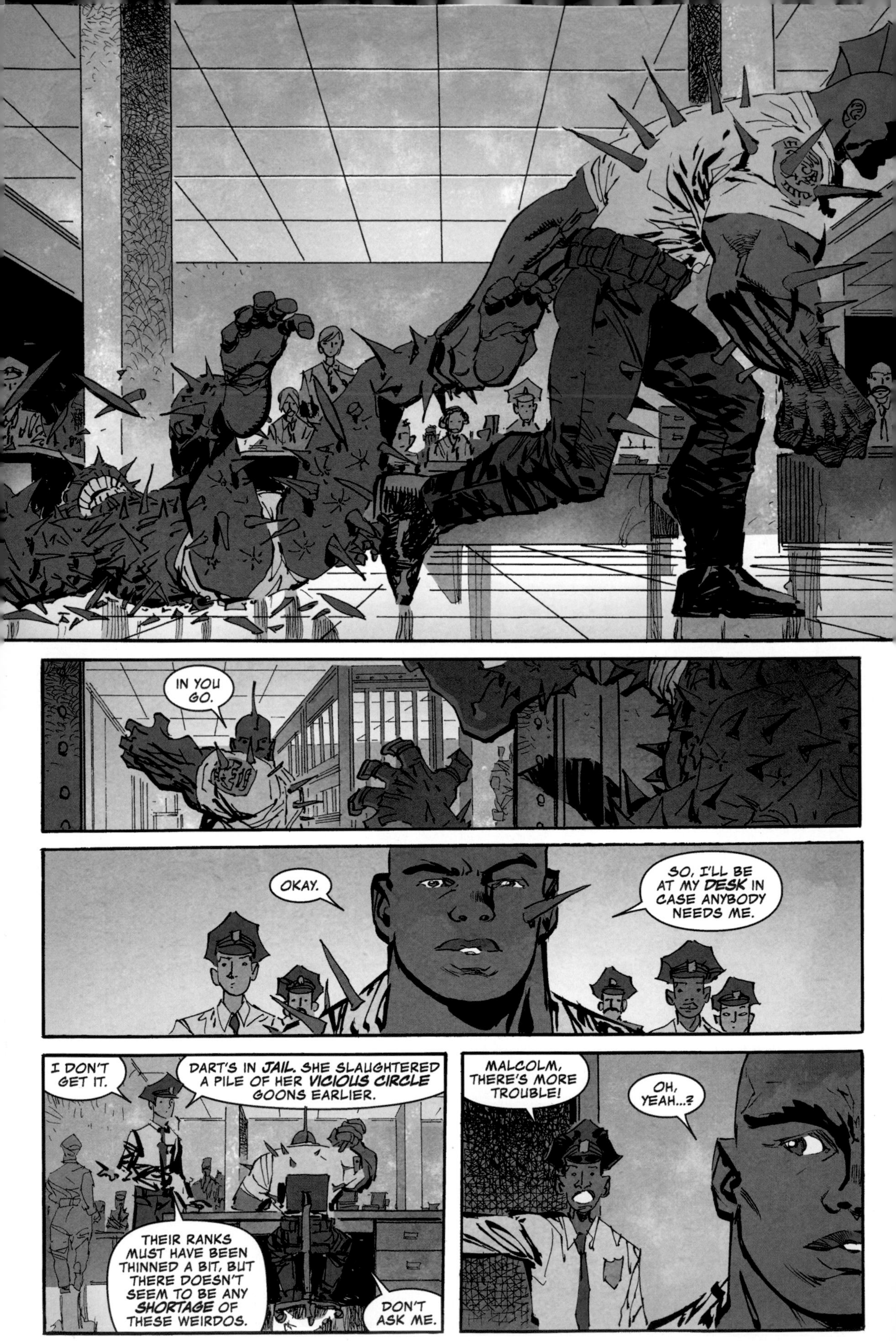
IN YOU GO.
OKAY.
SO, I'LL BE AT MY DESK IN CASE ANYBODY NEEDS ME.
I DON'T GET IT.
DART'S IN JAIL. SHE SLAUGHTERED A PILE OF HER VICIOUS CIRCLE GOONS EARLIER.
THEIR RANKS MUST HAVE BEEN THINNED A BIT, BUT THERE DOESN'T SEEM TO BE ANY SHORTAGE OF THESE WEIRDOS.
DON'T ASK ME.
MALCOLM, THERE'S MORE TROUBLE!
OH, YEAH...?

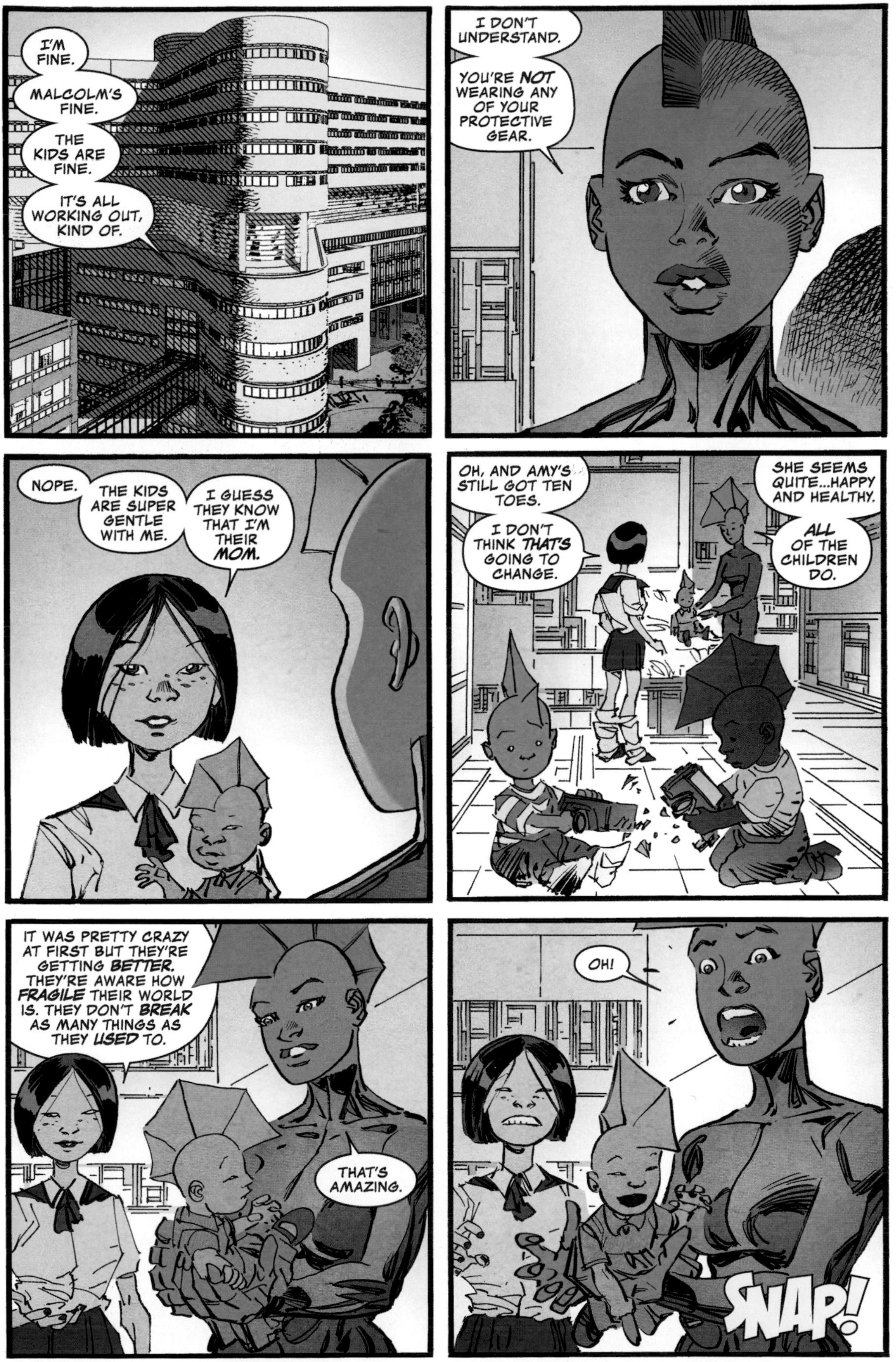
I'M FINE.
MALCOLM'S FINE.
THE KIDS ARE FINE.
IT'S ALL WORKING OUT, KIND OF.
I DON'T UNDERSTAND.
YOU'RE NOT WEARING ANY OF YOUR PROTECTIVE GEAR.
NOPE.
THE KIDS ARE SUPER GENTLE WITH ME.
I GUESS THEY KNOW THAT I'M THEIR MOM.
OH, AND AMY'S STILL GOT TEN TOES.
I DON'T THINK THAT'S GOING TO CHANGE.
SHE SEEMS QUITE...HAPPY AND HEALTHY.
ALL OF THE CHILDREN DO.
IT WAS PRETTY CRAZY AT FIRST BUT THEY'RE GETTING BETTER. THEY'RE AWARE HOW FRAGILE THEIR WORLD IS. THEY DON'T BREAK AS MANY THINGS AS THEY USED TO.
THAT'S AMAZING.
OH!
SNAP!

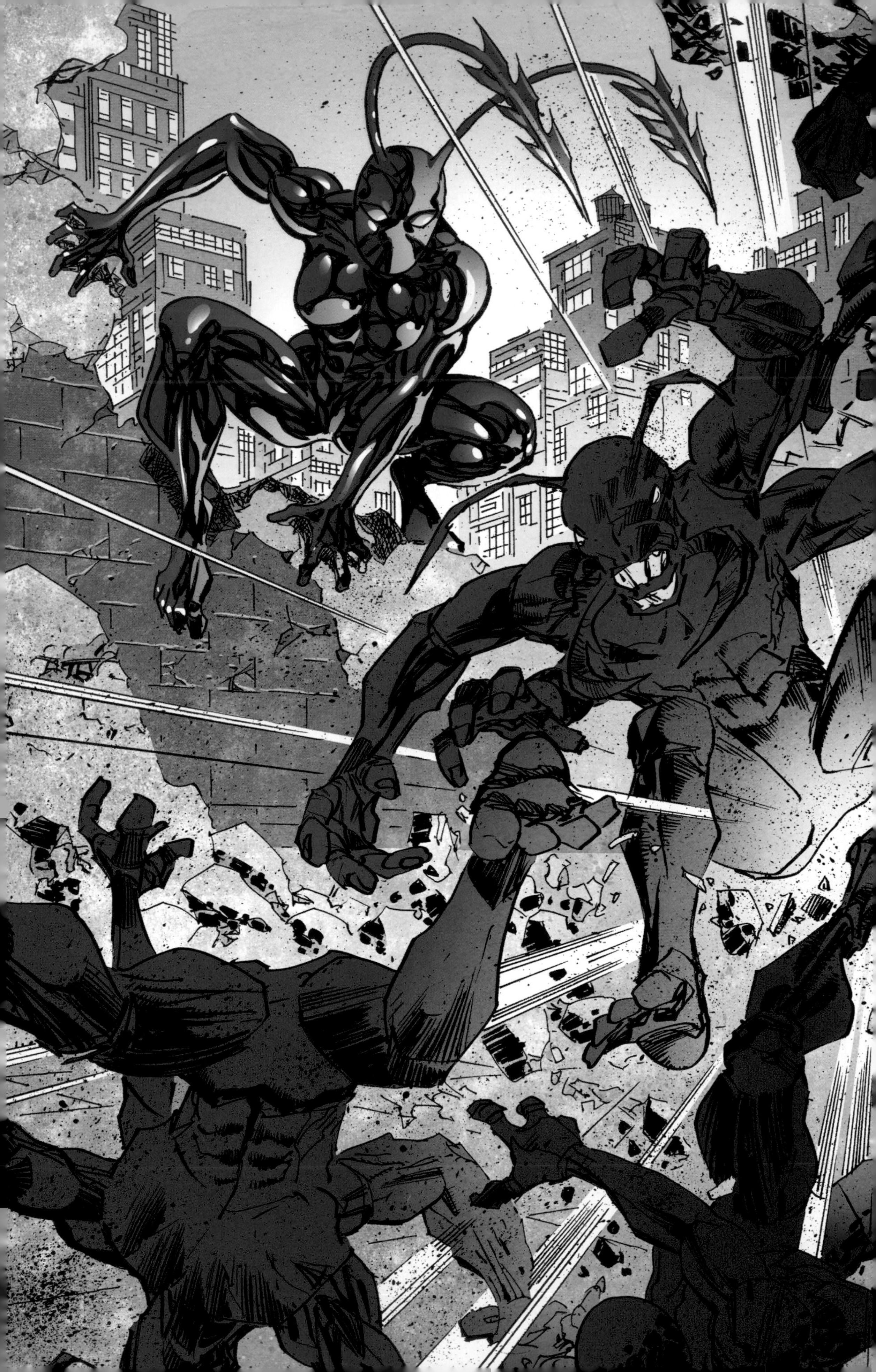

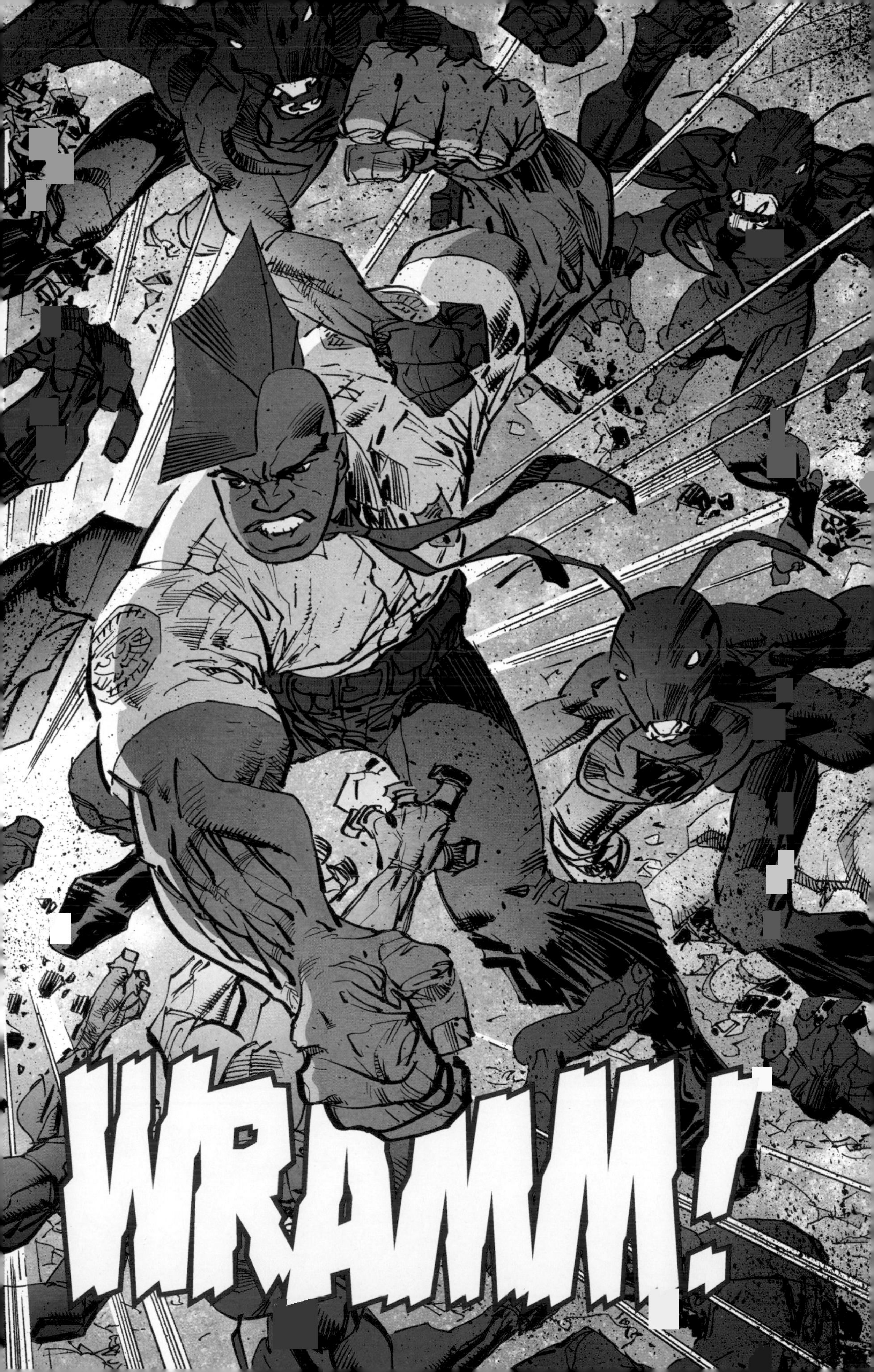
WRAMM!

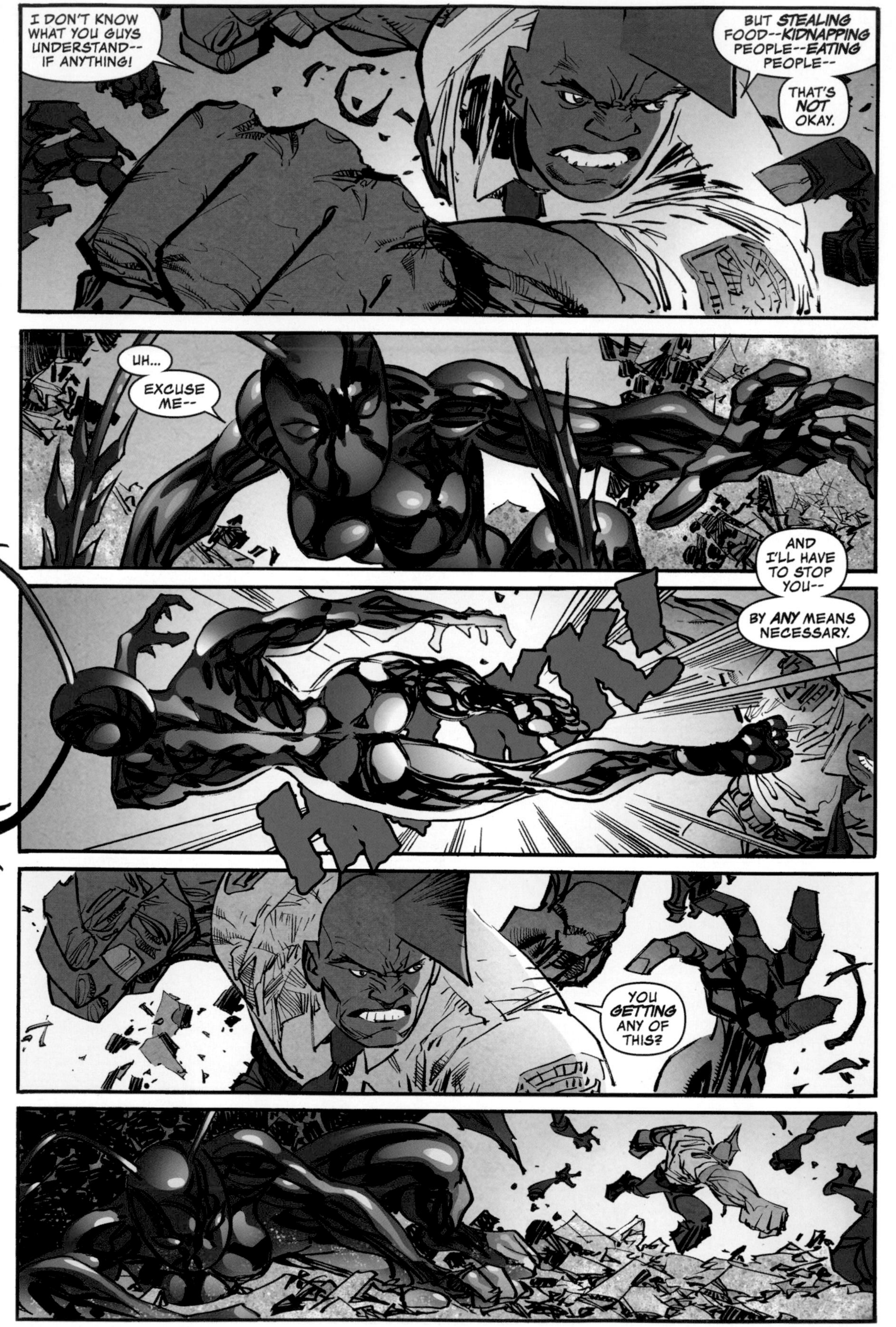
I DON'T KNOW WHAT YOU GUYS UNDERSTAND-- IF ANYTHING!
BUT STEALING FOOD--KIDNAPPING PEOPLE--EATING PEOPLE--
THAT'S NOT OKAY.
UH...
EXCUSE ME--
AND I'LL HAVE TO STOP YOU--
BY ANY MEANS NECESSARY.
YOU GETTING ANY OF THIS?

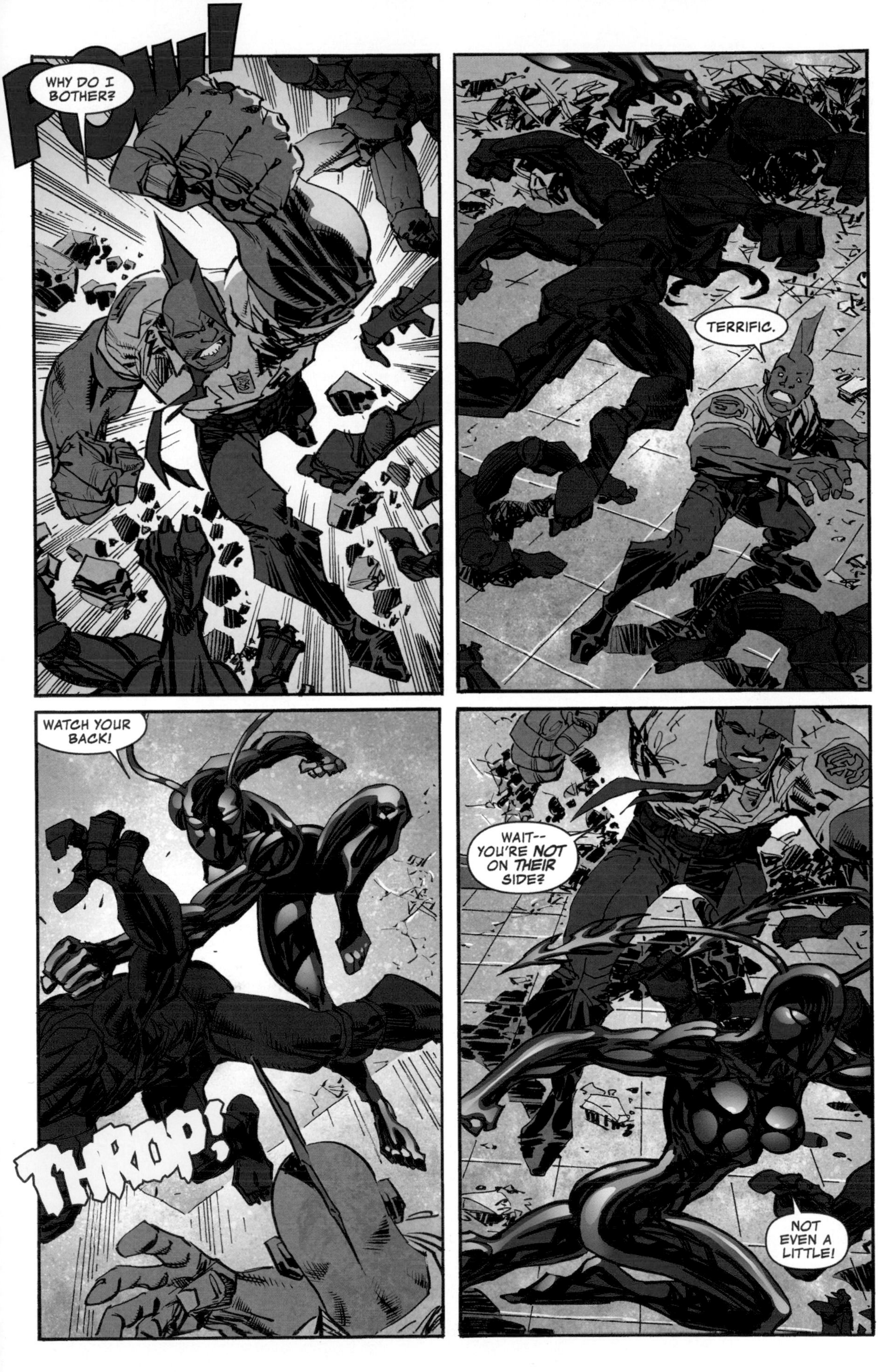
POW!
WHY DO I BOTHER?
TERRIFIC.
WATCH YOUR BACK!
THROOP!
WAIT-- YOU'RE NOT ON THEIR SIDE?
NOT EVEN A LITTLE!

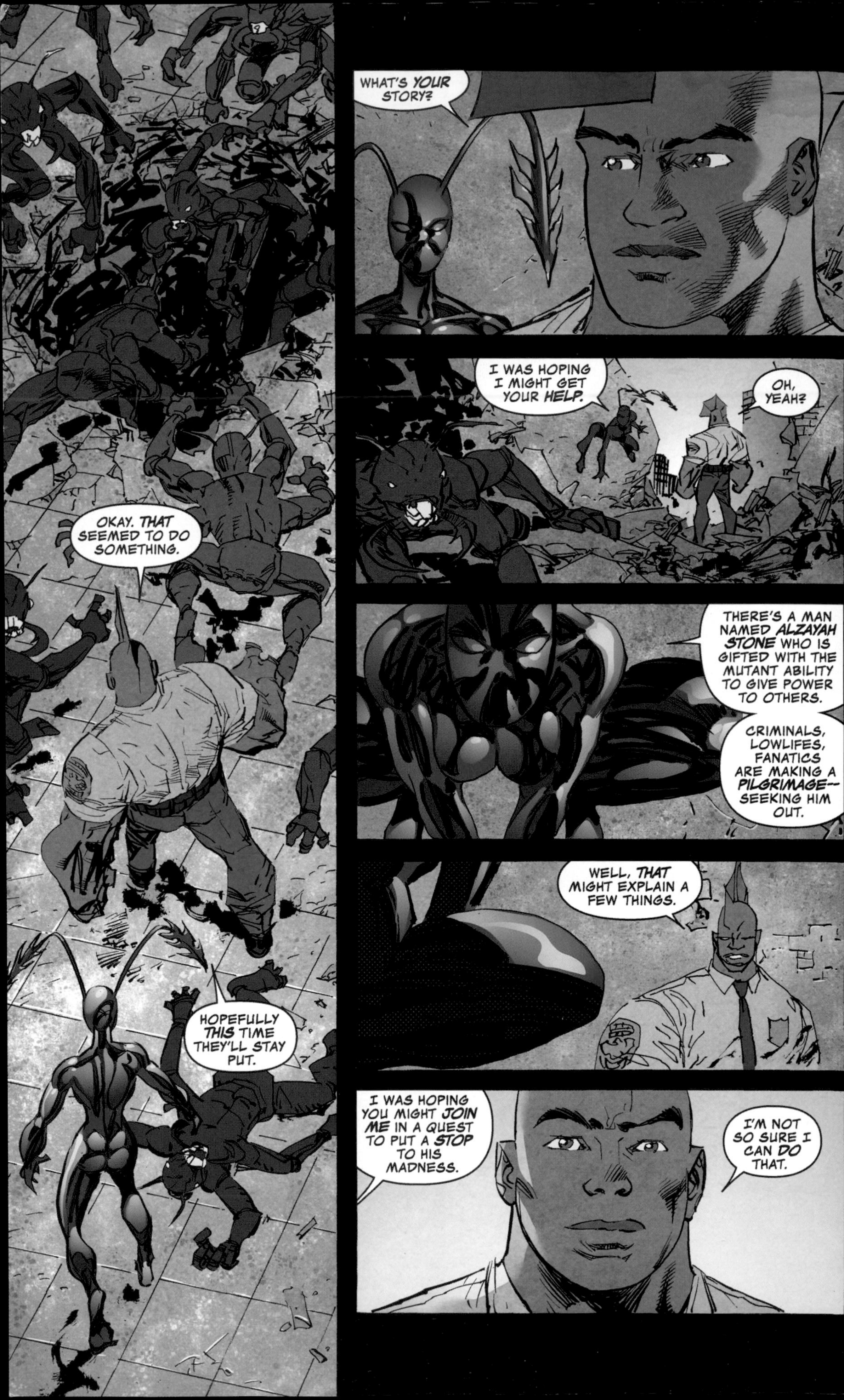
OKAY. THAT SEEMED TO DO SOMETHING.
HOPEFULLY THIS TIME THEY'LL STAY PUT.
WHAT'S YOUR STORY?
I WAS HOPING I MIGHT GET YOUR HELP.
OH, YEAH?
THERE'S A MAN NAMED ALZAYAH STONE WHO IS GIFTED WITH THE MUTANT ABILITY TO GIVE POWER TO OTHERS.
CRIMINALS, LOWLIFES, FANATICS ARE MAKING A PILGRIMAGE-- SEEKING HIM OUT.
WELL, THAT MIGHT EXPLAIN A FEW THINGS.
I WAS HOPING YOU MIGHT JOIN ME IN A QUEST TO PUT A STOP TO HIS MADNESS.
I'M NOT SO SURE I CAN DO THAT.

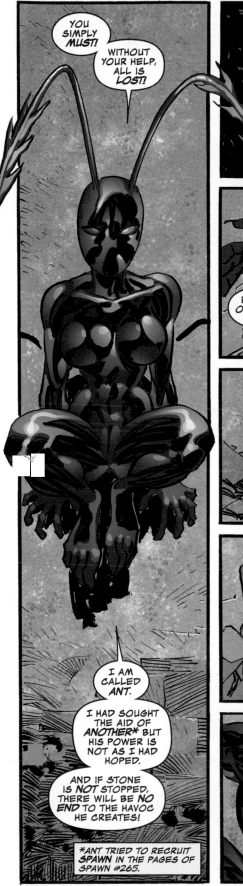

YOU SIMPLY **MUST!** WITHOUT YOUR HELP, ALL IS **LOST!**

I AM CALLED **ANT.**

I HAD SOUGHT THE AID OF **ANOTHER*** BUT HIS POWER IS NOT AS I HAD HOPED.

AND IF STONE IS **NOT** STOPPED, THERE WILL BE **NO END** TO THE HAVOC HE CREATES!

*ANT TRIED TO RECRUIT **SPAWN** IN THE PAGES OF SPAWN #265.

I HAVE NOWHERE ELSE TO TURN.

THAT MAY BE--

TOK!

BUT I HAVE OBLIGATIONS **HERE.**

I CAN'T GO RUNNING OFF TO-- WHEREVER, AND LEAVE CHICAGO **UNPROTECTED.**

I HAVE A **JOB** TO DO HERE--AND A **FAMILY** THAT DEPENDS ON ME.

I DON'T THINK I HAVE MADE IT CLEAR JUST HOW **DIRE** THE SITUATION IS.

THE VERY **PLANET** IS AT STAKE! LIFE AS WE KNOW IT HANGS IN THE BALANCE!

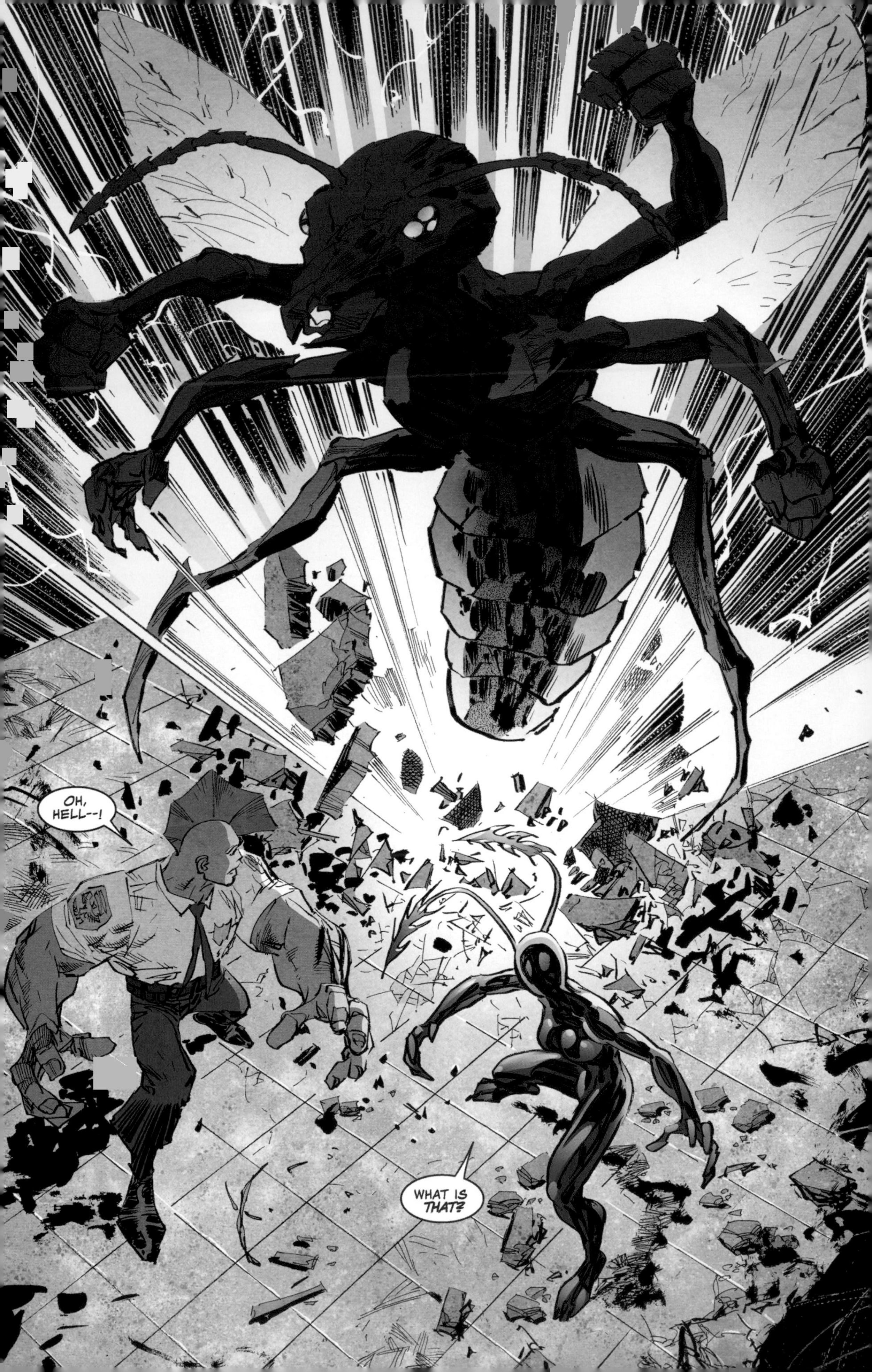
OH, HELL--!
WHAT IS THAT?

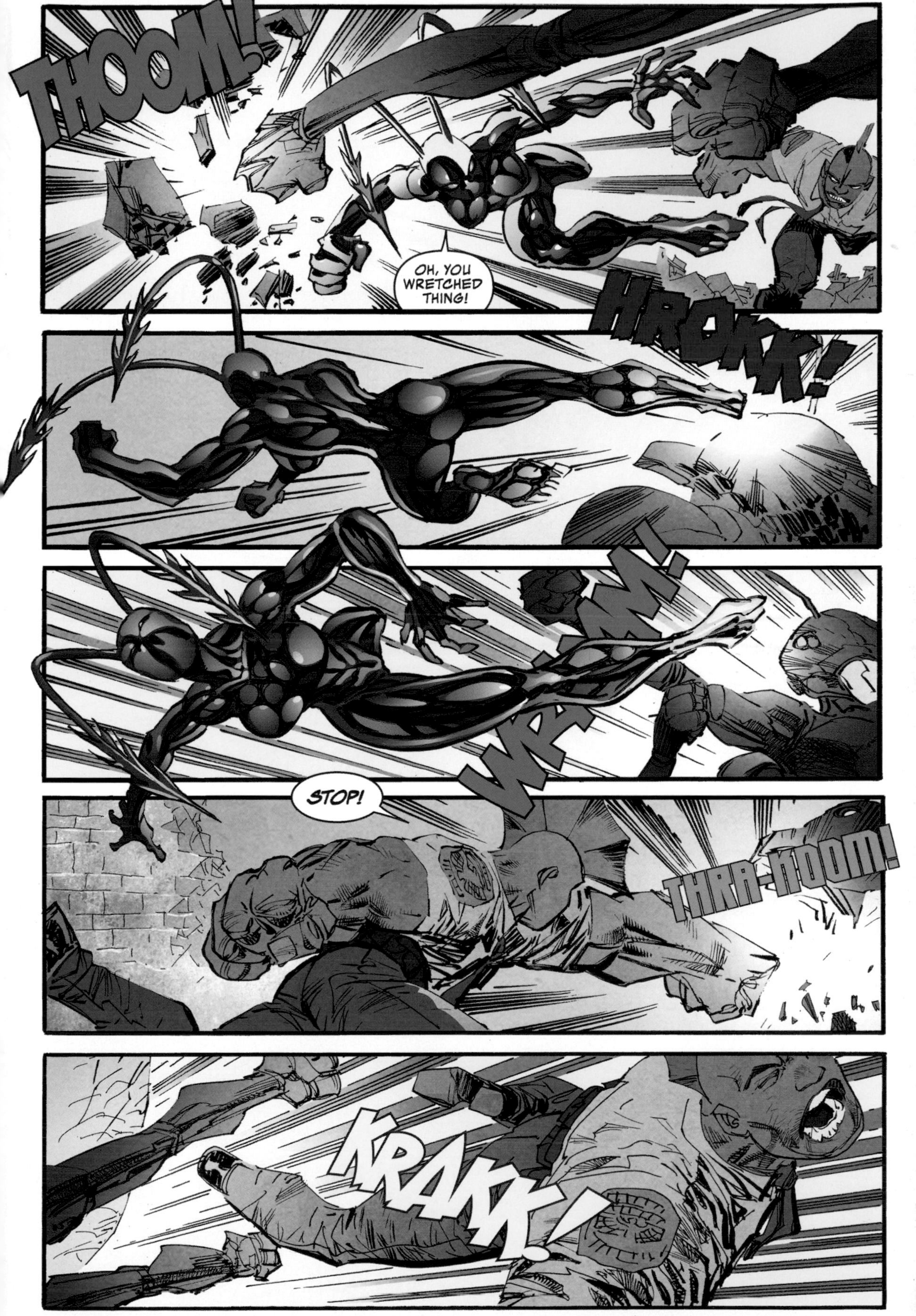
THOOM!
OH, YOU WRETCHED THING!
HROKK!
WRAMM!
STOP!
THRA-KOOM!
KRAKK!

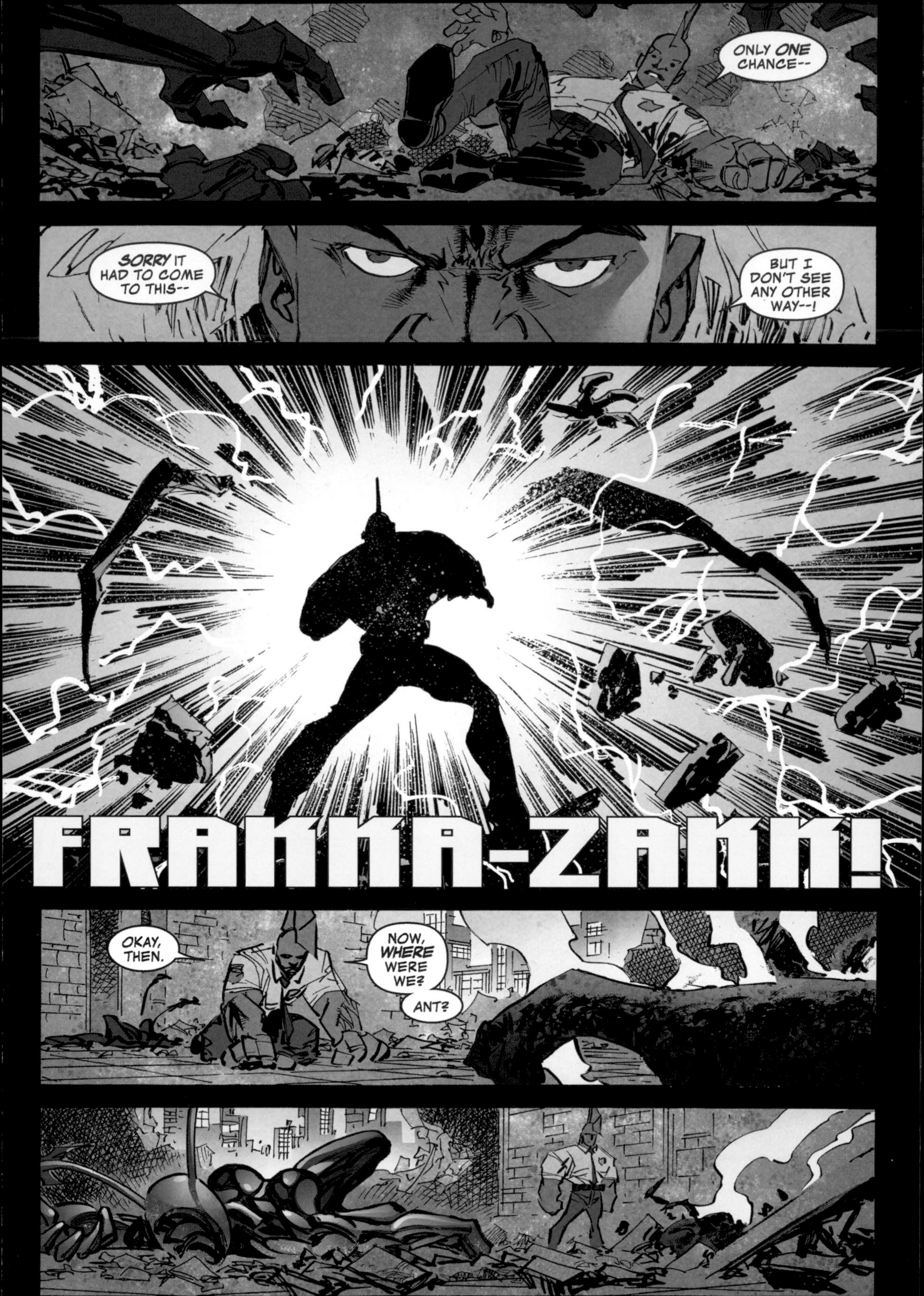
ONLY ONE CHANCE--
SORRY IT HAD TO COME TO THIS--
BUT I DON'T SEE ANY OTHER WAY--!
FRAKKA-ZAKK!
OKAY, THEN.
NOW, WHERE WERE WE?
ANT?

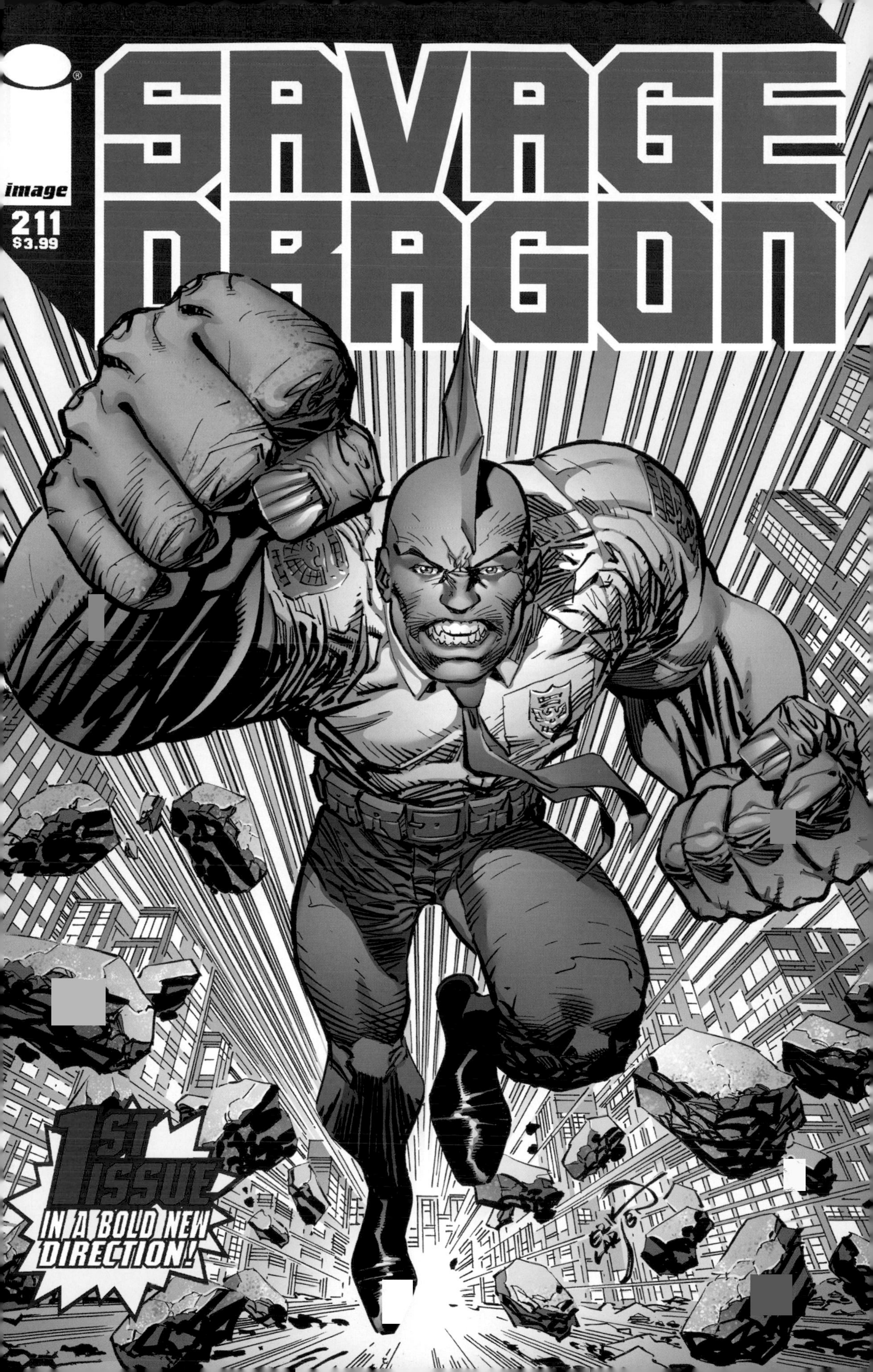
image
211
$3.99
SAVAGE DRAGON
1ST ISSUE
IN A BOLD NEW DIRECTION!

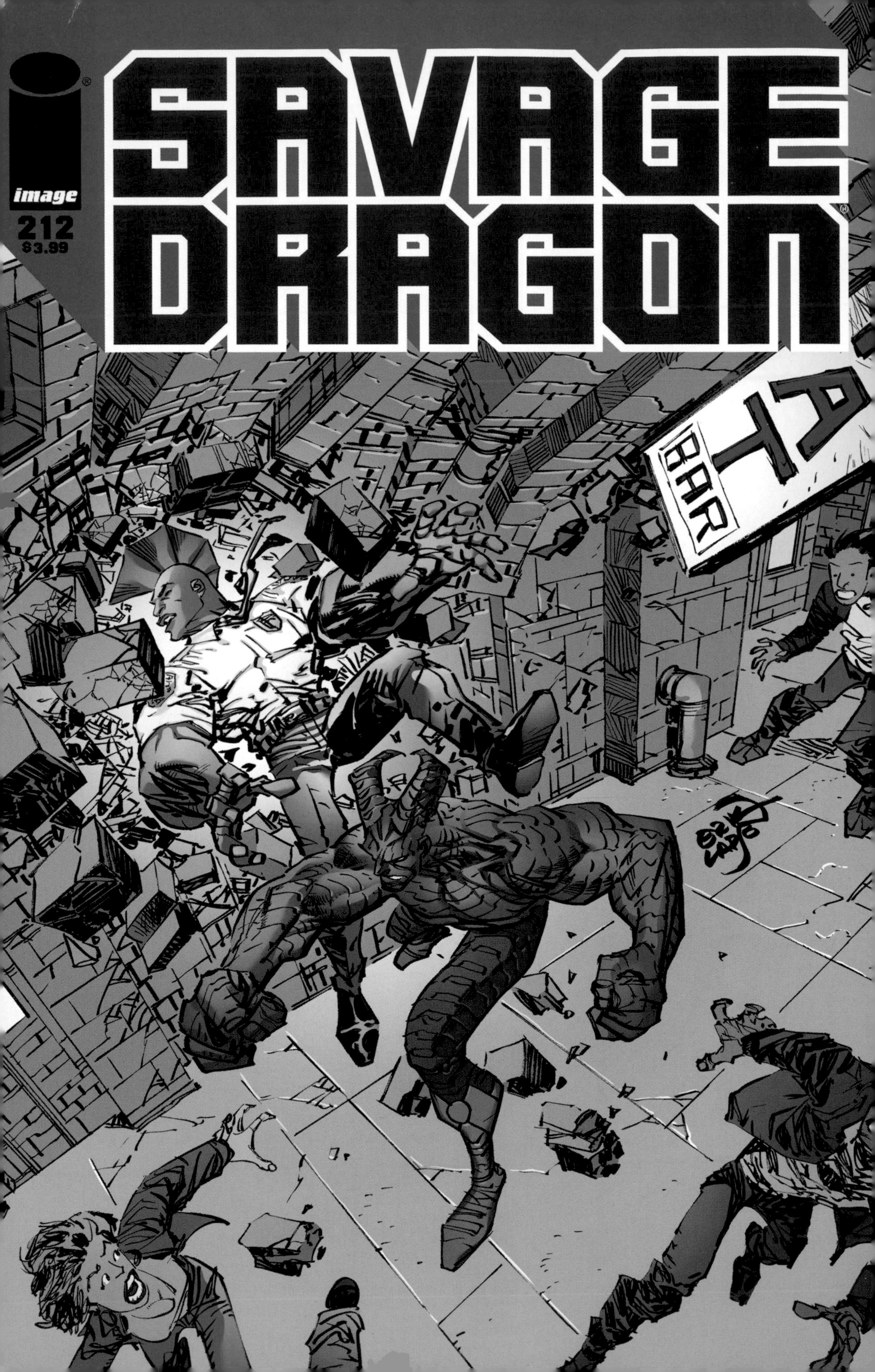
image
212
$3.99
SAVAGE DRAGON
BAR

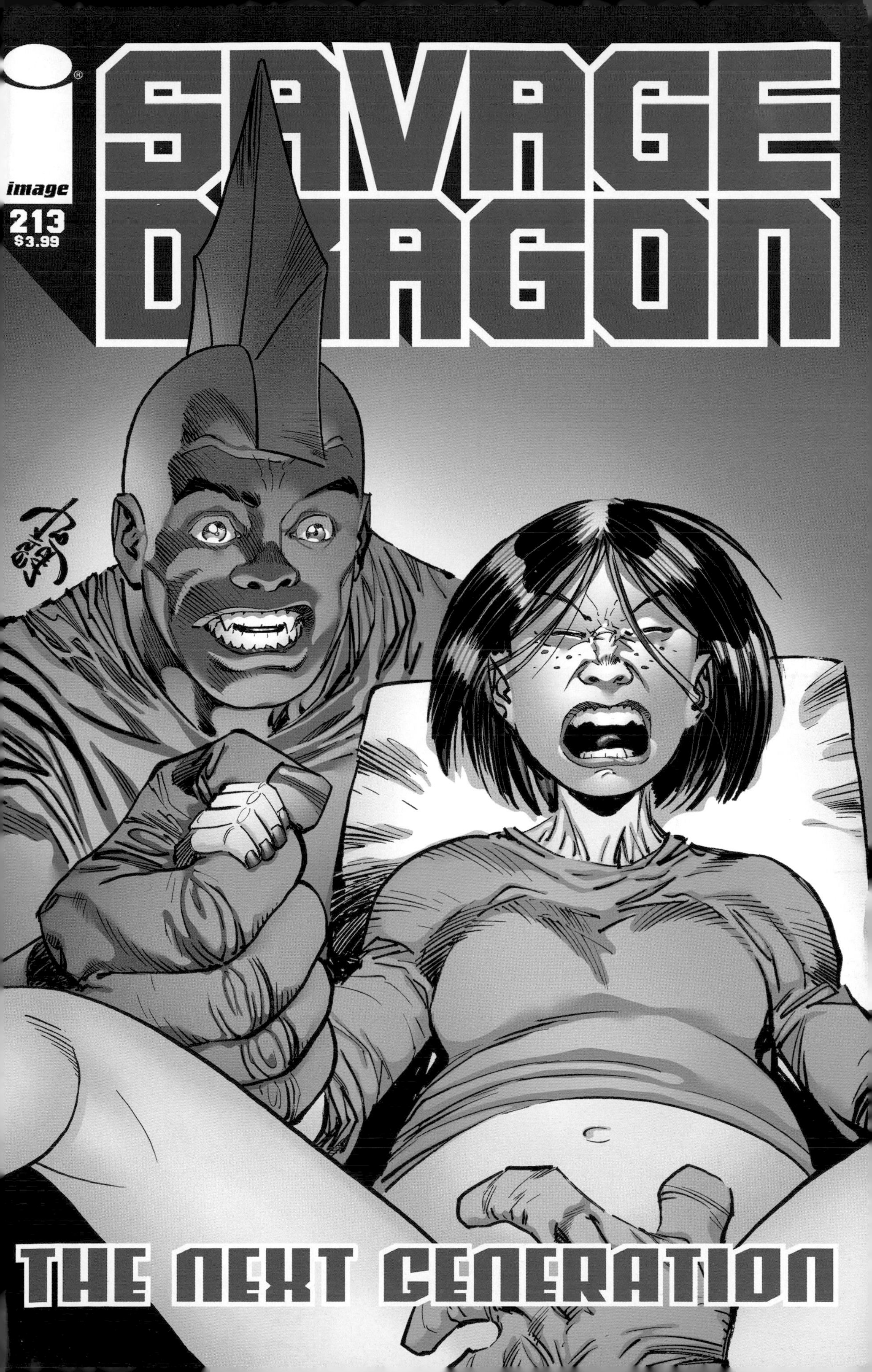
image
213
$3.99
SAVAGE DRAGON
THE NEXT GENERATION

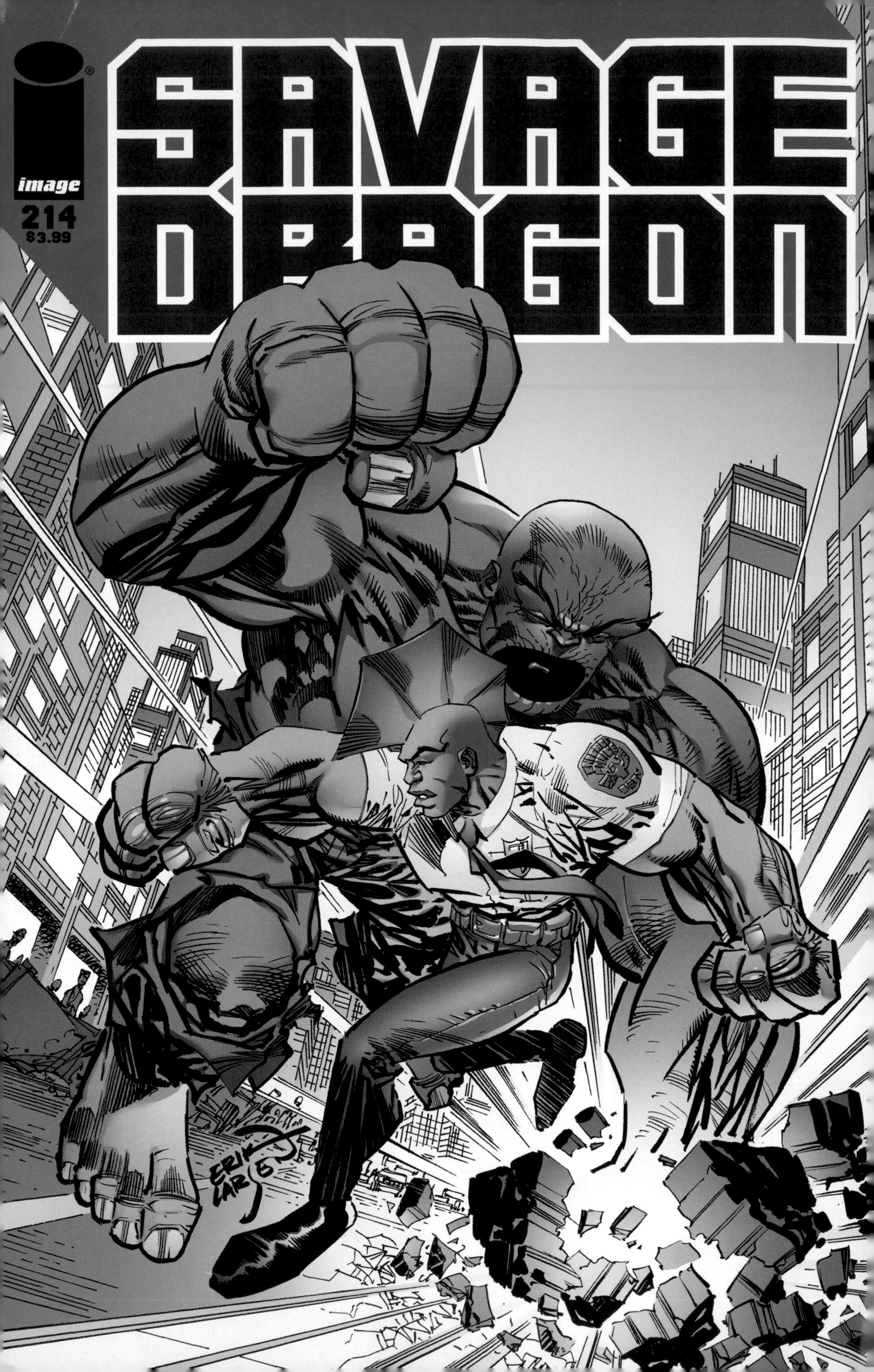image
214
$3.99
SAVAGE DRAGON
ERIK LARSEN

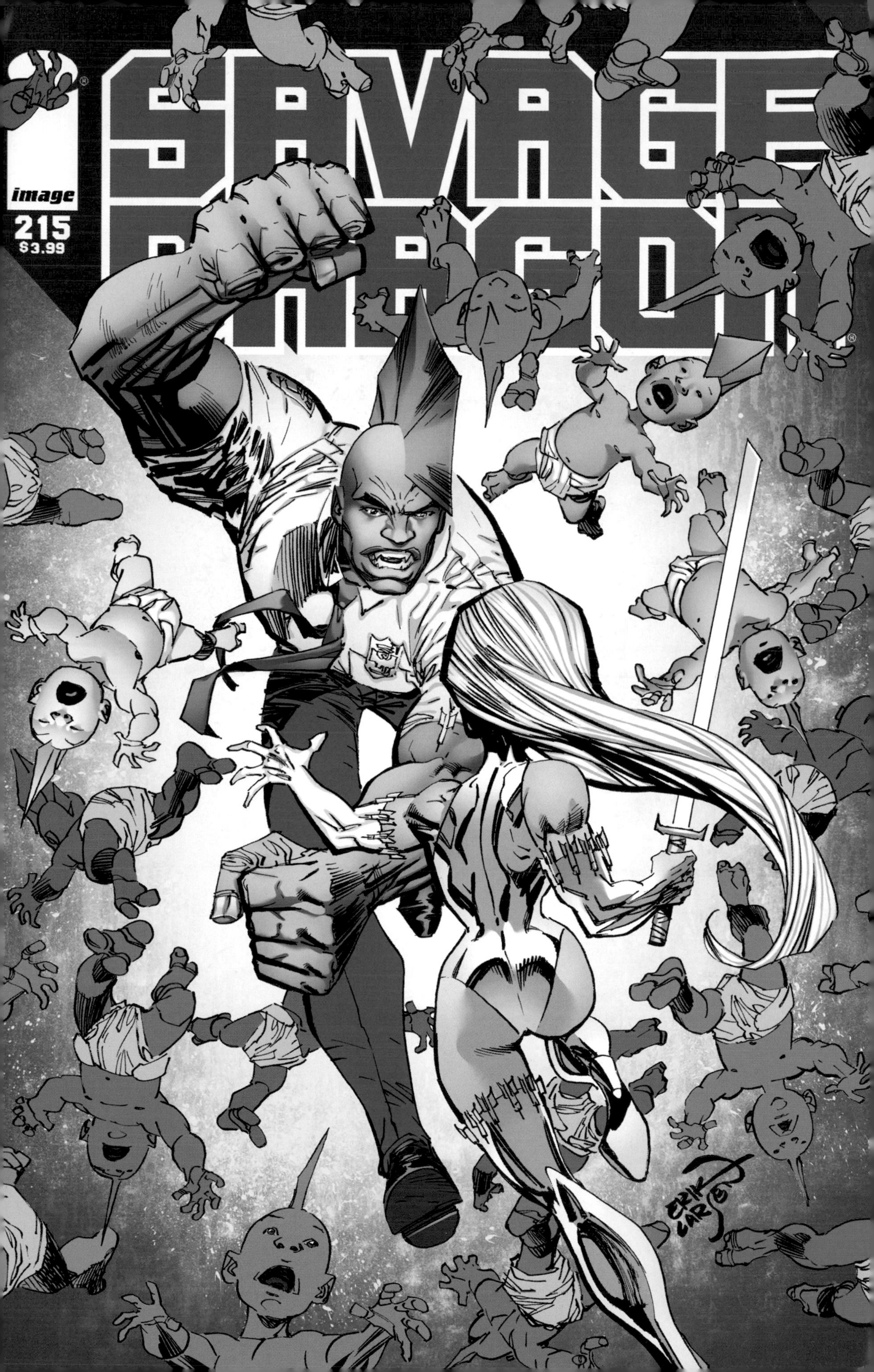

image
215
$3.99
SAVAGE DRAGON
ERIK LARSEN

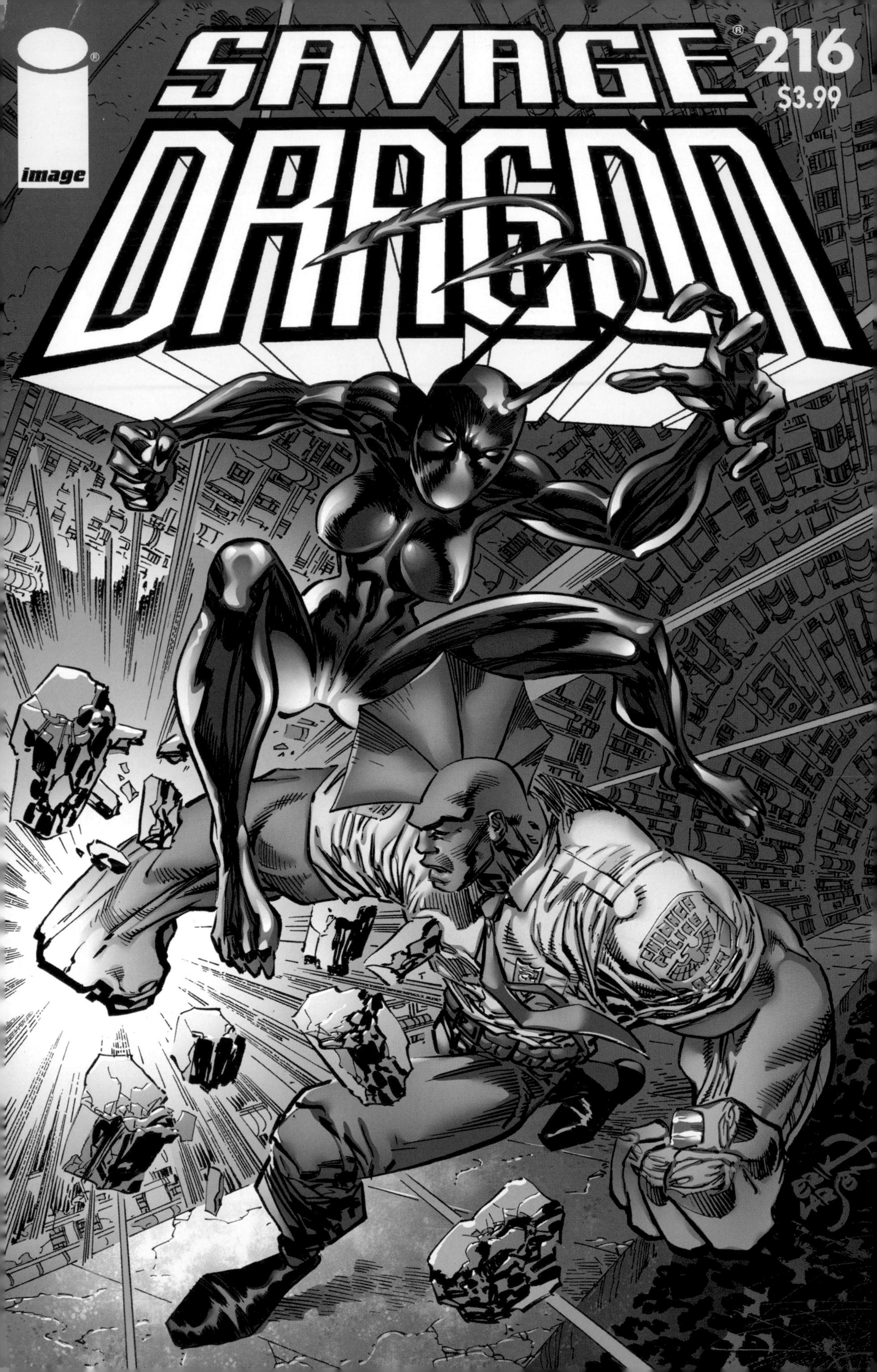
image
SAVAGE
DRAGON
216
$3.99

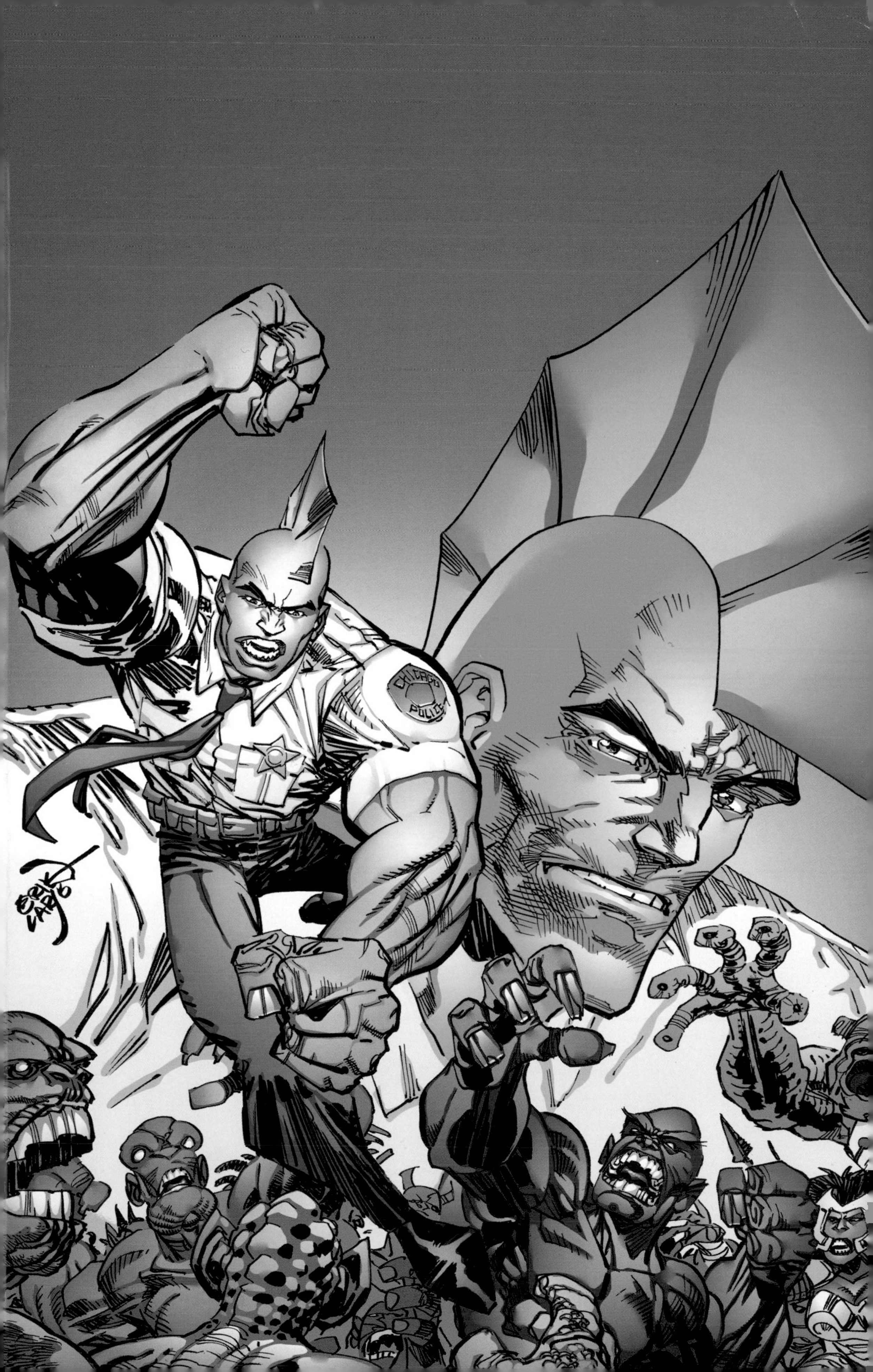
CHICAGO POLICE

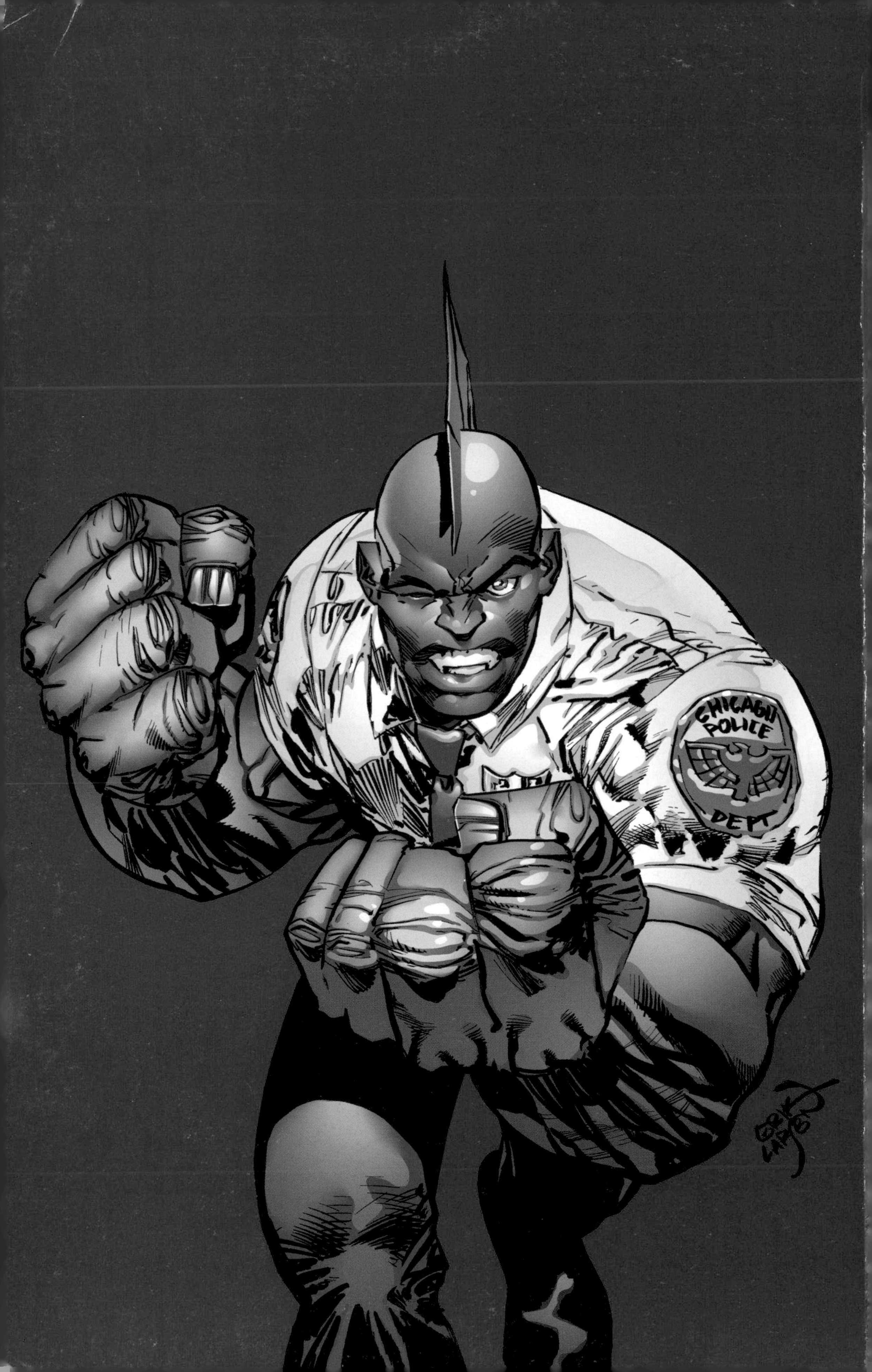
CHICAGO
POLICE
DEPT